THE NATIONAL ARMY MUSEUM BOOK OF

THE BOER WAR

Michael Carver, born in 1915, was commissioned into the Royal Tank Corps in January 1935, and was serving with the 1st Royal Tank Regiment in Egypt at the outbreak of the Second World War. Thereafter he served in armoured formations throughout the desert campaign in North Africa, towards the end of which he assumed command of the regiment, which he continued to do in Italy in 1943 and in the landings of Normandy in 1944. There, at the age of twenty-nine, he was promoted to command the 4th Armoured Brigade, finishing the war with them on the shores of the Baltic.

Since then he has held important command and staff appointments, at home and abroad, culminating in the posts of Chief of the General Staff and, as Field Marshal in 1973, Chief of the Defence Staff. He was created a life peer in 1977.

He has written thirteen books and edited two others, mostly of twentieth-century military history, as well as numerous articles and book reviews.

'A General Group' by 'Spy': *Vanity Fair*, 29 November 1900. From left to right:
Brigadier-General Herbert Plumer, Lieutenant-General Sir Archibald Hunter,
Major-General Hector MacDonald, General Sir Redvers Buller,
Major-General Robert Baden-Powell, Field Marshal Lord Roberts,
Major-General Lord Dundonald, Major-General Lord Kitchener,
General Sir George White, Lieutenant-General Reginald Pole-Carew,
Lieutenant-General Sir Frederick Carrington, Lieutenant-General John French.

THE NATIONAL ARMY MUSEUM BOOK OF

THE BOER WAR

Field Marshal Lord Carver

PAN BOOKS

in association with

the National Army Museum

First published 1999 by Sidgwick & Jackson

This edition published 2000 by Pan Books
an imprint of Macmillan Publishers Ltd
25 Eccleston Place, London SW1W 9NF
Basingstoke and Oxford
Associated companies throughout the world
www.macmillan.co.uk

In association with the National Army Museum

ISBN 0 330 36944 X

3 5 7 9 8 6 4

A CIP catalogue record for this book is available from
the British Library.

Typeset by SetSystems Ltd, Saffron Walden, Essex
Printed and bound in Great Britain by
Mackays of Chatham plc, Chatham, Kent

Foreword

The Royal Hospital Chelsea, the home of retired soldiers so famous through the world for their distinctive red uniforms, was the setting on 31 May 1962 for a parade of about 550 members of the South African War Veterans' Association. At that time there were ninety-nine In-Pensioners who had served in the Anglo-Boer War (1889–1902), of whom sixty-five were on parade for an inspection by Her Majesty Queen Elizabeth The Queen Mother, before a commemorative service in the Royal Hospital Chapel.

It so happened that just two years previously, in 1960, the National Army Museum (NAM) received its Royal Charter, which gives authority for the museum to collect objects and archives relating to the British and Imperial Armies in peace and war, including of course the Anglo-Boer War. As inevitably with the passage of time the veterans of the conflict passed on, so the collections of the NAM, located since 1971 on a site in Royal Hospital Road adjacent to the Royal Hospital, grew substantially. So extensive are those holdings now that the opportunity afforded by the hundredth anniversary of the outbreak of the Boer War in 1899 is being taken to focus attention upon and review the British Army's involvement in South Africa. This book is a contribution to achieving the aim of giving wider access to the relevant collections in the museum.

The National Army Museum Book of the Boer War consists of documents and photographs from the NAM's collections selected by Field Marshal Lord Carver, a distinguished soldier and writer on military history, who has himself composed the text, thus bringing to bear on the source material a significant personal perspective which will command respect. In all, extracts from some sixty-seven collections of documents are appearing in print, many of them for the first time, as well as photographs selected from the museum's extensive holdings.

It is worth remarking that there are two reasons in particular why we should recall the events of the Anglo-Boer War a century ago. The first is that the huge political changes in South Africa in the last decades of the twentieth century and the attitude of the World Powers to them invite comparison with the issues associated with the Anglo-Boer War and the interests of the Great Powers then in that struggle. The second reason is that in 2014 many countries in the world will seek to reflect upon the centenary of the outbreak of the First World War in 1914. In two respects at least, the Anglo-Boer War may be seen as a precursor to that more extensive conflict in that many of the Allied leaders in 1914 had gained their experience in the fighting in South Africa; while the preparedness of the British and the Imperial Armies in 1914 had been crucially influenced by the lessons learnt in the Anglo-Boer War.

Ian G. Robertson
Director, National Army Museum
18 December 1998

Contents

Acknowledgements

I wish to express my thanks to the following: to William Armstrong, of the publishers, for having suggested that I should write this book and his help while I was doing so, and to Nicholas Blake, my meticulous copy-editor: to the staff of the National Army Museum, especially to Dr Alan Guy, the Deputy Director, Dr Peter Boyden and Mrs Marion Harding of the Department of Archives, Photographs, Film and Sound and their assistants, and to Mr Keith Miller of the Department of Weapons, Equipment and Vehicles: to the copyright holders of the documents, from which I have quoted extracts, listed in the Index of Contributors, for their permission: to Timothy Ward and the staff of the Prince Consort's Army Library, Aldershot, for all the help they have given me over this and almost all my previous books; and to my agent, Bruce Hunter, for his help and encouragement over this book and ten of its predecessors in the last twenty years.

Preface

This book does not pretend to be a comprehensive or properly balanced history. It is an account of the Boer War as seen through the eyes of those participants whose letters, diaries or other papers are held in the archives of the National Army Museum, most voluntarily donated, some purchased. Although the narrative draws on other sources, all the papers quoted are from those archives, and all the illustrations are taken from the Museum's collection. It is inevitable therefore that the story is not completely balanced, although I have attempted to make it so as far as the material available has allowed. There is nothing from many of the principal figures, for instance from Buller, White or Methuen. However, that is compensated for by the papers of members of their staffs or their subordinates. There is only one contribution from the Boer side, which is not surprising as the Museum is concerned with the history of the British Army, and most of the papers of the Boer side are in South Africa.

For the view at the highest level, the papers of Field Marshal Lord Roberts and Rawlinson's diary have been invaluable. Lord Birdwood's diary is of limited value, partly because his position as brigade-major to Lord Dundonald was a fairly marginal one, partly because much of it is a rather bare chronicle of moves, as are several other diaries: of some value to the historian, but of little interest to the general reader. Much the same can be said of Baden-Powell's papers. Usable material at the level of battalion, brigade and division command is rare. As will be seen from the pages which follow, the best accounts are at the level of squadron, battery, company and below. The only papers of Kitchener's are the letters he wrote every week to Lord Roberts after the latter had left South Africa. They are revealing not only about how Kitchener viewed events in South Africa but also about his relationship with Roberts, who was then Commander-in-Chief in London. They seem remarkably subservient in tone, but that may have been influenced by Kitchener's keen desire to become Commander-in-Chief in India, an appointment for which Roberts could exert unique influence.

Balance is distorted also by lack of material covering some important actions, notably that at Nooitgedacht on 11 December 1900, when Major-General Clements's force was attacked by the combined commandos of Beyers, De la Rey and Smuts.

In spite of these gaps, a clear picture emerges of what life for the soldier was like in this messy and unnecessary war. Most of them were regulars or regular reservists – about 250,00 out of some 450,000 white soldiers who served there. They were supplemented by some 45,000 Militia, 36,500 Yeomanry and 19,500 Volunteers, 29,000 from colonies other than South Africa and some 52,000 raised in the latter.

These were the soldiers whose experiences are recorded in the following pages.

List of Illustrations

All are from the National Army Museum's collection. The numbers after the description are the Accession and Negative numbers.

Frontispiece. 'A General Group' by 'Spy'. *Vanity Fair*, 29 November 1900 (chromolithograph cartoon). (5608-99/21921)

Section One

List of Maps

Glossary

donga   gully

dorp   village

drift   ford

inspan   to harness a wagon or yoke animals in a team to a vehicle

kaffir   native African*

kloof   cleft or valley

kop or *kopje*   small or isolated hill

kraal   native village or collection of huts

laager   camp, bivouac or defended collection of wagons

nek   pass

outspan   to unharness animals, to camp

poort   gap

spruit   stream or watercourse

veld   open country

---

* Originally an Arabic word denoting an infidel. It became to be considered, like 'nigger', which occurs in some of the quotations, as a derogatory term, but at the time of the Boer War was in general use to cover Africans of any tribe.

1

THE PATH TO WAR

1806–1899

Sunday 10 December 1899 saw the start of the British army's 'Black Week' in South Africa. On that day Lieutenant-General Sir William Gatacre's 3rd Division suffered a humiliating defeat at Stormberg, the junction of the railways from Port Elizabeth and East London to Bloemfontein: two days later Lieutenant-General Lord Methuen's 1st Division suffered a more serious one at Magersfontein, failing to relieve Kimberley, and on Friday 15th Lieutenant-General Sir Redvers Buller, the Commander-in-Chief of the Forces in South Africa, on his way to lift the siege of Ladysmith, failed miserably in his attempt to cross the River Tugela at Colenso with Lieutenant-General Sir Francis Clery's 2nd Division. The cream of the British regular army had been stopped at heavy cost by a collection of Afrikaner farmers (*boers*), who seemed to have stepped straight out of the Old Testament.

South Africa had not been a happy battlefield for the army: Isandhlwana, partly redeemed by Rorke's Drift, in 1879, and Majuba in 1881, and now this triple defeat. How had it come about? The origins of the Boer War of 1899–1902 lay in the determination of the Afrikaner *Volk* of the Orange Free State and the Transvaal to retain the independence from British sovereignty which they had achieved by the 1852 Sand River and 1854 Bloemfontein Conventions. They were the descendants of the Dutch Calvinists, with some Germans and French Huguenots, who settled in the hinterland of the Cape of Good Hope when the Dutch occupied it in 1652. After Britain had acquired the Cape from the Dutch in 1806, during the Napoleonic Wars, these *boers* became dissatisfied with Britain's failure, as they saw it, to protect them, or let them protect themselves, against the African tribes with whom they competed for grazing. In 1834 many of them trekked northwards, some to the area between the Orange and Vaal Rivers, later to form the Orange Free State, and others to beyond the Vaal, which became the Transvaal Republic. Some moved into Natal, but the British government was not prepared to see that area become an Afrikaner province and annexed it in 1843, separating it in 1856 from Cape Colony, the whole area south of the Orange River, in which the great majority of the white population remained Afrikaner.

The Boers' determination to preserve their own way of life in independence clashed with Britain's grand imperial ambitions, which ran high in the second half of the nineteenth century. These were heightened by the discovery of diamonds at Kimberley in 1870 and by the replacement of Gladstone as Prime Minister by Disraeli in 1874. In 1877 the Afrikaner government of the Transvaal faced a grave financial crisis arising out of the construction of a railway from Pretoria to Delagoa Bay in Portuguese East Africa, while under threat from the Pedi and Zulu tribes on its borders. Under protest, they accepted a temporary submission to British authority, while their financial and security problems were sorted out, Paul Kruger, the Vice-President, dissociating himself from it.

The British victory at Ulundi in the Zulu War in July 1879 and over the Pedi in November removed the threat from them and the Transvaal's finances began to recover. Meanwhile legal preparations were being made at the Cape for the establishment of a Federation within the British Empire of Cape Colony and Natal with the Orange Free State and the Transvaal Republic. When Gladstone replaced Disraeli again in April 1880, Kruger, now President of the Transvaal, asked him what his intentions were, to which Gladstone replied that 'He could not advise Her Majesty to abandon her suzerainty over the Transvaal'. Led by Kruger, with Piet Joubert as his military commander, a great assembly of Boers at Paardekraal on 10 December 1880 decided to declare independence, besiege Pretoria and other towns with British garrisons and dispatch an army under Joubert into Natal before Major-General Sir George Colley, the commander of the forces in Natal, could be reinforced, in order to prevent him from marching to their relief. Four days later two companies (9 officers and 248 men) of the 94th (2nd Connaught Rangers), returning to Pretoria from the east, were intercepted at Bronkhorst Spruit, and when their Colonel rejected a Boer order to remain where he was were attacked, a third being killed and a third wounded before the rest surrendered, their Colonel and four other officers dead.

When Colley received the news, he set off north from Maritzburg with only 1,500 men to the pass through the Drakensberg at Laing's Nek where, on 28 January 1881, he met with a rebuff at Joubert's hands, as he did on 7 February at Ingogo, while Boers from the Orange Free State were promising support to Kruger, and the Governor of Cape Colony, Sir Hercules Robinson, feared that Afrikaners there might do the same. These events persuaded Gladstone that he should negotiate a peace. On 16 February Colley was instructed to offer Kruger an armistice and an invitation to peace negotiations. Independence would be granted, subject to British suzerainty in the form of control of foreign relations. Colley was to fix 'a reasonable time' for Kruger to reply. Although Joubert's representative said that it would take at least six days to get an answer, Colley, without reference to London, insisted on forty-eight hours. He thought he had discovered a key to Joubert's defeat in the occupation of an isolated hill at Majuba, from which he could outflank the Boer defences at Laing's Nek. On the night of 26 February 600 men, including three companies of the Gordon Highlanders, who had landed at Durban only a fortnight before, climbed the hill and occupied it without opposition. Colley himself led them, and, as dawn broke on 27 February, looked down on the Boer positions. Thereafter torpor prevailed until, at about midday, several hundred Boers, who had methodically made their way up the steep hillsides, attacked from all directions and overwhelmed Colley's men, killing 96, including Colley himself, wounding 132 and taking 56 prisoner, including Lieutenant Ian Hamilton of the Gordons, who was to renew his acquaintance with that corner of Africa nineteen years later. The sixteen-year-old Bugler W. H. Humphries of the 3rd Battalion The King's Royal Rifle Corps (60th Rifles), took part in the first of these battles, the one at Laing's Nek, and described it in an account he wrote of his army service, in which he rose to the rank of Company Quartermaster-Sergeant:

> The morning of the 28th [January] broke, contrasting greatly with its predecessor. The sun shone brightly, but not too warm, the air was as still as death, varied at intervals by slight gushes of wind, which came dancing over hill and dale. In short, nature appeared to have dressed her best, to witness the carnage which was to take place in the boundless arena before her.
>
> We were astir shortly after reveille had sounded and soon were in

a considerable state of excitement for all were aware that the enemy's position was to be attacked that morning. The camp represented a very different scene from what it had a few hours previously, when nought could be seen but the watchful out-post, patrolling to and fro. All now was animation, men running here, men running there, some getting their provisions, others seeing to their rifles. Artillery examining their guns, Cavalry looking to their horses and accoutrements, Sailors fitting their rocket tubes, while the discordant cries of drivers as they yoked their oxen, could be heard above all.

At about 7 a.m. the order was given to the Force to march off the ground: the 3/60th Rifles as advance guard, covered by two 9-pounder guns; the Mounted Infantry protecting the flanks; the Naval Brigade with their Rocket Tubes; and two Mountain Guns, manned by volunteers from the 3/60th Rifles; followed by the 58th Regiment* and Ambulance, composing the Rear.

We proceeded cautiously, skirmishing over each successive hill, the guns taking up commanding positions to enable them to cover the Force till we arrived about a mile from Laing's Nek, where a halt was ordered and from where the enemy could be seen in large numbers, swarming the hills right and left of the Nek. From the plan of battle it will be seen that the position held by the Boers was a most formidable one to be attacked by our small force, numbering only about one-third of their own. It extended from the square-topped mountain known as the Majuba on their right with its precipitous sides and intricate wooded kloofs which was about 2,000 feet above the plateau, to the round detached hill, or stone kopje, on their left. The Nek was commanded by hills at about 300 yards on each side which were fortified, while Table Hill, as it was called, which was the key of their position, was not less than 600 feet above the average level of the plateau on which we took up our position. The ground on which we formed was from 1,700 to 2,300 yards distant from most of the points occupied by the Boers. It was thought possible to take Table Hill with the bayonet. In aid of this movement a squadron of mounted men were to charge up the hill on the right, where there was some fairly good charging ground, to take the Boers in flank; but the 60th Rifles, and the Naval Brigade with their Rockets, occupied the whole dip in front of the Nek. From this point the

---

* 2nd Battalion The Northamptonshire Regiment.

Naval Brigade ultimately shelled the Boers out of a ravine in their front with their rockets. Three other companies of the 60th Rifles were employed to cover the 9 pounder guns, while the Natal Police covered the left, and the Mounted Infantry and 58th Regiment were held in Reserve ready to advance to the attack on the right.

At about 9.20 a.m. the engagement began by the Artillery shelling the heights and ravines, while the 58th moved into position. By about 10.15 the latter had reached their last cover. The Boers awaited them, without much firing as yet. By this time the mounted squadron, led by Major Brownlow, K.D. Guards,* and by Captain Hornby of the 58th Regiment, were charging up the stone kopje. They left the Force amidst the cheers of all, who watched breathlessly the result. As they neared the kopje a cloud of smoke and a storm of bullets issued out of the rifles of the concealed Boers, and in a few seconds half their saddles were empty, and riderless horses, with trappings bloody and bridles loose, were madly galloping rear-ward. Troop-Sergeant-Major Lunny of the K.D. Guards actually hewed his way into the Boer entrenchments, but fell dead, with six rifle balls in his body, while Trooper Venables, K. D. Guards, in leaping over the trenches, fell off his horse and was taken prisoner.

The crippled squadron retired, reformed, and again with brilliant valour charged up the hill, but nothing could withstand the storm of bullets. It fell back again with a loss of 17 killed and 32 horses killed, wounded and missing, and the triumphant shouts of the Boers followed them in their retreat.

. . .

As the Cavalry retired, the 58th Regiment were to advance and attack Table Hill which was the Key of the Boer position on our right of the Nek. They accordingly, under the command of Colonel Deane, the Chief Staff Officer, advanced in Quarter Column steadily towards the summit of the hill, and it is not surprising in such formation, they were soon suffering from a murderous fire from the enemy. We were more than surprised to see them taken up in such solid blocks, considering that our (Rifle) Colonel made us skirmish the whole of two miles, at ten paces interval, while leading the advance out to the position from Camp.

The first rush up the hill tried them severely. The ground was

* 1st (King's) Dragoon Guards.

steep, and the grass was slippery with the recent rains; but after a two minutes' halt and rest to gather breath, they advanced to a ridge between them and the edge of the ravine. No sooner did their white helmets top the green summit, and while they were rather crowded together, than a terrific volley from the front smote the leading companies, which were also enfiladed from the right flank. For five minutes the men endured this, returning as best they could the enemy's fire, the dead and wounded falling against and impeding the motions of those who were untouched as yet, till Colonel Deane called on the Regiment to Charge. At that moment his horse was shot and he fell. Springing to his feet, sword in hand, he shouted reassuringly, 'I am all right!' But the words had hardly escaped him when he fell again, and rolled over in agony, mortally wounded. Lieutenant Inman of the 60th Rifles, who was A.D.C. to Colonel Deane, soon fell by his side.

. . .

Major Hingsten of the 58th, who, with other officers, had kept to the front, cheering on their men, now asssumed the command, and gave the word to fix bayonets, prior to a rush; but he too fell mortally wounded. All this time the Boers had kept close within their trenches, while our men lay on the ground, taking a shot at them whenever a head with its broad-brimmed hat appeared; but when they started up to charge, the fire the Boers poured in was terrible and deadly indeed, at 200 yards range. There, Major Poole, R.A. and Lieut. Dolphine of the 58th Regt., were killed, and their bodies were found well in front of where their men lay in swathes, like grass beneath a scythe. Captain Lovegrove was wounded, and many N.C. Officers* and men were killed and wounded.

Reinforced from the rear, the Boers made their attack with such fury that the glorious black silk colours of the 58th, heavily covered with old honours, were nearly lost, and a large number of the officers were picked off by the enemy's select marksmen. Lieutenant Bailey, a mere boy subaltern, but a gallant one, who carried one of the Colors, on falling mortally wounded, was succoured by Lieut. Peel, who carried the other. 'Never mind me,' he exclaimed, while choking with blood, 'Save the Colors.' Peel then took both Colors, but fell into a hole, on which Sergeant Brindstock, thinking him shot, seized both

---

* Non-commissioned officers.

Colors, and bore them to safety. No words can sufficiently convey an idea of the gallantry of the 58th, charging up a steep hill, and their fatigue was so great that the officers and men could scarcely speak or move when they attained to the highest point they had been able to reach. At last they could do nothing but beat a retreat. This was covered by a fusilade from the Rifles who had been extended to cover their withdrawal, and a hot fire from the guns and rocket-tubes of the Naval Brigade, who, while the enemy was in the open, delivered some shots with splendid effect, which was known to have done incredible damage. The Rocket which is a kind of shell, creates great consternation when it is fired, and the roar it makes as it travels through the air and when it strikes an object, has a very demoralising effect. It has great penetrating power; it has been known to enter the earth to a depth of 20 feet at a distance of 1,260 yards. When the retreat began the Boers showed themselves defiantly and exultingly, and kept a constant fusilade till the fire of our shells and rockets cooled their ardour. On reaching the foot of the hill the men of the 58th Regiment refilled their pouches, reformed and were bravely prepared, if so ordered, to advance and again attempt to storm the position; but Sir George decided to withdraw.

At 11 56 a.m. the 'Cease Fire' sounded, and a flag of truce carried by the Church of England Chaplain (Rev. Ritchie) was despatched to the enemy's lines, to ask for time to bury the dead and collect the wounded, which was granted.

On 4 March Kruger accepted Gladstone's offer, and on 23 March provisional peace terms were signed. British garrisons in the Transvaal were withdrawn and the terms were confirmed in the Convention of Pretoria on 3 August.

The chances of this agreement producing a lasting settlement were undermined by two factors which influenced each other. One was the ambitious imperial dream of Cecil Rhodes, who gained a virtual monopoly of diamond mining at Kimberley, and the other was the discovery of gold in 1886 on the Rand in the heart of the Transvaal, in which Rhodes lost the leading role to his partner Alfred Beit. In 1884, under the London Convention, Kruger relinquished his claim to Bechuanaland, the key to Rhodes's northward drive, in return for Britain giving up its pledge to protect Africans in the Transvaal. By 1890, having tricked Lobengula of the Matabele into granting him a concession,

Rhodes had persuaded Lord Salisbury's Tory administration to grant him a Royal Charter for a Company to exploit the land of the Matabele and the Mashona over whom the former claimed authority. The discovery of gold in the Transvaal led to an influx of Europeans, known to the Boers as Uitlanders. While welcoming the money this brought him, Kruger feared that it would eventually result in the Boer *Volk* losing control of their own land and destiny. Strict limits were set on their participation in the administration of the Transvaal, and other restrictions also imposed which were a source of Uitlander complaint. In 1895 Rhodes, who had become Prime Minister of Cape Colony two years earlier, concocted a scheme which he hoped would, at one stroke, buttress his imperial ambitions and help to bolster the precarious finances of the Chartered Company, which had failed to find mineral wealth further north. The Uitlanders would be encouraged to rebel against Kruger and a force, provided by the Chartered Company, would arrive to support them, with the result that the Transvaal would again be annexed to the Crown. The outcome was a fiasco, Rhodes's colleague, Dr Jameson, prematurely dashing in from Mafeking on 29 December with 500 mounted police, while the Uitlanders remained passive. Kruger's men had no difficulty in rounding them up at Doornkop a few days later.

Before the subsequent inquiry in London, Lord Salisbury's Colonial Secretary, Joseph Chamberlain, managed, with some difficulty, to conceal his own involvement in Rhodes's plot; but he did not relinquish the grand imperial ambitions which he and his colleagues had inherited from Lord Carnarvon. However, he realized that they must be pursued by more regular methods than those of the swashbuckling Rhodes. In 1897 therefore he appointed as High Commissioner in South Africa Sir Alfred Milner, who shared his imperial vision, including that of bringing about a South African Federation, incorporating the Transvaal and the Orange Free State, within the Empire. Milner appreciated that time was not on his side. Kruger, re-elected President in 1888, was busy buying arms from France and Germany while growing richer from the goldfields. Milner planned to follow Rhodes's example in exploiting discontent among the Uitlanders. The issue on which it was to be forced was the representation of Uitlanders in the Transvaal's government: the method would be secretly to support a movement among the Uitlanders to demand British intervention to protect their rights as British citizens.

The shooting by Transvaal police of a British mining engineer, Tom Edgar, on 23 December 1898 sparked off the desired crisis.

A tortuous series of negotiations ensued in which Kruger tried to stave off the crisis by a series of concessions, while Milner forced the pace, backed by Chamberlain, but less firmly by Lord Salisbury's Cabinet. Milner asked for a reinforcement of 10,000 men, arguing that a show of force would double the strength of the forces in Cape Colony and Natal and, he hoped, make it possible to move a strong force to the north of the latter as a threat to the Transvaal. He also requested the replacement of the local Commander-in-Chief, Lieutenant-General Sir William Butler, whom he regarded as too weak and pro-Boer. Field Marshal Lord Wolseley, who had taken over as Commander-in-Chief in Whitehall from the Duke of Cambridge in 1895, wanted to mobilize an army corps and a cavalry division, calling up reservists to bring the force to a strength of 35,000, and send them, under the command of Lieutenant-General Sir Redvers Buller, to South Africa; but Lord Lansdowne, the Secretary of State for War, who was not on good terms with Wolseley, supported by the Cabinet, jibbed at that, arguing that the dispatch of such a force could precipitate a war before it could arrive, and that public opinion, and foreign governments, had not been prepared for such an eventuality, which might be interpreted as an intention to invade the Transvaal and the Orange Free State, forcing the latter, which might otherwise remain friendly, into the arms of Kruger. He also rejected Wolseley's suggested alternative, a concentration of the mobilized force on Salisbury Plain as a sign that Britain meant business. Chamberlain wanted to send Buller to replace Butler, but Wolseley, to Buller's annoyance, refused to let him go without his corps, and sent the ineffectual Lieutenant-General Sir Frederick Forestier-Walker instead, while Major-General Sir Penn Symons was sent from India to command the force in Natal.

No further decision about reinforcement had been taken when, on 28 July 1899, Kruger made another offer of concession. Egged on by Milner, Chamberlain's response was to raise a series of detailed questions about it, insisting that a joint inquiry must be established to determine whether or not this would give the Uitlanders 'immediate and substantial' representation. Kruger had not replied when Parliament went into recess at the end of the month and the government considered Lansdowne's proposal to reinforce Symons with the 2,000 men which he had originally said he needed to ensure the defence of Natal, although he had subsequently raised his demand to 5,000. 500 of them were to be transferred from the Cape.

Before any decision had been taken, Kruger, under pressure from Afrikaners in Cape Colony, agreed on 19 August to make further concessions, but rejected a joint inquiry. Milner advised Chamberlain to repeat the tactic of questioning detail, while whipping up support from the Uitlanders, Alfred Beit and sympathizers in the press and public in Britain and South Africa. The result was an uncompromising speech by Chamberlain on 26 August, a threatening dispatch to Kruger two days later, and a request for a Cabinet meeting to rule on Chamberlain's demand to Lansdowne for 10,000 troops to be sent. When the Cabinet met on 8 September, Chamberlain argued that the Uitlanders were being treated as 'little better than Kaffirs or Indians'; that the 'position of Great Britain in South Africa' was at stake, and that the dispatch of troops would prevent rather than precipitate war. He won his case.

On that day the Viceroy of India was told to send to Durban a cavalry, an infantry and an artillery brigade, while another infantry brigade was ordered to go from Britain. One infantry battalion was sent from each of Malta (1st Borders), Egypt (1st Royal Irish Fusiliers) and Crete (2nd Rifle Brigade), and a half from Mauritius (2nd King's Own Yorkshire Light Infantry). The total was 10,662 men. Forestier-Walker was optimistically ordered to provide transport locally for the whole force. All arrived before the outbreak of war, except for the 9th Lancers and two squadrons of the 5th Dragoon Guards, delayed in India by an outbreak of anthrax. They brought the total British army strength in South Africa, including locally raised troops, to some 27,500, of whom 18,500 were in Natal.

Lieutenant-General Sir George White, the sixty-four-year-old Quartermaster-General at the War Office, who had won a VC in Burma in 1852, was sent out to take over command, Wolseley rejecting Chamberlain's request that Redvers Buller, who from the Zulu War knew the area and the Boers well, should go. Wolseley insisted that Buller must remain in command of his corps, preparations for the mobilization and dispatch of which he failed to persuade Lansdowne to authorize. Buller was furious and wrote direct to Lansdowne, pressing the case for the dispatch of his corps and issuing a warning that White should not advance beyond the Tugela River, that is to Ladysmith and beyond, but remain on the defensive south of the river. Forestier-Walker was relegated to command of the troops in Cape Colony. White reached Cape Town, with Colonel Ian Hamilton and Lieutenant-Colonel Henry Rawlinson as his principal staff officers, on 3 October, to be told by Milner that Boer forces had concentrated on the frontiers of both Cape Colony and Natal; that Symons had moved a brigade up to Dundee, seventy miles north-east of Ladysmith towards Laing's Nek, and that the Afrikaners in Cape Colony were restive. Whereas earlier Lansdowne had taken the line that the only troops to be sent should be those needed to ensure the defence of the colonies against attack, he now switched to Milner's aggressive stance and on 3 October described the agreed strategy in these words:

> We have now definitely decided to adopt the Cape Colony–Orange Free State route. It is intended that 10,000 should remain in Natal, on which side it will make a valuable diversion. 3,000 should be allocated to the west, including the defence of Kimberley, and the main force will enter the Orange Free State from the south.

On the other side of the fence, President Steyn of the Orange Free State had been urging caution on Kruger, who was being pressed by Smuts to invade Natal before British reinforcements could arrive. Steyn was himself under pressure from more bellicose burghers like Christiaan de Wet, and at the end of September agreed to support Kruger in issuing an ultimatum. Kruger having mobilized his forces on 27 September and Steyn on 2 October, they presented an ultimatum to the British Agent at Pretoria, Conyngham Greene, on 9 October, two days after White reached Durban. They accused Britain of breaching the 1884 London Convention by interfering in the internal affairs of the Transvaal and massing troops on its borders. They insisted that the British Government should agree to arbitration on 'all points of mutual difference' and withdraw troops from the Republic's borders, and that all reinforcements that had arrived in South Africa since 1 June should leave, demanding compliance within forty-eight hours. This ultimatum forestalled one which Chamberlain was about to present to Cabinet and extricated him from the difficulty he faced in framing it in a way that could be publicly justified. There was no need for it now: Kruger had provided the justification, and there were no further doubts that Buller and his corps should be sent, the War Office having advised the Cabinet some time before that it would take three or four months for its deployment to be completed. Buller himself left Southampton on 14 October, greatly concerned that White's troops had already been deployed well beyond the Tugela.

The British army was ill-prepared for the war it was about to wage. In 1888 Edward Stanhope, then Secretary of State for War, had produced a memorandum for the Cabinet defining 'the general objects for which our Army is maintained'. After providing for support of the civil power in the United Kingdom, the requirements of India and those of 'all our fortresses and coaling stations' and the provision of two Army Corps of Regular troops and one of mixed Regular and Militia troops for home defence, 'subject to the foregoing considerations and to their financial obligations' it aimed at 'being able, in case of necessity, to send abroad two complete Army Corps, with Cavalry Division and Line of Communication', emphasizing that it was very unlikely that they would be sent to Europe and that first priority was home defence.

It is not surprising therefore that very little had been done to make the dispatch of even one army corps possible, until Major-General Brackenbury, one of Wolseley's favourites, became Director of Military Intelligence in 1886 and began to concern himself with mobilization plans: the call-up and movement of reservists and all that was needed to form divisions and make them ready for war; and, with the Admiralty, to dispatch them overseas. By June 1899 the special staff at the War Office, which he had established, had completed a mobilization plan for 'A Field Force for service in South Africa', and, on 20 September, they gave the Admiralty details of the force it was intended to send if Buller's expeditionary force was ordered out. A major omission in the mobilization plan was provision for the mobilization, including purchase or requisition if necessary, of horses. It had been assumed that any shortfall in the number of horses with units and remount depots could be made good from local sources on arrival. Ten days later the Admiralty received authority to take up the necessary shipping. On 7 October mobilization was ordered of the cavalry division, one army corps of three infantry divisions (1st, 2nd and 3rd: White's force was the 4th) with eight infantry battalions for the lines of communication, regular army reservists being called to the colours. 99 per cent of them turned up, of whom 91 per cent were passed as physically fit. The first troops (twenty companies of the Army Service Corps) had already gone on board the day before, embarkation of the rest starting on 20 October and being completed by 17 November, except for one cavalry regiment, delayed by horse sickness. On 11 November it was decided to mobilize another division (the 5th) and an additional brigade of artillery, the former being complete by 13 December, the latter by the 21st. Meanwhile, on 2 December, orders for the 6th Division to be mobilized were given: it was completed by 11 December and embarked between 16 December and 1 January 1900.

Two more divisions were to be mobilized after 'Black Week', which virtually denuded the United Kingdom of all regulars. The regular army's strength at the outbreak of war was 227,159, of whom 148,500 were infantry and 19,500 cavalry soldiers. 108,000 were in the United Kingdom, 68,000 in India and the rest scattered about the Empire in garrisons, the largest of which were in Malta (7,500) and Gibraltar (5,000). On mobilization 83,000 regular reservists could be called up. 'Auxiliary' forces consisted of 109,500 men in the Militia and its reserve, 10,690 in the Yeomanry, 224,000 in the Volunteers and 530 in the Honourable Artillery Company; but the Yeomanry and Volunteers were liable only for support of the civil power or home defence and could not legally be used overseas, although individuals could volunteer. The Militia, an ancient force originally raised by Lords Lieutenant by conscription, and later by ballot, for home defence, could also be used to supplement the regular army. By this time it had become a voluntary force, often seen as a back-door way into the ranks of the regulars, with the infantry battalions of which it was affiliated. When one of them was sent overseas on an expedition, its affiliated Militia battalion was occasionally called up to replace it, but that had not occurred for some time. By this time Militia units, or individuals, could be sent overseas if they volunteered. They did little training and their members tended to be either very young or rather old. Militia battalions were generally thought to be suitable only for line of communication duties.

There were also Militia units in the colonies, trained and administered by a small regular cadre: about 32,000 each in Canada and Australia and 7,700 in New Zealand. A firm decision had been taken that only white troops would be used in South Africa: the great potential of the Indian Army was not therefore available. Several British officers of the Indian Army, however, served as individuals in the British army or locally raised units and on the staff, and Indian water-carriers (bheesties) were also employed.

On the opposite side, intelligence estimated that the Boers could muster about 50,000 men, 30,000 from the Transvaal and 20,000 from the Orange Free State, but not all of them could be available for offensive operations. All men between the age of sixteen and sixty were liable to call-up into the Burgher Commandos, in three stages: first those eighteen and over and up to thirty-four, then those between thirty-four and fifty, and finally the sixteen- to seventeen- and fifty-one- to sixty-year-olds. Each 'Wyk' or electoral ward chose a 'field cornet', who was responsible for keeping a record of those available and seeing that on call-up they had clothing, a horse, a rifle and ammunition for it. He was helped by an assistant field cornet and two corporals. On call-up, the ward contingents assembled at the principal town in the district to form a commando and elected a commandant. Depending on the population of the district, a commando could be as small as 300 or as large as 3,000. Command was exercised in a very democratic manner and major decisions were taken by *Kriegsraads*, councils of war attended by all officers from the rank of corporal upwards. In the event the Transvaal raised 26,871 men initially, to which 14,779 were added later, while the Free State raised 21,345, to which 6,264 were added. Both states had a small regular force manning artillery, 800 men in the Transvaal, manning twelve fortress guns, thirteen obsolete mountain guns and twenty-one Maxim 'Pom-poms' (quick-firing 1-pounders), and 375 men in the Free State manning nineteen field guns, four mountain guns and three Maxims. Each state appointed a commandant-general as overall Commander-in-Chief and military adviser to the President. In addition 13,300 'rebels' from the colonies of Natal and the Cape joined the Commandos, as did 800 foreigners. There was also a Foreign Corps of 2,120, including 500 Irish, 320 Dutch, 200 Germans, 100 Scandinavians, 75 Italians, 50 French, 50 Americans and 25 Russians. The Boer forces eventually totalled 87,365.

2

TOWARDS BLACK WEEK

October to December 1899

Joubert crossed the frontier between the Transvaal and Natal near Laing's Nek with about 15,000 men on 11 and 12 October 1899. His main force, led by Commandant Erasmus's Commando of 2,000 men, followed the line of the railway southwards through Newcastle towards Dundee. On his left Commandant Meyer's 3,000 strong Commando moved south to the east of the Buffalo River, while Commandant Kock, with the Johannesburg Commando and German and Dutch volunteers, came in from the corner of the Free State south of Majuba and advanced parallel with Joubert on his right. By late on 19 October the forces of Erasmus and Meyer were converging on Dundee, the latter having crossed the Buffalo from east to west about fifteen miles north-east of the town, where Symons's force was encamped. He had four infantry battalions, grouped in Brigadier-General J. H. Yule's 8th Brigade, three of which had one mounted company, one cavalry regiment, Lieutenant-Colonel B. D. Moeller's 18th Hussars, with a squadron of Natal Carbineers, and three batteries of field artillery, the 13th, 67th and 69th, each of six 15-pounder guns.

Soon after dawn on 20 October Meyer's men were seen on Talana Hill, two miles east of the town, from where they opened fire with a 75mm Creusot gun, to which the British artillery replied, although outranged. Symons decided to deal with Meyer before he could link up with Erasmus, whose leading troops were believed to be just north of Mount Impati, a few miles north of the town. His plan was for a concentrated attack by three of Yule's battalions directly up Talana Hill after a bombardment by two of his field batteries. This left only one battalion, the 1st Leicesters, and one field battery to guard Dundee against the threat from Erasmus. The 2nd Dublin Fusiliers were to lead, the 1st 60th Rifles to pass through them and the 1st Royal Irish Fusiliers to take the final objective. A smaller hill, named Lennox, was to be kept subdued with artillery fire. The attack was launched at 7.30 a.m. and the infantry gradually worked their way up in the face of intense fire from the Boers' effective Mauser rifles, firing smokeless ammunition. As they struggled to the top, they came under shrapnel fire from their own artillery, which caused severe casualties and halted them, allowing the Boers to withdraw. Symons had intended that his cavalry should prevent this, but he had given Moeller a free hand and no orders about timing. The latter had passed round behind Talana Hill and, by the time the fight for it was over, had disappeared behind Mount Impati, where, two days later, he was surrounded and forced to surrender. Meyer's men mounted their ponies and trotted away, not even being fired at by the British artillery, who mistook them for the 18th Hussars. Casualties in the attack had been heavy, 51 killed, including the commanding officer of the 60th, Lieutenant-Colonel R. H. Gunning, and 203 wounded, including Symons, who died a few days later.

The action at Talana Hill was reported to Ladysmith as a victory, but White was rightly concerned that Joubert's forces were more numerous than his own, which were divided between Dundee and Ladysmith. Early in the morning of 21 October he asked Major-General John French, who, with his staff officer Major Douglas Haig, had just arrived to command the cavalry, to send a reconnaissance force to the north-east, where it was reported that the railway and telegraph line to Dundee had been cut at Elandslaagte, fifteen miles up the line. French discovered that the Boers were occupying the station and telegraphed to White for infantry in order to attack them. They were in fact Kock's Commando, about 1,000 strong, which had diverged from Joubert's main force and crossed the Biggarsberg fifteen miles west of Dundee. White sent up the 7th Brigade, the command of which he had given to Ian Hamilton, the first train carrying the 1st Manchesters and the second the 2nd Gordons and 1st Devons. French's cavalry consisted of a squadron each of the 5th Lancers and 5th Dragoon Guards and five squadrons of the Imperial Light Horse, as well as some of the Natal Mounted Rifles. Artillery support was provided by two 15-pounder batteries of the Royal Field Artillery and one of the Natal Artillery, giving French, who was in overall command, 1,630 infantry, 1,314 cavalry and 552 gunners with eighteen guns against Kock's 1,000 men, supported by only three 75mms. They were occupying a slight ridge south of the station. Hamilton's plan was for the Devons to attack it frontally, while the Gordons and Manchesters, with the dismounted Imperial Light Horse, worked round Kock's left flank. The attack was launched at 3.30 p.m. under the shadow of an approaching thunderstorm. and met with volleys of rifle fire which brought all the battalions involved to a halt, until the arrival of the storm provided an opportunity for the Gordons, Manchesters and Imperial Light Horse, spurred on personally by Hamilton, to advance again and clear the crest of the ridge. Now it was the turn of the cavalry, but not before a counter-attack, led personally by Kock, had thrown back some of the Gordons and the Imperial Light Horse, who, in their turn, charged forward again, while the Boers withdrew. As they rode away, French's 400 cavalry charged and charged again, inflicting heavy casualties. Kock himself was among the 60 dead. British casualties were 50 killed and 213 wounded.

James Macqueen was a civilian transport contractor, called in to reinforce White's transport. He was sent up to Elandslaagte to help collect the wounded, and described the battle in his diary:

21st.

Reported enemy is at Elandslaagte. Apaher has gone out there. Went out there in afternoon: it is 17 miles from Ladysmith; got there 4.30 p.m., found Natal Mounted Rifles, who with Natal Volunteer Artillery were on left flank, guarding Railway; an engagement has proceeded all day, but of a desultory character, – only our Volunteer Artillery were on the scene at first, and enemy's artillery overmatched them. At 4.30 p.m. the fight is proceeding on flat, 1 mile to right of station. The enemy are falling back on Kopjes in front of station, and gain that position a little before sundown, – the position is strong & commands a sweep of the entire country to the front – Our artillery doing good practice, and infantry now moving to attack Kopjes, they are half battalion Gordons, half battalion Devons, 2 companies Manchesters & the Imp'l Light Horse. Our crowd have taken up positions at station on left front of Kopjes. The fighting is most determined, it is getting dusk & our artillery ceased firing. The enemy is making stubborn resistance & our troops under a withering fire; – they fire volleys in return. Darkness is creeping on & we can not discern much; for some 3 minutes a terrible fire was sustained by enemy & then all is still. Our infantry have charged position and gained it; then we hear cheers, and can faintly see a part of enemy

clearing off on left side, but the 5th Lancers are stationed near by: –
some of enemy galloped off near us, & we gave chase, but were
stopped. It is pitch dark now – We are all ordered to guard station,
– presently a loud cheer is heard to our left, – this is the 5th Lancers
returning from the chase, but we were not certain. I stood to arms.
At 9 p.m. volunteers were called for to go & seek the wounded. I
went as one, leaving my horse at Station. It is a miserable drizzling
night, a faint moon flickering giving a ghastly light to the grim
occasion. In gaining the Kopjes we find small clusters of our men
with prisoners & wounded, also bearer parties with lamps are spread
over the field looking for wounded; saw a few dead Boers, also Boer
Red Cross people. The Demon of Avarice was also at work, looting
the baggage wagons & horses, mules, rifles etc. I touched nothing,
but loathed the brutes who began looting, instead of looking after
wounded. I returned to Station at midnight, and got order to start
for Ladysmith as it was feared Boers of Free State Commando might
intercept us.

Although Kock's commando had been thoroughly trounced, the
presence of Joubert's main force immediately north of Dundee prevented
White from sending Yule either supplies or reinforcements. Troops to
provide the latter could in any case not be spared, as a new threat to
Ladysmith had developed in the advance of Free State forces under
General Prinsloo down the railway from Harrismith and the Klip River
valley. Joubert was methodically closing in on Yule, while bombarding
Dundee with a 'Long Tom', a Creusot 155mm gun firing a 94lb shell,
taken from one of the Pretoria forts. After some hesitation, Yule accepted
the advice of his subordinates to seek White's permission to withdraw
by the only route open, southwards in the direction of Helpmakar.
White agreed and Yule's dispirited brigade set off during the night of 22
October, marching by night and resting by day. Joubert made no attempt
to pursue them, and, hungry, weary, sodden with rain and caked with
mud, they reached Ladysmith on the 26th, bringing White's numbers
there up to 13,000, supplies for which were arriving by every train from
Durban.

Before this, on 24 October, White had tried to prevent a junction
between Prinsloo's force and Joubert's by inflicting a defeat on the
former before the latter could arrive and possibly interfere with the
return of Yule's brigade. White himself commanded the force, which

consisted of the Gloucesters, Devons and Liverpools, with half of the 2nd 60th Rifles, the 5th Lancers with a squadron of the 5th Dragoon Guards protecting their right flank. He intended to occupy some hills out to the north west, but the Boers got there first and the attempt failed at a cost of 12 killed and 102 wounded, the commanding officer of the Gloucesters, Lieutenant-Colonel E. P. Wilford, being among those killed. In spite of this failure, White pinned his hopes on dealing Joubert what he called 'a knock-down blow'. He rejected a withdrawal to the Tugela, although by then it might not have been opposed by the Governor of Natal, Sir Walter Hely-Hutchinson, who had become concerned that so few troops remained south of the river to cover the capital, Maritzburg, which could be threatened if Joubert by-passed White at Ladysmith.

On the day after Yule's men reached Ladysmith, Joubert's leading elements were reported as being only four miles east of the town and others were closing in from the north. White gave Hamilton permission to attack the latter, but changed his mind at the last minute. Two days later, when the water supply had been cut off, White decided to employ both his brigades to attack Pepworth Hill, four miles to the north-east of the town, on the west side of the railway from Elandslaagte. Joubert's vanguard had occupied it and appeared to be building a platform for a Long Tom. White's plan was for 8th Brigade, now commanded by Colonel Geoffrey Grimwood, with 1st Leicesters, 2nd Dublin Fusiliers, 1st and 2nd 60th Rifles and 1st Liverpools, to make a night approach march round to the eastern flank and attack at dawn on 30 October from that direction, while Hamilton's 7th Brigade (Gordons, Devons and Manchesters) created a diversion by advancing directly against Pepworth Hill, which it was then to attack. Artillery support was provided by the 15-pounders of 1st Brigade Royal Field Artillery, reinforced by the recent arrival of a naval gun detachment of four 12-pounders and two 4.7in guns, commanded by Lieutenant the Hon. Hedworth Lambton. The cavalry would then sweep round the eastern flank and drive the fleeing Boers up against a column which White sent on another night march round the western flank to Nicholson's Nek, five miles away. This consisted of Lieutenant-Colonel F. R. C. Carleton's Royal Irish Fusiliers and the Gloucesters with a battery of mule-carried mountain guns, but no cavalry. Lieutenant-Colonel Sir Henry Rawlinson of the Coldstream Guards, who was serving as a Deputy Assistant

Adjutant General (DAAG) on White's staff,* had argued against the force going out so far, but was overruled.

The result of the whole operation was a disaster. The Boers had moved to new positions east of the railway and attacked Grimwood's vulnerable right flank as he launched his men against empty defences, driving them into a panic retreat, which also infected French's cavalry. Carleton's force, without its artillery which had been scattered when its mules panicked under fire on the night march, was left isolated and forced to surrender. Rawlinson wrote in his diary:

> This has not been a successful day. As a matter of fact we were so greatly outnumbered that it would have been impossible for us to hope for success in the open field against a mounted and tactically very mobile force. But we have any way made the attempt and induced the boer to shew his numbers and guns. His artillery is really surprisingly good. Now we shall have to sit down in Ladysmith and stand an investment and bombardment, which is very unpleasant and tantalyzing though not dangerous. . . . Really Ladysmith is one of the most indefensible localities I ever came across. It is like the bottom of a tea cup with one side broken out and a large basin outside the tea cup.

Captain Christopher Balfour of the 60th Rifles arrived in Ladysmith on 30 October, having landed at Durban the previous day. In a letter to his mother in the form of a diary, he describes the day:

> On arrival hear that a big battle is to come off, the attack is to begin at 5 a.m. Pitch dark and no one to tell me where my regiment was. Wandered about with 2 other men and eventually found Head-quarters Officer. Met C. in C. (Sir G. White) just starting. Saw one of his staff who gave me a cup of tea and told me I couldn't possibly get to my regiment which had left the evening before at 9.30 to take up position and attack Boers at dawn. Told me to join our baggage train. After a good deal of wandering eventually found it under the command of Birch (The Queen's) attached to us also Douane our Quarter-master. Went with them into the town (I found them in Ladysmith Camp). Heard the first shot at 5.15 when a shell from their 40-pounder burst near the station. Left the baggage and went

---

* The General Staff had not yet been formed. All staff officers on headquarters were considered to be members of the Adjutant-General's Department.

with Douane to a hill at the N. end of the town and watched our gunners shelling the enemy. No one could tell me where the Rgt was so I couldn't join them. Went back into the town to find if any news. None. Went up again alone to see if I could find the Battn. Joined them when they got near and found they were our 2 battns and 2 other Rgts. Their retreat was covered by the Artillery who behaved splendidly. The news they gave me was as follows. They were ordered to take up a position before dawn. They got there after a very tiring march of 6 hours. The Boers must have got information for at dawn they found Boers in position on three different Kopjes with artillery in position, they held on from dawn at 5 till 12 noon under terrible fire and shell fire and then when the hill on their right was deserted by the Leicesters (they got orders) they found they were enfiladed and likely to be cut off. Gen. Hunter, Chief of Staff, then ordered a retirement. Our losses, 1 officer killed, poor Forster who only arrived 2 days before, 1 wounded, Major Riddell, 9 men killed, 14 wounded, and 40 missing who are all probably wounded or dead in the hands of the Boers. 1st Battn 2 officers killed, Major Meyers, 2nd-Lt Marsden, 1 wounded, Lt Johnson. I don't know how many men. This makes 16 officers 1st Battn hors de combat in a fortnight's fighting. It's awful. This is the account of the right brigade. The left apparently walked into a trap. We can get no definite news but they were caught and surrounded in a defile. Most of them have straggled back chiefly without arms. What is true can't tell but disaster in some form. We are in a very tight place and expect to be in a state of siege directly but thank God got up two 6″ guns [*sic*] from the 'Powerful' who ought to keep their heavy guns in check. Expect to hear any day that the railway has been cut. Enemy moving round both our flanks. We must hang on and wait for the Army Corps which ought to have been here months ago, a wicked waste of life has consequently ensued. There are thousands of Boers round who have every modern weapon, officered by foreigners. The accounts of escapes are marvellous. Every one well and keen but frightfully done up from overwork and want of sleep. Our men actually slept when holding position and had to be kicked awake to make them fire. The last of the Battn was in 7.30 p.m. nearly 24 hours on the march or fighting having lost the Maxim and 1st Reserve ammunition mules.

After this setback, it would still have been possible for White to have withdrawn to the Tugela, although it would have meant abandoning or destroying a great pile of stores; but he was too depressed to make such a bold and harsh decision. He did nothing, and three days later, on 2 November, the railway and telegraph line to the south were cut. Rawlinson's comment was:

> I can't say I was altogether sorry for the constant flux of telegrams of all sorts and descriptions combined with the long cipher messages that had to be coded and decoded gave me very little time for real military work and no time at all for sleep. Sir George has been very much worried lately. The loss of the Royal Irish Fusiliers and Gloucestershire Regiment weighed on him very much.

In spite of this pressure, Rawlinson found time, a few hours before the lines were cut, to go up in the observation balloon. He describes the experience in his diary:

> I went up in the Baloon [sic] 1600 feet. Beautiful view of the whole surrounding country weather quite still and clear. Didn't feel a bit sea sick but inclined to hold on very tight. The Boers seem to be scattered all over the country not in great numbers anywhere. Joubert's camp is visible on the left of Pepworth hill and about ½ a mile further back – difficult to spot guns from the Baloon as it rocks about so and keeps revolving round so much that one cannot keep ones glasses steady. I spotted a large Bivouac on the bank of the Klip river near Smith's crossing – on this side of a hill near the top. On my way down one of the guns from Bulwana hill put a shell through the baloon at about 8000 yards – it was a wonderful shot but must have been rather a fluke. Did not hurt baloon much made clean hole bang through it – It came down rather faster after it was hit but did not bump me on the ground – I kept the shell to make an ink pot of when I get home.

Colonel Frank Rhodes, brother of Cecil, had once served in the Royal Dragoons, been a war correspondent at Omdurman, and was a participant in the Jameson Raid. He, with Jameson himself and another ex-Raider, Sir John Willoughby, had made their way to Ladysmith, expecting to join a victorious army on its way to Pretoria. They now found themselves besieged in Ladysmith, where Rhodes gave some help to White's intelligence staff, as well as providing his friends with

local volunteers, the commanding officer of the Loyals, Lieutenant-Colonel R. G. Kekewich, having been appointed garrison commander, which did not prevent Rhodes from acting as if he was responsible. On 5 November Rhodes sent a message to Milner saying: 'If you do not advance at once from Orange River you will lose Kimberley'. Milner's fears of an Afrikaner uprising in Cape Colony were revived and his first demand to Buller was to clear the Boers out of the colony, including Kimberley.

When Buller had sailed from Southampton, he had assumed that White would be holding Natal and that his own corps of 47,000 men would assemble in Cape Colony before advancing up the railway to Bloemfontein and on to Pretoria, where Kruger and Steyn, their capitals occupied and their forces defeated, would have to accept his terms. Logistics alone dictated that such an advance could not begin until January at the earliest. Meanwhile the situation in Natal was critical. White had supplies to last him for two months, but there were only two battalions south of the Tugela and, unless they were reinforced, Joubert, by-passing Ladysmith, might even reach Durban. Buller reluctantly decided that he must split his corps. Lieutenant-General Sir Francis Clery's 2nd Division, the first due to arrive, would be diverted to Durban, while Lieutenant-General Lord Methuen's 1st, Lieutenant-General Sir William Gatacre's 3rd and French's Cavalry Division would disembark at the Cape as planned. Methuen would move to De Aar and advance from there to relieve Kimberley; Gatacre, based at Naauwpoort on his right, would secure the two railway lines leading to Port Elizabeth and East London, and French would act as a general reserve for the Cape, while Buller himself went to Natal to direct operations leading to the relief of Ladysmith. He left for Durban on 22 November.

On 9 November Joubert had held a council of war outside Ladysmith. He offered three choices: to attack Ladysmith, to divide his forces between besieging Ladysmith and defending the Tugela against a relieving force, or to drive south in the hope of reaching Durban before reinforcements could arrive. Although he was depressed by his casualties – over 600 – and was having difficulty in keeping his men from returning home, he was inclined towards the last, which was strongly urged by the young Louis Botha, who had replaced Meyer, but was opposed by Prinsloo, who said his men would not participate in it. Botha had his way, although the force which crossed the river at Colenso numbered only 1,500 Transvaalers and 500 Free Staters. By the evening of 14 November they had reached Chievely, twenty miles north of Estcourt, which was held by most of the 2,300 British soldiers left in Natal. Joubert intended to by-pass it, which he and Botha did, making a wide detour on both flanks after capturing an armoured train on which Winston Churchill, acting as a war correspondent for the *Morning Post*, was travelling. The first of Clery's troops started disembarking at Durban on 12 November, and by the 22nd, when Joubert's force had concentrated again at Willow Grange, ten miles south of Estcourt, the leading brigade, commanded by Major-General Henry Hildyard, had reached that area, the second being some twenty miles behind. Hildyard attacked in a thunderstorm, suffering 86 casualties and inflicting few. Botha wanted to press on, but Joubert, who had been injured when thrown from his horse, refused, and on 25 November the Boers set off back to prepare defences on the Tugela at Colenso, driving 2,000 looted horses and cattle with them, Botha taking Joubert's place.

Away to the west Lord Methuen had moved 8,000 men of his division up to Orange River Station, the bridge which took the railway over the river to Kimberley, seventy miles beyond. They consisted of the Guards and the 9th Brigades, the Highland Brigade being left behind to guard his long lines of communication six hundred miles back to Cape Town across the desolate Great Karoo. His artillery consisted of sixteen 15-pounders. Although he had some good infantry, he was short of three things, transport, mounted troops and intelligence. He had only 190 of the 367 mule wagons he had been promised, which limited the extent to which he could move away from the railway. He had fewer than 1,000 mounted troops, only the 9th Lancers, some locally raised mounted infantry and Major Rimington's 'Tigers', a force of 200 colonial 'guides' on whom he was largely dependent for intelligence. There was little of that, partly because Rimington's scouts were easily picked off in the open country by the Boers' Mauser rifles. Besieging Kimberley and facing Methuen were some 8,000 Boers, commanded by the Transvaaler General Piet Cronje, whom Prinsloo, back from Natal, had now joined. They included 700 Transvaalers under Koos De la Rey and were supported by six or seven Krupp 75mm guns and four 1-pounder Maxims, colloquially known as pom-poms. Methuen's troops crossed the Orange River bridge on 21 November and met the first Boer position at Belmont, twenty miles beyond, two days later, manned by Prinsloo's men. Methuen

attacked with both brigades, one of which, the Guards, contrary to
Methuen's intention, found itself making a frontal attack which resulted
in nearly 300 casualties. The Boers, having themselves suffered 150,
withdrew without interference to their next position, twenty miles on, at
Graspan, where, on 25 November, the pattern was repeated.

Two days later, Methuen approached the Modder River, about ten
miles beyond which he believed the Boers to have withdrawn to the
Spytfontein kopjes, halfway between the river and Kimberley. Methuen
planned to make a twenty-five-mile march in a wide arc to the east to
outflank them there; but mounted patrols reported that some of the
enemy, perhaps as many as 4,000 (it was actually 3,000), were digging in
on the far bank of the Riet River and the Modder which joined it just
above the bridges, which had been blown. Methuen thought the numbers
exaggerated, but nevertheless decided that it was unwise to start the
march away from the railway before this force had been dealt with. He
therefore prepared a frontal attack astride the railway: to the east of it,
Major-General Sir Henry Colvile's Guards Brigade against Cronje's
positions on the south bank of the Riet above its confluence with the
Modder, and, to the west of it, Major-General Reginald Pole-Carew's 9th
Brigade against De la Rey's positions on both banks of the Riet and,
further west, against Prinsloo's men at Rosmead's Drift. All sixteen 15-
pounders were in support, as well as four naval 12-pounders. Cronje's
guns did not cover Prinsloo's position. At 4.45 a.m. on 28 November the
infantry advanced. Had Cronje's men held their fire until the Guardsmen
were close to the river, as they had been ordered to, the result might
have been devastating, but they opened up when, at about 7 a.m., the
leading troops were 1,000 yards away, with the result that the Guardsmen
went to ground and lay there for hour after hour, unprotected in the
open, suffering severely from Cronje's guns, a hail of Mauser rifle fire,
thirst and sunburn, unable to make their way forward. Meanwhile
Methuen's artillery pounded away at the Boer trenches.

On the other side of the railway, however, Pole-Carew's men, having
also been pinned down for several hours, were on the move. On the left
they were out of range of Cronje's guns, while Prinsloo's men were
subjected to constant artillery fire. Soon after eleven o'clock those
companies of the Loyals that Kekewich had not taken with him to
Kimberley led the 1st Argyll and Sutherland Highlanders in driving
Prinsloo's men back across the river at Rosmead's Drift. They then began

to advance eastwards along the north bank towards De la Rey. The latter drove them back to the Drift, as Pole-Carew's artillery fired shrapnel over them by mistake. But as this long battle died down at the end of the day, Cronje's men east of the railway had had enough and withdrew from the Riet and across the Modder as well, leaving in the lurch De la Rey, himself lightly wounded and his son dying. They had suffered only 80 casualties to the British 460, which included Methuen himself, slightly wounded in the thigh, and his chief of staff, Colonel Northcote, dying. As the moon rose, the rest of the 9th Brigade crossed to join their comrades, followed by the Guards. Lieutenant E. Longueville was regimental transport officer of the 1st Coldstream and described his experience in the battle in his diary:

Nov. 28th.

I was woke up at 4 am by hearing them loading the waggon over my head. On making enquiries I found that it had been decided that we should march to Modder for breakfast; so got up and we had some coffee biscuit and jam. We marched off at 5.15 am and went about three miles. On coming over a rise we could see the line of the river marked by trees, but there was a lot of mirage. Suddenly firing began in front and they stopped the transport. I rode on to the Field Hospital and sat down to watch. From there I could see the Scots Guards and the 1st Bn Coldstream going up the reservoir on the right. I went on a bit further and found our ammunition carts with sergeant major Wright; he said that the carts could go no further and that he wanted some men to carry up the ammunition by hand. I galloped back to the transport (dropping and losing my glasses on the way), and brought up all the spare men. When I got back I found the carts had moved away. Some cavalry were dismounted close by so I went and asked them if they had seen the carts; but they knew nothing about them. At this moment a segment shell arrived and the cavalry galloped off. I went on a bit further; but as I had'nt [*sic*] the faintest notion where the Battalion was, and could see no sign of them I took the men back. We waited all afternoon getting different orders every few minutes: nobody knew where anybody was, or what they were doing. At last Warner who was D.A.A.G. (B), settled (heaven knows why) to take all the food wagons to the left of the line, and off we went. They shot at us a bit when we started; but luckily it got dark almost directly, and we got to the lower ford without mishap. Here we found a mixed lot of men of all corps, and Warner finding that instead of the whole Brigade being there, there were only some 40 or 50, went off and I did not see him again. I was told that there were some more of our men over the river, so I got across the wall guided by sergeants Plackett and Edwards. It was pitch dark and about three inches of water running over the top of the wall, I didn't half like it for I did not know that there was only a six foot drop – it looked like a precipice – on one side, and that the river was quite shallow on the other. When I got over I found Gen. Pole Carew and Newtown Butler with about 600 men of all sorts. I gave them my reserve rations and finding an old boat on the river I punted back and with great trouble took over a load of bread and oat, assisted by sergeant Barter, brigade clerk, who turned up from I don't know where. It was a most perilous voyage, we nearly upset several times and were almost carried over the wall. Then we ran aground and I made Barter get out and walk and push.

Lieutenant Harry Pryce-Jones was also with the 1st Coldstream and described his experiences in a letter to his mother, dated from Modder River Railway Station on 1 December:

On Tuesday [28 November] we started at 4 a.m. and met the enemy at 6.30 at Modder River, they were heavily entrenched, in a very strong position, about 5000, we fought from 6.30 a.m. till dark about 7 p.m., the enemy still being in the village, but we decided to capture the place the next morning early, but when we paraded at 3 a.m. we found the enemy had fled. I personally had a rough day of it, as I swam the river twice with Col. Codrington & a few others to find we were cut off & the Boers were on us, so we swam back, I absolutely ruined all I had on me, including watch, camera & glasses, 2 of my company were nearly drowned. We had to haul them out, so you will probably see it in the papers – after that (about 11 a.m.) we attacked the village & got within 500 yds, when we ran short of men and ammunition & so could not advance. I can assure you the Bullets were swarming round us, our escape was extraordinary as we (my company) only had 9 wounded – when we retired, I found myself in command of about 150 men, who I took to a fort where the Scots Guards were & there we spent the most miserable night imaginable, having had nothing to eat since dinner the night before: we were only dressed in Khaki, so we were icy cold – we paraded at 3 a.m. &

finding the enemy gone, we had breakfast, how I ate!!! we then proceeded to hunt for dead & wounded, who kept on pouring in until 4.30, when we marched through this village (which was absolutely riddled with Bullets) & found that we had to go on outpost for the night. It rained hard, so we spent another night without sleep, however yesterday we settled down here & had a most ripping wash & brush up & eat like wild beasts. Our Battalion has been marvellously lucky, as you will see by the papers. It was impossible to wire to you though I knew you would be anxious. Poor Col. Stopford & Earl (2nd Batt) were killed, the former by a shell & the latter shot at 1700 yds – Hill (Scots Gds) was at Vaughans with me & I am afraid he'll lose his arm & heaps of others I know are wounded. The Boers must have lost heavily, we have about 60 wounded here, & about 200 dead horses, they put about 150 into the river, hoping to poison it we suppose – yesterday 400 cigarettes arrived from Bert, oh! How delighted I was, please tell him I am *more* than grateful. I gave 100 to Follett, who offered me £2 for them, but of course I refused, so you may imagine that cigarettes are at a premium here – we are going to stay here for 7 days, & then continue to Kimberley, I'm afraid we have another big fight in front of us, we are all pretty sick of it, as it is killing work, the sun absolutely boiling all day and at night it is very cold. . . . . we are the luckiest, only having 1 officer wounded & about 20 men killed & 50 wounded so far but who knows what may be in store for us!! I have a lot of experiences, which I will tell you of when I return, but have never been in real danger, altho' bullets & shells have been *very* close – in fact too close to make you feel comfortable. The shells are the worst, they smother you in dust, if you are within 20 yds, & often kill or wound you within that distance, in fact the whole thing is just luck. Yesterday I looked at myself in the glass for 1st time for 10 days I was astonished at the others, but I simply roared at my appearance, I believe if I came to Dolerw, you would send me round to the Backdoor!! my face is all burnt & peeling & *very* grimy, & I have quite a beard, about which I get chaffed, as it is very long at the chin & cheeks, but there is a vacuum of hair about my jaws!!!

Captain W. L. Foster was on the staff of the Commander Royal Artillery of the 1st Division and described the battle from the gunner's point of view in his diary:

Nov. 28th.

How different a day to what we expected. Left camp at 4 a.m. with 2 Batteries artillery, 9th Lancers, M.I., N.S.W. Lancers (20 strong), North Lancashires & half battalion Northamptons & 1 Field Coy RE.

Before we had proceeded 2 miles from camp we heard that the enemy were strongly entrenched at Modder River with strong parties out on each flank; so word was immediately sent back to camp for the whole division to advance. I galoped [*sic*] on behind Col Hall & the General (Methuen) who went on to reconnoitre the position from about 2800x we saw the enemy standing outside the houses of the village looking at us. I was then sent back to bring on the 2 batteries of artillery, one battery started to shell the entrenchments at about 2800x & the 18th Batty was sent off to the right to shell a farm which the MI [Mounted Infantry] were trying to capture soon three of the enemy's guns galoped off to our right & opened fire. Both batteries immediately opened on them & from what I could see their Gunners deserted their guns & made off. The General at once sent me away to get a Squadron of Lancers & go for the guns. Hurrah said I, now 'I'm in for a nice little Cavalry charge.['] Unfortunately I had to go 3 miles to get a squadron as the Lancers were away on the extreme right & by the time I reached them the battle had so changed as to make the charge absolutely impracticable. So after telling the 9th Lancers the General's message I returned to the Col who told me that the General was across the River with 2 or 3 battalions away on the left flank & that the Boers were 'off'.

To my dismay tho' on return to the centre [?], we found the Guards' Brigade & 5th Brigade [he must have meant 9th] retreating under a perfect hail of bullets which also whizzed round us.

The two batteries came into action at 1700x for about 10 minutes but then as the infantry continued to come back the Colonel ordered the batteries to limber up & galop in 500x further. My own thought & I am pretty sure all of us were of the same opinion, was that none of us would ever leave that position unwounded for the bullets, shells & the small 1 lb shells from the automatic gun was simply awful. I went in with the 75th battery to whom I had taken the Colonel's order to advance, and the guns had scarcely been unlimbered before Major Lindsay, Capt. Farrell & two or three gunners were wounded in the 75th, also about 8 horses were shot & a driver was killed. Altho' the Infantry who were in the line with us were lying down & would not raise their heads even to fire, the Gunners of both batteries stuck magnificently to their guns & poured in shell after shell. Never again I hope shall I experience so many shells & bullets fizzing by me & the bullets seem to strike the ground all round me & beyond me. There the batteries stayed for about 4 hours. About two hours after this we heard the General Pole-Carew had got across the river, so the General ordered me to tell the 3rd Coldstreams who were in the firing line, in line with the batteries to move off to the left to reinforce the 9th Bde on the left. They got up & as the Boers began to pour in a tremendous fire instead of moving to our left they moved to the rear. The General then sent me to rally them & was wounded just after I left him, not severely tho'. The stragglers of two or three other regiments had joined them in the retreat and it was a good hour before we could prevail on them to move up again to the ford on the left. Till 7 pm I was continually taking messages from one part of the field to another, generally under fire & I found that if I did not galop hard the Boers always tried to pick me off. The 62nd battery luckily came up about two o'clock in response to a galoper that I had sent back to them to say that they were urgently required. They had marched 33 miles that day & had done the last 12 miles at a trot. This shows what Artillery will and can do. They immediately went into action & did a good service. At about 6.45 two batteries drew off under a very hot fire from the Boers, the 62nd still remaining in action to wait till dawn. For about an hour previous to this the three batteries had poured in a tremendous bombardment with a view to a bayonet attack by our infantry at dusk, but the latter were too done up to carry the attack out. A great pity as we should have captured 14 Boer guns & given them a good taste of cold steel. I was employed till about 9 p.m. trying to get the batteries their food & supplies, then the 18th Battery very kindly gave me something to eat & I lay down absolutely exhausted.

Never before in the history of the Regiment have the batteries done braver & more yeoman work. The advance into 1100x at a galop was nothing less than grand, & the way the batteries stayed there and plugged in shell after shell, while the infantry alongside would not raise their heads to fire, was magnificent. The long march of the 62nd is also worthy of the greatest admiration. Our casualties in all three Batteries was 5 men killed, & about 20 wounded, while about 80 horses were either killed or wounded. Four officers were wounded.

It was merely Providence that brought anybody out of the 18th & 75th from the close position, unwounded.

Cronje and De la Rey withdrew, not to the Spytfontein kopjes, but, at the latter's suggestion, to positions immediately in front of Magersfontein Hill, astride the railway six miles beyond the Modder. De la Rey thought that Methuen would expect them to occupy the high ground and that positions at the foot in front of it would take the British by surprise, as those on the south bank of the Riet had done. Prinsloo's unreliable Free Staters would be placed in the centre, where they could not easily reach their horses to get away. Cronje was reinforced by men who had been besieging Mafeking, bringing his strength up to 8,200, of whom 6,000 were mounted.

Methuen now brought up Major-General Andrew Wauchope's 3rd Highland Brigade, of which the four battalions were the 2nd Black Watch, 1st Argylls, 2nd Seaforth and 1st Highland Light Infantry, a total of 3,500 men. In spite of the urgency of relieving Kimberley, he thought that the Guards and 9th Brigades needed rest; that he needed fresh troops, and that he should not attempt a further advance until the bridges over the Modder had been repaired. Kekewich in Kimberley had signalled by searchlight that he had enough supplies to last forty days. By 8 December the bridges over the Riet and Modder had been repaired and Methuen planned that Wauchope's brigade should march towards Magersfontein during the night of the 10th and attack the Boers there at first light, after a bombardment delivered by twenty-four field guns, four naval 12-pounders and one naval 4.7in gun, the British answer to the Long Tom, known as Old Joey after Joseph Chamberlain.

As dawn was almost breaking on 11 December, Wauchope's leading troops, still marching in column, were only 1,000 yards from Magersfontein Hill and even closer to the forward Boer defences. His brigade-major, Major Benson, represented to him that it was time to deploy into open order. Wauchope, fearing that this might cause a loss of direction, refused. So they marched on until, at a range of only 400 yards, they met the withering fire of the Boer Mausers. After an initial panic, in which the commanding officers of the Black Watch and the Argylls were killed, some order was restored and the battalions regrouped and deployed, but were pinned down. As at the Modder, they lay there for hours in the open, scorched by the sun, as the guns behind them blazed away and Methuen sent up the Royal Engineer Captain Harry Jones in his captive balloon to see where Cronje's defences lay. Jones spotted a gap to the east of Magersfontein Hill, but, before Methuen could direct any troops there, it had been filled by Cronje's mounted infantry. Instead, he sent the Guards to the right of the Highlanders to face the Boers manning defences between this gap and the Modder, but they made no attempt to attack them. The 9th Brigade was held back to secure the area round the Modder bridges.

Early in the afternoon the commanding officers of the Seaforth (Lieutenant-Colonel James Hughes-Hallett) and of the Gordons (Lieutenant-Colonel George Downman) found that some Boers were trying to work their way round their flanks and ordered a readjustment of their positions to meet this threat. But the Highlanders had had enough, and the readjustment turned into a rout which infected the whole brigade, in the course of which many casualties were added to those already suffered. The tally was 902, to the Boers' 236, and included Wauchope himself, found dead only 200 yards from the Boer defences.

Private Fred Bly of the 2nd Seaforth Highlanders described his experiences in his diary:

10 Dec 99.

At 2 pm we moved forward and almost as soon as we commenced to march it began to rain heavily and continued nearly all night. At 4 pm we got well in sight of the enemy position, and our artillery at once commenced shelling them and continued a heavy shrapnel [*sic*] fusilade until dark. During the whole of that time in which the Boers must have suffered severely they never replied with a single shot, in fact I began to think they had left their position. About 7.30 we anchored down for the night, H Coy being put out as 'picket' about 200 yds in front of the regiment. What a horrible night. Wet through to the skin and 1 Blanket between 2 men shivering with cold & the rain coming down in *torrents*. One can guess what it *must* have been like. At midnight the Highland Brigade moved forward to within 700 yards of the enemy, but without troubling to let poor old H Coy of the S.H. know anything about it. So until about 4 a.m. we laid still. Just as day was dawning the silence was broken by rifle fire from the enemy who opened a murderous fire from the Hill straight in front of us. Just at that moment a mounted officer rode up and told my Captain (Clark) that the Brigade had gone on & we were to join them. The Captain gave us the order and we moved forward. In a few minutes the bullets began to 'Whiz' around us so thickly that we had to lay down and take as much cover behind bushes &c as we could. The first man hit was Mr Millan and directly after that S. McLeod was killed. There were 4 of us laying behind a bush, when one of our Maxim Guns came up and opened fire quite close to us, which naturally drew heavy fire down on us. I was talking to old Dudley Miller when suddenly he shouts Oh 'I'm Hit' within a yard of me. This rather scattered our little party behind the bush leaving me and poor old Dud who was shot through the thigh. I pulled out his dressing & bound him up the best I could, and as there were no stretchers or Doctors about had to leave him and go on with the company. We advanced about 50 yards at a time by rushes then laying & keeping as much out of sight as possible. About 8 o'clock we were within 250 yds of the enemy's trenches and there were stuck for hours as we could not get any further as our artillery were firing over our heads and dropping the shells just in front of us. There we lay for hours, the Boers 'pinking' away at us, every time we moved or exposed ourselves in the least, every now and again hitting one of us. It was 'awful'. About 11 o'clock the Captain was killed, just after my poor old Chum Jeremy Jenkins was shot through the chest. A short time before he had asked me if I was alright. About one o'clock there was a lull in the firing & I had a look around and saw dozens of our poor chaps lying dead & wounded all round me moaning for water but I had none & was gasping for a drink myself. The enemy soon spotted me and sent a shower of bullets in my direction ploughing up the ground all around me, so I quickly lay down again, & stuck my nose in the sand. About 3 o'clock a large body of the enemy managed to get round our right Flank and opened a heavy fire so that we were between two fires. Then the fire from the hill in front got heavier until we were almost surrounded by a regular hail of bullets. I quite gave myself up, thinking it utterly impossible to escape much longer.

Presently some-one, God knows who it was, passed along the order to retire & our own troops got up and ran away. This was disastrous, for as we exposed ourselves the Boers dropped our fellows in dozens. We had to get through a wire fence, and in doing so several fellows got stuck in it including myself, and were shot down. Poor old Douglas was shot in the Spine & died shortly afterwards. I managed to get through after a struggle, and ran on. I remember saying to a fellow of the Blk Watch 'This is a fine affair chum'. He said 'Yes you're right' & gave a yell and fell over shot in the thigh. I did not like to leave him so I dressed his wound and got him on my back & carried [him] until I had to stop for a rest done up. However with the assistance of one or two more men at last got him to the Red Cross waggon where we found hundreds of others. Here I met Frank Bolton and was glad to hear he was alright. We were now out of rifle range of the enemy who now opened fire on us with shell. But our artillery kept playing on him not giving their guns much chance. After a while we managed to get the regiment together (or what was left of them) and the roll was called and we found more than half the officers and over 300 men of the regiment were killed wounded or missing. We next got some water and food and a lot of rum which livened us up a bit. We were then told we could lay down and go to sleep if we liked which I did notwithstanding the awful events of the day I slept very soundly on the bare ground.

Lieutenant Longueville's diary records his experiences on that day:

At 4.30 am we moved on a couple of miles and waited: just as it got light a tremendous fusillade began in front, this was the highland Brigade being surprised while deploying. The firing was tremendous and we wondered what on earth was going on. I rode on and had a look at things. It was quite a different country to what we had lately been in, long grass with mimosa trees scattered about. Some distance on I found a doctor dressing some wounded highlanders under a cart, from them I heard all about the disaster. I then went back to the transport. The Gordon highlanders were there and I was talking to some when they were ordered to advance. They went forward, and were also cut up, and we took the mules back to the river to water. When we returned I went forward again to see if anything was wanted. I went up a slight rise to where G Battery R.H.A. was in action, and found the Colonel, Steele, Campbell and a mixed lot of men, most of the battalion being extended just in front; there seemed to be a bit of a lull in the battle. The guns were fired every few minutes (they fired 1153 rounds from that battery that day), and the boers occasionally replied. At this point we were about level with the corner of the hill, the boer trenches being thrown back, and I could see the boers moving about in their trenches quite distinctly under the kopje; but in front there was rising ground and too many bushes to see anything. Steele had a touch of sun and was very seedy. While I was there a man came in and reported Winchester's death. Everyone was very hungry and thirsty I helped to keep order at the water cart for a bit and then went back to the waggons. Grindel was seedy so I sent him back. We decided to put each battalion's rations on a separate waggon and try to get them up to them. To do this we drew the waggons up on a nice grassy spot and began to take out the mules and sort things. Just as we were in full swing bang came a shell knocking over two highlanders who were standing by and hitting the Colonel's old mare which I was looking after in the hind fetlock. This was immediately followed by another so a retirement to a safer place was ordered, and those waggons inspanned and galloped off as I have never seen waggons gallop before or since. My waggon being more or less ready by this time I stopped it in the bush and then turned back to go up to where the head quarters of the battalion were with the guns. I got along all right until I came to a large open space where I found the Lancers laying out bivouac with their lances stuck in the ground to mark their lines. Just as I reached them two shells pitched amongst them, so they jumped on their horses and galloped off; one officer leaving his sword behind which I picked up and afterwards returned. I made the men jump on top of the waggon and ordered them to turn it round and gallop, as we were getting the shells which had been prepared for the cavalry. But a buckwaggon with ten mules is an unwieldy vehicle, and in turning we must needs stick on an antheap. I talked loud and long to the nigger drivers and the odd soldiers I had with me jumped down; between us we pushed the wheel over the beastly antheap and then went off like blue blazes! We were none too soon as they put a shell into the antheap before we had gone 200 yards. I saw that it was useless to try to get a waggon up by daylight so I waited until it got dark when I took up what was wanted and brought back Winchester's body. I slept for a few hours half way to Modder, as I went straight back to bury him with Stopford, as we thought we should probably go on next morning. It was a fearfully cold night as a cutting wind sprang up. One had to walk about to keep warm, as of course we had no blankets. I got into Modder River at daylight, routed out a parson –

Hill – and made the cooks dig a grave. While they were digging the parson and I had some food. When we had finished I hurried back to the battlefield fully expecting that we should go on; but I found a retirement had been ordered and we returned unmolested to our old camp. The Grenadiers covered the retirement.

Harry Pryce-Jones wrote an account of the battle to his mother on 13 December:

Well! here I am with a whole skin after going through our fourth & worst fight. I will give you an account as best I can. We left here [Modder River] on Sunday night at 6.0 p.m. where it was pouring with rain, & marched across the river about 2 miles where we tried to sleep until 12.30 when we paraded & marched off, of course it began to rain & we were drenched, we lost our way as it was pitch dark, but eventually at 4.15 a.m. we heard the first shot about ½ mile away, so we halted for further orders. The firing continued hard for ½ hour, then turned out to be the Highland Brigade, who marched within 200 yds of enemy's trenches in quarter column. No one knows why! With the result that they lost 800! & 53 Officers, as you must know by the time you get this letter. Poor Gen Wauchope was shot in two places & killed, also 3 Colonels & 1 Second in command – Well! we proceeded to form up. I was in the firing line, we advanced in extended order, meeting these wretched Highlanders, quite disorganized, in 2s & 3s without helmets or rifles – Suddenly we were fired at & a shell burst among the company on my right, wounding poor Follett in the stomach, he was taken away on a stretcher, & seemed very cheerful; as he waved to me in passing – we never moved from that position all day until it was dark, except I had to get some ammunition & distribute it, we were sniped at every time we moved, but we were marvellously lucky, only losing 7 men, one man was shot twice through the helmet, another had his rifle smashed to bits – Col Codrington was wounded twenty yards behind me & remained with my company all day, he was very slightly touched – Sterling, next company on my right was wounded twice, & Lambton next company to Sterling was wounded in knee at 7 a.m. & was left there until 1 p.m. the next day, as there were no stretcher bearers & he could not be found, Beckwith, too, was the next company to me on my left – he was wounded in arm & thigh.

The enemy slackened their fire from 5–6 p.m. but when it got dark, they suddenly began, they simply poured shots into us & we returned the fire, of course we could see exactly where they were from the flashes, but they were in trenches & we were simply lying in the open. I really gave up all hopes & only prayed that I should be finished off without pain. We were ordered to cease fire & retire, had the enemy advanced we *must* have been annihilated, as they were 800 opposite our 100 & only about 300 yards away. Well! we retired with No 3 Beckwith's company & marched about 3 miles to the Field hospital, where we spent the most awful night, no water or anything & it was bitterly cold, sleep was out of the question – at 3 a.m. we paraded & found 2 more of our companies – by degrees we collected ourselves & at 12 p.m. we marched here, forming the rear guard of the guns & cavalry who were firing all the morning. We got back here at 5 p.m. & are now quite comfortable.

Captain Foster described the battle in a letter to a friend on 18 December:

Last Monday week's fighting was too awful for anything & I shall never forget the sight of the Highland Brigade after their terrible slaughter. As they came streaming back into our guns, they were no longer men, they had no nerves, did not know where they were – We tried to rally them, all the Monday, but it was no good & some of the sights & things that happened people in England I am glad to say do not know of. Some day, if I come back alive, I will tell you all about it. One regiment the Black Watch came back with 6 officers left out of 29 & the Seaforths had 10 officers killed & 8 wounded. I attended the funeral of the Highland Brigade officers, & all these regiments were utterly unnerved. How I came out of the Modder River battle alive, I don't know. I expected every minute to be stretched out as the bullets & shells were whistling all round me for 12 hours. I don't like the bullets & shells a bit but I believe nobody else does – If you are standing still doing nothing, you keep on thinking where you are going to be hit. We had 12 horses killed the other day & it was simply marvellous how the enemy's shells burst right in the middle of the battery & yet sometimes hit nothing. The life is precious hard. For over a fortnight we slept in the open every night, with one blanket only, & some nights were very cold. I find an ordinary saddle makes an excellent pillow, but the ground is awfully hard. During the Modder fight I had to get a gun across the river, very hard work as we had to wade about 3 ft 6 in & the river is nothing but rocks.

Methuen hoped that, as they had done at Belmont, Graspan and the Modder, the Boers would withdraw to lick their wounds, but, when Captain Jones rose in his balloon next morning, he reported that they were still there.

Every morning in Kimberley Lieutenant-Colonel Kekewich climbed to the top of the 155 foot high tower of scaffolding erected on top of the main diamond mine, from which he could see as far as the north side of the Spytfontein kopjes and Magersfontein Hill, in the hope of detecting signs of Methuen's approach. Since the town had been surrounded on 14 October and the Boer demand for surrender rejected, it had suffered no attack, only occasional bombardment by field guns. Kekewich knew nothing about plans for relief until, on 23 November, a message from Methuen arrived by African runner which, when decoded, read: 'General leaves here [Orange River Station] with strong force on November 21st and will arrive Kimberley on 26th, unless delayed at Modder River. Look for signals by searchlight.' Feeling that he ought to take some action to distract the Boers as Methuen approached, he asked Major H. Scott-Turner, a 'Special Officer' like Baden-Powell, in command of his 800 mounted troops, to attack Carter's Ridge to the south-east of the town, from which one of the Boer guns fired. This they did at dawn on 25 November, causing 28 Boer casualties and taking 32 prisoners at a cost of 7 of their own men killed and 25 wounded, but did not succeed in taking a gun. A repeat performance on the 28th proved a disaster. The ridge had been reinforced and Scott-Turner's force lost 24 killed, including himself, and 32 wounded. Every day therefore Kekewich climbed to the top of his tower and looked anxiously through his binoculars for signs of a Boer retreat and Methuen's advance, but the events of 11 December at Magersfontein determined that he looked in vain.

*

On that day, in Natal, Buller decided on his plan to evict Botha from the positions he had occupied astride the demolished rail bridge over the Tugela at Colenso. He had difficulty in making it, as he had only a vague idea of where the Boer defences were and how many men manned them. Attempts at reconnaissance forward of Frere, ten miles south of the river, had been driven back by Boer mounted patrols. At Frere he had 19,000 men in four infantry brigades and two regiments of cavalry with some locally raised mounted troops. Buller therefore decided on a wide outflanking move to the west to cross the river at Potgieter's Drift, some fifteen miles upstream of Colenso. He informed White by heliograph that he had chosen that route, although it was a longer way round which might not benefit from White's offer to send a mounted column out as far as Onderbrook, ten miles north of Colenso, to draw off the Boers facing Buller. However, a day after making this decision, Buller received bad news from the Cape: not only that of Methuen's failure at Magersfontein, but also that Gatacre had suffered a severe loss, about 600 men missing and captured, at Stormberg, where a column on a night march to recapture the railway junction had lost its way. Colonel R. E. Allen of the East Yorkshire Regiment was Gatacre's AAG and gave an account of this action in his diary for 10 December:

> First shot fired by Boers from the top of the hill at 3.45 am, the 7th Royal Irish Rifles who lead [*sic*] the column of route at once rushed forward half going to the left from which there was no fire and siezing a Kopje half to the right to the main position but it was too steep – The 2 batteries came forward & endeavoured to come into action one gun came to grief in a ditch & had to be abandoned all the team was shot. Mounted infantry came forward & endeavoured to get round the boer right flank. our infantry made no progress & had nothing to shoot at. Soon the Northumberland Fusiliers & some of the Irish Rifles retired rapidly across the open to a position some ½ mile in rear & on this ridge the guns took up their position & came into action – A retreat was then decided upon & covered by the Mounted Infantry & the two batteries – We reached Molteno about 11 am losing another gun stuck in a ravine quicksand – the infantry were simply dead beat before they came into action, had not a kick in them – I think a large number of the R.I. Rifles & N. [Northumberland] Fusiliers simply laid down where they first rushed to & remained there till taken prisoners – They were up at 4 am in the train at 1 pm & marched 16 miles or so all night – exhausted men cannot fight.

Second Lieutenant John Preston was with the Royal Scots in the same brigade, but his battalion did not take part in the operation. He gave an account of it in a letter to his uncle on 18 December:

On the same date [9 December] General Gatacre took the North-umberland Fusiliers, Irish Rifles, two field batteries, & some of the Cape Rifles, to Molteno in order to make a night attack on Storm-berg, where he lost 672 killed, wounded & prisoners also two guns. His reasons for failing were these (1) He had not reconnoitred the direction he was going to march in properly previous to his attack (2) His guides lost their way & he had to march 16 miles from Molteno instead of 7 (3) He had no patrols or scouts out in advance of his column, his troops were marching in fours unaware of the proximity of the enemy when they were attacked (4) That his attack did not come as a surprise it is said that a Boer Commando watched him leave Molteno (5) His troops were exhausted. On Saturday morning they got up at 3.30 A.M. & had a field day in the early morning & at midday they had to wait 3 hours at the station before they were able to entrain when they got to Molteno they had to march 15 miles before they reached the enemy, they had no food since Saturday morning. (6) The attack instead of taking place at 11-o-clock at night took place at about 4 A.M. (7) The excellent cover the Boers had, no one saw more than three or four Boers. Since then we have been reinforced by another battery & the Derbyshire regi-ment. Our losses lately have been very heavy owing chiefly to our bad scouting.*

Milner was calling for reinforcement, and in the light of this bad news Buller decided that he could not take the risks entailed in being separated from his railway line of communication by the distance (and therefore the time) which his plan to move by Potgieter's Drift involved. He was in any case short of transport and would have to leave one of his brigades at Chievely to guard his railhead base. If, while he was away to the west, Botha left his defences at Colenso and cut him off from his base, he might finish up like White. He therefore decided to opt for a straightforward frontal attack on Colenso and helioed White accordingly. He did not rate his chances of success highly. Although in a cable to Lansdowne on 15 December, he signalled, 'Today I am advancing to the attack and trying to force the direct road. I fully expect to be successful but probably at heavy cost', in a dispatch sent to the War Office the day

* John Preston was to die of enteric fever on 27 June 1900.

before, he wrote, 'From my point of view, it will be better to lose Ladysmith altogether than to throw open Natal to the enemy'.

On the evening of 14 December he gave out his orders to put this into effect. The principal problem was how to get across the river. The only 'drifts' believed to be fordable at the time were the Old Wagon Drift, half a mile upstream of the demolished railway bridge at Colenso and just downstream of the iron road bridge which was still intact, the Bridle Drift four miles further upstream, a mile west of where the river made a loop to the north-west, and Robinson's Drift, a further three miles upstream. Botha's 4,500 men occupied defences covering these, dug in close to the northern bank: the Free Staters and the Middlesburg and Johannesburg Commandos opposite Robinson's Drift; the Ermelo Commando opposite the Bridle, the Zoutpansberg and Swaziland Commandos covering the loop, in which, unknown to Buller, there were two drifts, one at the north-western point and one on the eastern side; the Heidelberg, Vryheid and Krugersdorp Commandos in the main positions at Colenso and the hills behind; and the Wakkerstroom and Standerton Commandos on the hill of Hlangwane, four and a half miles east of Colenso and south of the river. On 13 December, when Buller's attack appeared imminent, the garrison of the hill, found by the Zoutpansberg and Boksburg Commandos, declared it untenable and left it; but a stern telegram from Kruger himself resulted in these two commandos being chosen by lot to reoccupy it.

Buller's plan was for the Royal Dragoons, commanded by Lieutenant-Colonel John Burn-Murdoch, to cover the left flank, while Colonel Lord Dundonald's 3rd Mounted Brigade, with the 13th Hussars, several squadrons of locally raised Light Horse, two regiments of Mounted Infantry, Bethune's and Thorneycroft's, the Mounted Infantry Company of 2nd King's Royal Rifle Corps, and one battery of field artillery protected the right and, if possible, occupied Hlangwane. Hildyard's 2nd Brigade was to make the main attack on the Wagon Drift and Major-General Fitzroy Hart's 5th (Irish) Brigade the Bridle. The other two brigades would be held in reserve, Major-General Neville Lyttelton's 4th between Hart and Hildyard and Major-General Geoffrey Barton's 6th (Fusilier) Brigade east of the road and railway between Hildyard and Dundonald. Colonel Charles Long's artillery was to open the battle with a preliminary bombardment by twelve 15-pounders and four naval 12-pounders, backed up by two longer-range naval 4.7-inch guns, all under

Long supporting Hildyard. Lieutenant-Colonel L. W. Parsons, with two batteries of 15-pounders, supported Hart.

The leading brigades advanced at dawn on 15 December, but Long was determined to get his guns into action as far forward as possible and went ahead of Hildyard and sited his two batteries just east of Colenso Station, only 1,000 yards from the Boer positions north of the river, the six naval guns under Lieutenant F. C. A. Ogilvy behind him. On the left, Hart led his brigade (2nd Dublin Fusiliers, 1st Inniskillings, 1st Connaught Rangers and 1st Borders) towards Bridle Drift, marching, like Wauchope's at Magersfontein, in close order. His operation was to be fatally flawed by an inaccurate map and what was probably a misunderstanding by the African guide, accompanied by an interpreter, who was supposed to be showing him the way to the Bridle Drift. Hart's orders were 'to cross the river at the Bridle Drift immediately west of the junction of the Doornkop Spruit and the Tugela' and after that to advance east towards Colenso, clearing the north bank of the river. Unfortunately the map showed the Doornkop Spruit as joining the Tugela at the western base of the loop and the Bridle Drift as being close to its junction with the river, and also another loop west of that, which did not in fact exist. The spruit actually joined the river at the eastern base of the loop and the Bridle Drift was a mile west of the small donga on the southern bank of the river at the western base of the loop. Hart's northward advance took his brigade, correctly, across the Spruit from east to west, but when, at about 6.15 a.m., having been warned by the Royal Dragoons that the river was strongly defended, he approached the southern bank between the Bridle Drift and the western base of the loop, his guide protested that this was not leading to the drift, perhaps because he came from a kraal at the point of the loop where there was a drift. Hart, realizing that the map was inaccurate, accepted his advice and, leaving one battalion to line the river bank, redirected the others to the right and into the loop. By that time they were under Boer artillery fire, and soon under rifle fire also from both sides of the thousand-yard-wide loop. Hart himself was bravely trying to get men whose units had become jumbled up together in the confined space up from the ground to fight their way forward to the drift at the head of the loop.

Meanwhile Parsons's guns, sited to cover Bridle Drift, were out of range of the Boer guns firing onto the loop and could give Hart only limited support. Buller saw all this from his field headquarters on 'Naval

Gun' Hill, two miles south of Colenso village, and sent one galloper after another to Hart to tell him to extricate his troops from the loop. He was even more concerned when he saw where Long had sited his guns, which were soon under intense enemy fire before Hildyard had even started his approach to Colenso village. It was not long before they ceased firing, those crews not killed or wounded taking refuge in a nearby donga. The naval guns had come into action half a mile behind, out of range of Boer rifle fire, when the African drivers of the oxen which pulled them panicked. Buller rode over to try and sort things out and met two gunner officers, who told him that all twelve 15-pounders were out of action; that their crews had fought to the last man and round and were all killed or wounded (which was not true) and that the naval guns were also out of action (which was not true either). Buller rode on to see Hildyard and decided that the whole action had to be called off. Even if Hildyard could get across the river without artillery support, he would be in a precarious position, Hart having failed to cross upstream and turn the flank of Botha's strong positions on the far side. If, by trying to press on in these circumstances, committing the other two brigades as well, he suffered further casualties, he might not just fail to relieve Ladysmith, but seriously prejudice the defence of Natal. He therefore limited further action to telling Lyttelton to help extricate Hart and getting Hildyard, helped by Barton, to try and recover Long's guns and rescue the surviving crews.

It was still only 8 a.m. when Buller made this decision. He rode on to a large donga behind the gun positions, while Hildyard pushed two battalions, the Queen's and the Devons, forward into Colenso village, from which they might attempt a rescue. Buller was himself hit in the side and badly bruised by a bullet. As he exhorted some of Barton's infantry to go forward to recover the guns and a corporal and six men volunteered, he turned to his personal staff and said: 'Some of you go and help.' Three did so, Captain H. N. Schofield, an ADC, Captain Walter Congreve, the Press Censor, and Lieutenant Frederick Roberts, son of the Field Marshal, who had been on his way to join White. Schofield and the corporal succeeded in bringing two guns back, but Congreve and Roberts were wounded, the latter dying later that day, being posthumously awarded the Victoria Cross, which was also awarded to Congreve.* When further

---

* These were two of the three occasions on which father and son were awarded the

attempts to bring the guns in only led to more casualties, Buller called off the attempt to do so from that direction. Further attempts to rescue them by Hildyard's infantry from Colenso village were also called off, and Clery decided that he could not leave the two battalions there by themselves during the night in order to try again under cover of darkness. Later in the afternoon some Boers came across the river to the small donga where the crews were sheltering and allowed the stretcher bearers to remove the wounded, who included Long and several other officers. The commanding officer of the Devons and those of his men who had reached the donga from Colenso were marched off into captivity. With Lyttelton's help, Hart's battered brigade was extricated from the loop in mid-afternoon.

Captain Henry Warre of the 3rd 60th Rifles described the action in a letter to his father, the Reverend E. C. Warre, who, having been a master and chaplain at Eton, was Honorary Colonel of the 4th (Eton College) Volunteer Battalion of the Oxfordshire Light Infantry:

> I feel almost too depressed to give you an account of our doings but I know you will like a report & one's personal experience. Friday's battle may be called a Reconnaissance in force or anything else you like but as it was carried out there are two words which I think will express it better viz. 'Severe Check' & I expect I shall be right in thinking that at home it will be thought so too. To begin with for 2 days before the fight our big guns did a little shelling but on the Thursday only a few Boers were driven out & I fancy it was thought that a great many had trekked – so much for the intelligence – (Another point on this matter – there have been hardly any officer patrols (cav) down towards Tugela). I was warned for outlying Pic't Thursday & went in at 6 pm. Orders came about 8 to parade 2 next morn & were altered to 3 am. The Bge [Brigade] in Reserve & to be near the guns. We moved out and shortly after 4 am & getting close up to the Naval guns by dawn in Q'er [Quarter] Column. The first gun fired at 5.30 am by my watch & apparently the searching the trenches with gun fire was not thought necessary as the Inf'ry attack began 6.30 am, Hart's Irish B'ge to go across the river on our left & Hilyard's [sic] B'ge to make a frontal show towards Colenso Bridge. About 6.30 shells came into us so we opened into extended to single

---

Cross, Roberts's father having gained it in the Indian Mutiny in 1858 and Congreve's son winning it in France in 1916.

rank at Col'n distance. About this time Long in command of the
Artillery moved his battery into a position which really caused the
trouble. Without any ground scouts he galloped up to within easy
rifle range of shelter trenches & a small covert & their horses were
knocked over & men mown down on coming into action. The guns
were left & the limbers were taken out of action, the men flogging
and spurring their horses with shells bursting just behind them.
About 7 am ½ our B'ge (1st RB & Durham L.I.) went down to
support Hart's B'ge on left. This B'ge had as far as we c'ld learn
moved in *Q'r Column without any scouts out* & got within 1000 yds
of the trenches. Here they were caught both with gun & rifle fire but
extending continued to move towards the river: the rifle fire was
incessant & it is said the Dub Fus [sic] fired 240 rounds a man
(McGrigor says this is wrong but they averaged 76 per man through
the B'ge). I dont think they ever really got across the river in any
force. On the right of all Barton's B'ge formed for attack & the cav'y
or most of it was there. Hilyard's B'ge was now told to go on to what
seemed a suicidal attack & the only reason anyone can think of is
that they were wanted to try & drown the fire of the enemy in order
that an attempt to extricate the guns could be made. We moved out
to the right & advanced down towards the place our left resting on
the rail'y & the Scottish Rifles on our left – Before we got into rifle
fire the retirement was made & we lost no men & were out of one of
the worst shows possible. It was before we advanced that poor Freddy
Roberts* Congreve RB & Schofield RA made their most gallant
attempt to save the guns. I did not actually see it myself but I heard
that they rode on with the teams & were met by a most murderous
fire. It is said that a shell burst under Freddy's pony. He was hit 3
times & the most wonderful thing Schofield got off & saved two guns
out of the 10 [sic]. The Boers came out and took Congreve but let
him go as he was badly hit & I suppose Freddy was unconscious &
they paid no attention. Anyhow he was not in Hosp'l till late in the
evening & must have been lying out in a very hot sun all day. We
covered retirement of Hilyard's & Barton's Brigade & many came
through us knocked about. Retirement it [sic] was carried out
magnificently the men coming back sullenly & with no hurry – at
one time viz during the retirement of naval guns to a back position

---

* Also an officer of the 60th Rifles.

the shells came pretty quick but only 2 or 3 of them burst & they didn't matter tho' I cannot say I prefer them to rifle fire although the latter is much more dangerous. As for the Boer shooting, I fancy it must be wild in the extreme as the roar of their rifle fire was terrific. On the naval guns opening again they didn't fire much & we got back to camp about 3.30 in a miserable state. The losses I have heard put to 1098, & a Boer next day said they lost 800 men. I couldn't sleep that night thinking over everything & of poor Freddy but I had to be up for Picquet at 2.15 am & was on all day until relieved at 8.30 in the evening; but to return. I got away from my Picquet about 4 am & went to the Hosp'l close at hand to see Freddy – I found him on the train in a terrible state & I am afraid in pain. I had heard he was to be recommended for V.C., but couldn't say so as it was a report but a thing like that would have cheered him. His pluck was extraordinary & he said Good bye warrior we'll meet again soon. I must say I thought he was dying at the time, it was terrible. I cld'nt take his hand but just caught hold of his elbow & I think he moved it as an acknowledgment as he cldn't speak at the moment. The doctor practically gave me no hope. I cannot say how sorry I am for Ld Roberts & Lady Roberts & his sisters, it must be a horrible blow.

Another participant in the battle was Captain H. F. N. Jourdain of the 1st Connaught Rangers in Hart's Brigade. In his diary for 15 December he wrote:

Got up 2.30 am and packed waggons at 2.45 am. Got breakfast of tea and dry biscuit at 3 am. Fell in 3.40. Marched on the Brigade parade at 4.5. Marched off B'gde parade at 4.20 down towards the Tugela River. While we were marching in Mass of Quarter Columns, The Brigadier (Maj-Gen Fitzroy Hart CB) in front, then the 2nd Royal Dublin Fusiliers, 1st Connaught Rangers, then the Border Regt, and lastly the 1st Inniskilling Fusiliers. At 4.50 a shell fell about 20 ft from the leading coy of the Dublin Fusiliers. We were ordered to deploy at once the Border Regt to the right, & our Regt & the Inniskilling Fusiliers to the left. This we did as soon as possible, but the guns of the enemy were on us & shell after shell fell near us. The Dublin Fusiliers then advanced in extended order to the River Bank & we came behind them. The Dublin Fusiliers then moved to our right & we had the bank to ourselves with the Inniskilling Fusiliers on our left. The fire at this point became very heavy, & man after man fell down, & was carried out. The first man Inbrady of E Coy, who was shot in the foot, unlaced his boot, put a bandage on the ankle, & ran on to join the firing line. After over an hour of sitting still and being shelled & fired on, without being able to reply, we moved in file under a heavy fire to the right, and came into the fire aimed at our maxim. We then lay down for a time. This was about 10.30 am. A staff officer at this point ordered us to retire, which I did. I had then about 25 men of my regiment, & one or two others. We had to cross nearly ¾ of a mile of open country, with a perpetual rain of shells & bullets. We reached a partial cover & joined Capt Robertson's details which he had collected. We were told by Col. B. H. Hamilton to hold this position, which we did for nearly an hour. Numbers of men were struck here. A tree close by drew the fire of the enemy upon ourselves. [Under/near] this tree a good many men of the Inniskilling Fusiliers & Border Regt collected but were scattered by the shells of the Boers. The Colonel* was hit in the lungs & had one finger shot thro'. While Major Barton was tending him, he was struck the second time. A man named Livingstone of my coy while carrying the Col was struck in the neck, but refused to drop the Col. Pte Caughlin, servant to Pomeroy, was badly hit in five places in the thigh, in the legs, shoulder & arm, we were ordered to retire from this position towards the drift in the stream. We did this exposed to a heavy shell fire & reached the river† & lined the bank. We were ordered to retire but Sarsfield refused to do so. We stayed by the river about half an hour. After the Rifle Brigade & other details had retired through us, we crossed the drift, this was about 12.35. We got over & retired leisurely still exposed to shell & rifle fire, but not suffering much casualties . . .

We then marched back to camp, which we reached about 2.40 extremely done up, dirty, thirsty & tired. Here Molony had some tea on the brew, & I demolished many cups . . . The men pitched their tents & lay down to rest. I was much struck by the manner in which my coy proceeded to pitch our tent before any of theirs. A man of my Coy, Cox by name, gave me some water, when I was very thirsty, before he had had a drink himself. There were numerous instances of great pluck, Cowey was very fine carrying messages in the middle

---

* Lieutenant-Colonel J. G. Brooke.
† Probably the Doornspruit stream, not the River Tugela.

of a terrible fire – I walked with one man shot thro' the leg, who talked quite cheerfully with me. I saw one man walk into camp with bullet wounds thro' both legs. There was a man who had part of his hand shot off, who was carrying a rifle, and went along quite gaily. When I was retiring with part of my Coy, I met our Colonel in great pain, he asked me how I was, and if I was still unhurt. One man of my Coy was shot through the Canteen on his back, one man had his rear brace pierced by a bullet, but did not enter his back. I saw one man had his back pierced by a bullet come to the medical officer next day & show him in a most casual way. One was shot thro' both legs, sat down & blazed off all his 150 rounds at the invisible enemy. The bullet wounds were very round & neat. Young Brooke of ours was shot thro' the chest, the knee & the arm. Two men of my Coy Leonard & Kennedy were sitting on either side of me at the first shelter, were both hit before they had gone 20 yards.

Buller's total casualties were 143 killed, 755 wounded, many of them not seriously, and 240 missing, mostly captured, only 5 per cent of the force. It was by no means a disaster, but it was, as Buller described it in his cable to Milner and the War Office, 'a serious reverse'. Unfortunately for him he also sent another personal cable to Lansdowne, in which he said: 'My failure today raises a serious question. I do not think I am now strong enough to relieve White. Colenso is a fortress, which, if not taken on a rush, could only be taken by a siege ... My view is that I ought to let Ladysmith go, and occupy good positions for the defence of South Natal, and let time help us.' In sending this, he had been influenced by a telegram from Lansdowne telling him that, as a result of Magersfontein, Lieutenant-General Sir Charles Warren, who was about to reach the Cape with his 5th Division, should replace Methuen. Buller mistakenly took it to mean that the 5th Division, which he had intended should come to Natal, would instead be held in Cape Colony. Announcement of his failure naturally spread gloom in Ladysmith. Rawlinson recorded:

Another telegram from Buller rather more lugubrious than the first – asking what we can suggest! Saying he cannot take Colenso but writing to say either what his losses are or what is happening in other parts of the country. Says he simply cannot march more than 10 miles a day in this weather and that he is short of water where he is

– altogether taking a very gloomy view of the situation and saying he may be able to advance again in three weeks time. This is all very pleasant reading for us!!!! If he cannot force the passage of the Tugela he had better give up the show and sue for terms for it's no good going on pretending to fight and then not attacking the enemy because you think he is too strong – This is no time to sit down and say 'I'm beat' or 'I can't' – the thing *must* be done at all costs or the blow not only to England but to the whole British Empire will be one from which she will not easily recover – get up big naval guns, set [sic] the Howitzers out bring all the heaviest artillery you can to bear on the Boer, and if absolutely necessary let the Basuto and Zulus slip or send for Gurkhas and [indecipherable] from India – Do anything in fact but don't sit down and say 'I can't' the word does not belong to the vocabulary of the true soldier.

The failure at Colenso, following on those of Methuen at Magersfontein and Gatacre at Stormberg, caused a sense of deep shock at home. In the near half-century that had passed since the Crimean War and the Indian Mutiny the British public had become accustomed to a string of easy victories over unsophisticated opponents, although not without the occasional setback. Few songs had been more popular than G. W. Hunt's music hall ditty:

> We don't want to fight,
> But, by Jingo, if we do,
> We've got the ships,
> We've got the guns,
> We've got the money too.

But, in spite of all those, a collection of primitive farmers had defeated the cream of the British regular army, part of which was ignominiously shut up in Ladysmith; and all this just as everyone was getting ready to celebrate the last Christmas of the nineteenth and the first New Year of the twentieth century. Lord Salisbury's government was shaken and Lansdowne was sparked into uncharacteristically vigorous action. Ever since the crisis arose, Field Marshal Lord Roberts, the sixty-seven-year-old hero of the 1880 march from Kabul to Kandahar, had been pestering Lansdowne that he, rather than Buller, a favourite of his great rival Wolseley, should be sent to South Africa; and, when Buller was sent, that he should replace him. On his return from India in 1893, he had been mortified when Wolseley was chosen to succeed the Duke of Cambridge as Commander-in-Chief at the Horse Guards and at being fobbed off with a peerage and the rank of field marshal to compensate for being shunted off to the command in Ireland, from where he constantly expressed his criticism of Wolseley's reforms. On 8 December he had sent a letter to Lansdowne, which began:

I am much concerned to hear of the very gloomy view which Sir Redvers Buller takes of the situation in South Africa. There is, of course, no disguising the fact that we are engaged in a very serious war – one that may task our resources to the utmost, and the manner in which the difficulties, inherent in such a war, can be overcome depends almost entirely on the confidence of the Commander in being able to bring it to a successful conclusion.

As I have, I think, often remarked to you, it is impossible to gauge a General's qualities until he has been tried, and it is a regrettable fact that not a single commander in South Africa has ever had an independent command in the field. It is the feeling of responsibility which weighs down most men, and it seems clear, unless I am much mistaken, that this feeling is having its too frequent effect on Buller. He seems to me overwhelmed by the magnitude of the task imposed upon him, and I confess that the tone of some of his telegrams causes me considerable alarm. From the day he landed in Cape Town he seemed to take a pessimistic view of the position, and when a commander allows himself to entertain evil forebodings, the effect is inevitably felt throughout the Army.

I feel the greatest possible hesitation and dislike to expressing my opinion thus plainly, and nothing but the gravity of the situation and the strongest sense of duty would induce me to do so, or to offer, as I now do, to place my services and experience at the disposal of the Government.

The difficulty of making this offer is greatly increased by the fact that, if it is accepted, I must necessarily be placed in supreme command, and to those who do not know me I may lay myself open to misconception. But the country cannot afford to run any avoidable risk of failure. A serious reverse in South Africa would endanger the Empire. I might not be able to avert it, but experience of command in war ought to help to this end. Already there are signs of the rebellion being on the increase, and, unless this can soon be checked, it will scarcely be possible to prevent its spreading to the surrounding Native States.

Lansdowne politely rejected this offer; but when news of Magersfontein and Colenso reached London he quickly changed his mind. Going behind the backs of Wolseley and the eighty-year-old Queen Victoria, who also favoured Buller, Lansdowne, in collusion with Arthur Balfour (who was deputy to his uncle the Prime Minister, Lord Salisbury), persuaded the latter to appoint Roberts to command the forces in South Africa, Buller remaining in Natal as his subordinate. Salisbury agreed on condition that he took with him as chief of staff the forty-nine-year-old Major-General Lord Kitchener, who had so effectively organized the campaign to avenge Gordon in the Sudan, culminating in his victory the previous year at Omdurman, where he still was. On 16 December Lansdowne summoned Roberts to the War Office, where he had to break the news to him of his son's death at Colenso. Buller received the news with grim resignation. By appointing these two popular heroes, the Salisbury administration hoped to escape most of the criticism caused by what rapidly became known as 'Black Week'.

On his return to Dublin that day, Roberts telegraphed to Lansdowne his proposed plan of campaign. Methuen should withdraw to the Orange River, abandoning attempts to relieve Kimberley and Mafeking. Ladysmith should 'be approached by a turning movement. There should be no more direct attacks. All our efforts should be devoted to massing troops in Cape Colony so as to enable us to enter the enemy's country in proper strength.' On the day he sailed from Southampton in the *Dunottar Castle*, 23 December, Roberts sent a cable to Buller, based on the agreement he had by then reached with Lansdowne and Balfour. In it he stressed the importance of the original plan. He assumed that Buller, having been reinforced with Warren's 5th Division, would be holding an 'entrenched camp' at Chievely, and would use the rest of his force to

turn the enemy's strong position on the Tugela. If that succeeds, I imagine it would be desirable to evacuate Ladysmith and hold the line of the Tugela. In same way, if Methuen relieves Kimberley, he should fall back to the Orange River. A certain amount of food, arms and a very small increase in the garrison would make Kimberley thoroughly secure.

All available force should then be concentrated for the advance to Bloemfontein. One of the problems Roberts had to deal with before he left was pressure from the Duke of Connaught that he should be employed in South Africa. Roberts pointed out that there was no command post available suited to his rank and royal station, and that that of chief of staff had already been filled by Kitchener, who joined him at Gibraltar. The government also took immediate steps to raise more troops. On 16 December orders were issued to mobilize a 7th Division and four more artillery brigades, the former embarking between 3 and 18 January 1900, the latter between the 21st and 27th; and, once Roberts had approved, an additional cavalry brigade was mobilized and was embarked between 8 and 17 February. On 19 January the mobilization of an 8th Division was ordered and it embarked between 12 March and 18 April.

This exhausted the supply of regular troops in the United Kingdom, the defence of which was now left entirely in the hands of 'auxiliary' forces. Fortunately there was no direct threat to the country at that time and Ireland was quiet. The government now turned to these forces as a further source of troops for South Africa. Thirty-five Militia battalions asked to volunteer and all but four did so: three of those were Irish and the fourth was composed almost entirely of Highland Scottish fishermen, who feared for their livelihood. Legislation was also introduced to allow men from the Yeomanry and Volunteers to serve. Each Yeomanry regiment was encouraged to form a company of volunteers, these companies being brought together to form battalions of the Imperial Yeomanry and infantry battalions to form Volunteer companies. There was an immediate response, and by 27 January 10,731 volunteers for the Imperial Yeomanry had been enrolled: the final total reached 35,500. In addition private individuals were encouraged to raise volunteer units, the Lord Mayor of London raising the City of London Imperial Volunteers, consisting of two companies of mounted infantry, an infantry battalion and a four-gun artillery battery, and also the City of London Yeomanry (Roughriders). Lord Lovat contributed his Scouts and Lord Strathcona raised a regiment of horse. The Earl of Dunraven raised a battalion of 'Sharpshooters' which became the 18th Battalion of the Imperial Yeomanry, succeeded by the 21st and 23rd Battalions, their members, on return from South Africa, forming the 3rd County of London Yeomanry. Similar volunteer units were raised in the colonies,

Australia contributing 16,378 men, Canada 7,289 and New Zealand 6,416. This was in addition to the 52,414 raised in South Africa itself. It was expected that these volunteers would serve principally as mounted infantry rather than as traditional cavalry. Many did so, but as mounted infantry units were raised by other means, many of the Yeomanry units served as normal cavalry. When the nature of the war changed after the capture of Pretoria in June 1900, many infantry units either formed their own mounted companies, as some had done since the beginning of the war, or were converted into complete battalions of mounted infantry, as were the 5-in howitzer batteries of the Royal Field Artillery. But few of these reinforcements had reached Lord Roberts when he set off from Cape Colony to relieve Kimberley at the beginning of February 1900. On the 4th of that month he reported to Lansdowne that 'the effective strength of fighting men in Cape Colony, exclusive of seven militia battalions and the garrisons of Mafeking and Kimberley, was 51,900' and that in Natal it was '34,830, of whom 9,780 were in Ladysmith'. In terms of fighting men, he still did not have a significant numerical superiority over his opponents, and they enjoyed a qualitative superiority in several respects.

3

BOBS TO THE RESCUE

January 1900

Kruger's immediate response to the victories of 'Black Week' was to urge Cronje and Botha to take the offensive and cut off Methuen and Buller from their rail lines of communication before reinforcements could arrive; but both protested that they were not strong enough to do so in the open country in which both the British forces lay. Kruger had to face the possibility of a long drawn out war of attrition, to which the industrial resources of the Transvaal, perhaps with some foreign help, could make a valuable contribution. Meanwhile the isolated British garrisons of Mafeking, Kimberley and Ladysmith could be dealt with, although, if they were eliminated, Roberts would not have to make efforts to relieve them and could concentrate on a direct advance to Bloemfontein and Pretoria. The decision was made to deliver the first blow against Ladysmith, which was under sporadic bombardment by two of their Long Toms.

Morale there had suffered a severe blow when news of Buller's failure at Colenso reached the garrison. Rawlinson was not too worried about the garrison's ability to deal with an infantry attack, but was concerned that if the Boers were not under pressure on the Tugela they would transfer guns to reinforce the artillery of the besieging force; but he was more concerned at the state of health of the soldiers, as he wrote in his diary on 16 December:

> I do fear enteric. It may so reduce our forces that there will not be enough sound men to man the defences and there is sure to be trouble over Intembi camp, which the Boers will try and force us to withdraw. We *must* refuse or we shall be frightfully hampered with the sick, women, civilians &c. As it is I reckon we shall have at least 1000 more sick by the middle of January.

When Ladysmith was first surrounded, Joubert had offered to hand over 98 wounded men who had been taken prisoner at Dundee, but White had at first refused to accept them, saying that they should be treated as *hors de combat* and allowed to go down the railway to Maritzburg, as should any women and children who wished to go. Joubert refused, but agreed that all wounded and sick from Ladysmith could be treated at a hospital which White had established at Intembi on the railway four miles south of the centre of the town, where it was two miles outside the British defences and immediately below the Boer positions on Mount Bulwana. That arrangement continued throughout the siege, the only occasion when there was any threat of it being interfered with being when there was an argument about sick returning to duty within the garrison. That was settled and they were allowed to do so. That Rawlinson's fears were justified is shown by the sick state of 19 December (see pages 58–9).

Rawlinson also recorded his reaction to Buller's message:

> It is not encouraging for a beleaguered garrison who have already been shut up here in Ladysmith for nearly 7 weeks. It implies that he cannot relieve us and must wait for the siege train which will take a full month to come out. Well! I suppose we can 'stick' it all right if he will keep some of the enemy employed meanwhile on the Tugela but if he lets the whole lot come back on the top of us we shall have a tough fight to hold our own.
>
> After all we can only fight to the last and when food and ammunition are finished we must surrender but it ought not to come to this till Feby unless enteric & horse sickness decimate our ranks. I think I would get rid of the Cavalry somehow or other; the only thing against is 'Can we spare the men?'. I am a little doubtful of this.
>
> Sir George has replied to Buller saying that our information points to the Boers having withdrawn from Colenso and that we can easily hold out for another month as far as provisions go but that we might be overwhelmed with Arty if the enemy were permitted to withdraw their guns from Colenso.

Before this, there had been both military and civilian criticism of Sir George White's passive strategy. He appeared to be content to sit and do nothing until the garrison could be relieved, calculating that there was enough food to last until the end of January, perhaps longer. Rawlinson deplored the lack of any offensive spirit, and had managed to persuade White to take some offensive action to distract the Boers from Buller's attack, but it was limited to raids on the guns threatening Ladysmith. In the early hours of 8 December 600 men of the Imperial Light Horse and Natal Carbineers successfully attacked a Long Tom and a 4.5in howitzer on Gun Hill, two miles east of the defences, blowing up both guns and removing the breech-blocks and sights. An attack by the 2nd Rifle Brigade on a 4.5in howitzer to the north-west three days later was less successful. The gun was blown up, but the Boers intercepted the raiding party, which lost 9 killed and 52 wounded fighting its way back. Sergeant Alfred Rumbold of the battalion gives his account of the action:

Dec 10th.

The Boers were exceedingly quiet yesterday, but we gave them another surprise to-night, also a taste of the bayonet for the first time. About 10.15 p.m. five companies of the 2nd Rifle Brigade left camp 420 strong to take or destroy a big gun two and a half miles out, and commanding one of the strongest positions in the enemy's lines, called Surprise Hill. It is exceedingly steep and on account of its great height overlooks the whole of our camp. The Boer gunners on this hill have been having some fine fun lately, making things very warm indeed for us. So we go out anticipating great sport, although it is the least bit of sport some of the poor bounders get in this world. We reach the Railway about 800 yards away from Surprise Hill at about 11 p.m. The moon is up, so we wait two hours for it to get quite dark. When everything is ready, at a whispered word we move off, leaving one company on the line for reserve. We get to the foot of the hill without any noise whatever, leaving one company here as supports. The remainder start crawling up the Hill like a phantom army. We get about thirty yards from the sentry and turn two companies outwards. These lay down keeping perfectly still, Whilst the other company rushed for the gun. The Boer sentry challenged, pulled a string which rang a bell and fired his rifle at us. The Colonel shouted 'Fix Swords' [bayonets] at the top of his voice. The sentry was instantly run through. Then over the parapets we go, right into the sleeping Boers. Then the sport commenced, everyone went under that got in our way and I may say that if there was anything approaching the inferno it was that night on Surprise Hill. Then we lay down and fired into the Boer position, and waited for

Daily Return of Sick of Troops on Active Service in NATAL, Dated 19th December 1899 at Ladysmith

		Commissioned Officers – Strength									Warrant & NC Officers & Men – Strength								
		Remained last Return	Admitted into Hospital	Transferred from other hospitals	Died In Hospital	Died Out of Hospital	To Duty	Otherwise	Transferred to other Hospitals	Remaining in Hospital	Remained last Return	Admitted into Hospital	Transferred from other hospitals	Died In Hospital	Died Out of Hospital	To Duty	Otherwise	Transferred to other Hospitals	Remaining in Hospital
I. General Diseases	Small Pox										202	12		4		4			210
	Other Eruptive Fevers		1							1	21	1				8			18
	Enteric Fever	5								5	189	26		3		1			202
	Other continued Fevers										7	6				1			6
B	Cholera										2								2
C	Dysentery										3								2
D	Malarial Fevers																		
	Erysipelas																		
	Syphilis																		
	Gonorrhœa										26	4				4			20
	Other Diseases	1							1		6								6
	Parasitic Diseases										1								1
	Scurvy																		
	Debility	3								2	10					2			10
	Rheumatism	1					1			1	13					2			8
	Other Diseases	2								2	1								4
II. Local Diseases	Diseases of Nervous System										20					2			1
	Diseases of Circulatory System																		19
	Diseases of Respiratory System																		
	Diarrhœa																		
	Other Diseases of Digestive System																		
	Diseases of Urinary System																		
	Other Local Diseases																		

III.

IV — Injuries General—
Sunstroke
Exhaustion
Other General Injuries
Injuries, Local
" in Action

Poisons

Not yet diagnosed ... 7 | 3 | 10 | 27 | 15 | 3 | 1 | 21 | 14 203 | 265

Total ... 46 | 4 | 49 | 960 | 99 | 7 | 39 | 21 | 992

N.B. — This form is equally applicable for Returns by Medical Officers in charge of hospitals and by Principal Medical Officers.

Remarks:

Cases of Enteric Fever Remaining

5th Dgn Guards	5	1 Leicestershire	2	2 Diffle Bde.	18	Natal Mtd Vol.	5
5th Lancers	9	2nd Gloster	2	1 Gloster	6	Carbineers	30
18th Hussars	4	Roy. Engineers	4	1 K.R.R. Corps	6	Mounted Rifle	7
19th "	41	1 Royal Fus:	1	P.A. Hospl "	1	Border "	18
21st Batt R.F.A.	6	1 Liverpool Bg.t	14	1 Sod Q	3		
53rd " "	1	1 Devon "	2	1 Light Horse	9		
				1st Ind Fus:	3	Regularcy	7
						Total	202

The sick report for the garrison of Ladysmith, on 19 December 1899, the forty-eighth day of the siege. Ladysmith was finally relieved on 28 February 1900.

the Engineers to blow the gun up. They were rather a long time about it as the gun failed to go off at the first charge causing us a lot of delay. They eventually succeeded, and we took different parts of the gun and started retiring, with not a man hit. But whilst we had been waiting the Boers had got round us with the intention of cutting us off. Then the sport commenced again. With our bayonets fixed we went through them, and a very rough time of it they had; likewise ourselves, for we cut through and through them suffering heavily. We got through the first lot all right, then we came across about another forty, in a donga. I fancy we killed every one of these. We eventually reached the railway leaving sixty killed and wounded on the hill. Taking everything into consideration, I think we had a most delightful night. We make a glorious name for ourselves, and I for one, should have been very sorry to have missed it. The following morning I was watching through my glasses the Boers and our wounded lying side by side, when one of the Medical Officers, who had been attending the wounded started to leave the Boer lines, with the white flag, and the red cross on his arm. The Boers started firing on him from all directions as he was crossing an open space, ignoring the white flag. He was under terrible fire for about three minutes, then he reached our lines in safety, thanks to the crack shooting of the Boers. Some few minutes afterwards the same officer returned to the wounded with stretcher bearers. The Battalion gets a splendid letter from the Brigadier, also one from Sir George White, V.C. congratulating us on our splendid feat of arms.

A picture of what life in Ladysmith was like for civilians was given by W. H. Gilbert, an army schoolmaster, who wrote a diary in the form of letters to his mother:

19th Dec.

The last 2 days have been terribly hot, so much so that yesterday the thermometer was 105° in the shade. Fancy working & writing as I have been! By the way we have had bad news. An official announcement states that Genl Buller has failed to make good his attack on Colenso, & therefore we will not be relieved for some time. This news puts one in the 'dumps' for I don't mind saying I'm about sick of this siege. It's getting monotonous in the extreme. Yesterday morning the Boers did the greatest damage to the Volunteers by a chance shell. While they were cleaning their horses a shell burst, killing 5 of the men & 11 animals. The troop belonged to Dundee, all lads, one of the men being only 16 yrs old. To make things sadder in his particular case, his father is away out here in Fugitive's' Camp, so that the presence of even a parent while he was dying was in vain, for of course the Boers allow none to come into the Town under penalty of being fired at. Again, as a funeral party was passing the Head Quarter Office, a shell burst, knocking the corpse off the carriage & wounding two of the followers. Horrible, isn't it? Our provisions are getting very scarce. Matches cannot now be bought in the shops, nor coffee, tobacco, jams, pickles & other necessaries. A tin of condensed milk went the other day for 10s 7d. Really, our Xmas dinner will be a poor one this time. I was down town yesterday morning & whilst in a shop espied some lemon peel which I pounced upon for a shilling's worth. I did enjoy eating it. Queer things one has to do now in the shape of living. I don't think I will ever again grumble at dry bread for tea, or complain if there's no milk in the jug. Another thing too, all my khaki uniform is worn out, & it's impossible to obtain any, as Tommy even has to wear patches. The stores are completely empty. Matches were yesterday 1s/6d a dozen if obtained anywhere.

22nd Dec.

The Boers are evidently beginning to use their guns properly. This morning at 7 while some of the men of the Gloster Regt were eating breakfast, a shell burst on one of the sangars with terrible results, killing 7 men & wounding 10 others. Those who witnessed it say it broke right in amongst them. All this afternoon shells shrapnel especially were flying. A huge fragment fell on the top of the office where I am working, which is about 100 yds from the Glo'ster camp. Luckily it bounced off. Right along in front of the road we could see the huge things exploding.

In his next letter he describes Christmas Day:

Well, this is how I spent Xmas Day.

Yesterday of course was a day of peace, & we calculated the Boers would say 'ditto' today, so imagine my surprise this morning about 5 to hear heavy musketry fire at one of the outposts. The beggars also flung a few shells. It quite upset our Church Parade. In the office we had about 200 papers printed with 'Hark the herald angels sing' & 'Come all ye faithful', for the service, but you see they were useless,

as it was highly dangerous to mass troops then. I was up at 6 a.m.
When I found out the state of affairs, I trotted off to the English
Church in the Town for the 8 o'clock Communion ceremony. It
would have done any one good to have had a view of the communi-
cants. There were generals, staff officers, & regimental ones represented beside the ordinary rank & file. But what touched me more
was to see six Kaffirs participate in the solemn rite. As you may guess
the function was very impressive, especially so, when the venerable
archdeacon, whose locks are white as snow, read those beautiful, &
to my mind, matchless prayers, for the troubles we are passing
through. His prayer for those heroes gone, was deeply felt by the
fervent 'Amens' which went up.

Another account of Christmas Day was given by Frank Rhodes in his
diary:

   Xmas Day 25.
Boers fired a musketry salute carrying it on right round the hills
about 4.30 am. Long Tom fired a few shots night and morning but
they were fairly quiet all day – Sir George is evidently much better;
Hunter is looking seedy: Hunter gets telegrams 'The Gypies are
coming' from Pink & Silline [?] Sir George told me he does not
believe Ld Roberts and Kitchener are coming He thinks some of the
Boers who fight against Buller Colenso Way return here behind
Bulwana at night. Our Xmas trees were an enormous success, 4 Great
Britain (self) Australia (Davies) South Africa (Col Durtnell) Canada
(Maj Doveton) 250 children Durtnell and Davies worked indefatig-
ably Mullins and Wade better also Dugdale – Col Dick Cunningham
thinks health among the troops is in the main a question of the men
getting properly boiled and filtered water: the Gordons are very
particular about their water and they have got no sick Jameson's
[illegible] that Methuen has got Cronje in a tight place. '*I wonder*'
106 in shade so Durtner says. A lot of private Xmas Helios going
thro and we hear the Lyddite Howitzers are at Estcourt. I think they
are 5 inch Howitzers – Shells coming over as Communion service
was going on on Caesar's Camp today – Pearce and Abdy 11 Hussars
dinner, Soup, Mutton, Goose, Champagne excellent dinner.

Sergeant Rumbold's complaint was not the meagre rations nor the
shelling, but the lack of fighting. In his diary for New Year's Day he
wrote:

Things are getting very trying, and the same old things happen every day. If we could only get a little more fighting it would be so much more pleasant for us all. We are all longing to do something. The Boers fired a *Feu-de-Joie* at us from all their big guns round Ladysmith. We think it is in return for the salute we gave them on the Prince of Wales's birthday.

He did not have to wait long for his wish to be granted.

The result of Kruger's pressure for offensive action was seen on the night of 5/6 January 1900. The naval gunners, protected by 100 men of the Imperial Light Horse, were in the process of moving two 12-pounders and the 4.7in nicknamed 'Lady Anne' to a new site at the south-west corner of the hill called Platrand, which formed the southern-most sector of the defences, commanded by Colonel Ian Hamilton. As they did so, the Boers attacked both there and at Caesar's Camp on the eastern end of the hill, two and a half miles away. By dawn Hamilton's men, mostly Manchesters and Gordons, were being driven back from the crest of the hill by some 2,000 Boers. White was ill with fever, and Rawlinson, with White's chief of staff, Major-General Sir Archibald Hunter,* organized a counter-attack, supported by all the artillery that could be mustered, employing the Rifle Brigade, both the 1st and 2nd Battalions of the 60th Rifles and two reserve companies of the Gordons. They stabilized the position, but suffered heavy casualties every time they tried to drive the Boers back from the crest. Christopher Balfour described the action in his diary:

Jan. 6th.
Most eventful day, at 3.30 a.m. heard heavy rifle fire on Wagon Hill but thought nothing but the Boers usual 'Waphenshaus'. At 4.30 a.m. we got the order (4 coys 1 K.R.R. 4 coys 2 K.R.R.) to turn out and reinforce the 3 coys 1st K.R.R. on Wagon Hill. Left Dawson City at 4.45. Reached Wagon Hill at 6 a.m. Tremendous fusilade going on. As soon as we got there 'G' Coy moved off at once into firing line and 'C' Coy in support on Right. At 7.30 a.m. half H. Coy moved forward under Tod whom I never saw again. At 9 a.m. I had orders to move my Coy along the right under the crest and report to

---

* He had come out with Buller as his chief of staff, but was with White when Ladysmith was cut off and was forced to remain there.

Gen Hamilton. He told me to go on cross the 'Howitzer Gully' at the
bottom climb the hill on the other side and wait as a support till
further orders. Did so, and reported myself to Major Milner-Walnut
92nd,* who ordered me to put ½ coy in support with him and ½
coy under me was to creep up the slope of Howitzer Gully and when
I heard a bugle, charge ! I got my Coy in position and waited for
signal. While waiting I put my head over the rock to look round and
promptly got a bullet through my helmet which went so close that it
cut some hair off! Thank God that bugle never sounded for there
was a party of Boers who kept firing at our flank. Got some bread
and bully [beef] pluckily brought by Transport. About 1.30 p.m.
Major Walnut came to see me and told me I would soon have to
creep higher. At 2 p.m. a tremendous fusilade broke out again, it was
then I heard that the Boers again took the point of the hill, killing
poor Walnut, Digby Jones and many men. I then got orders to go up
the hill on to the crest. This I did with a party of Boers firing into
my left flank. So I drew back a section on my left to keep them busy
and went on with my other section. Thank the Lord there was a team
of oxen and a wagon left by the working party of the R.E. who were
surprised. These protected me a little and there were a few small
(very small) rocks one could get one's head behind. Here I lost 2
killed and 4 wounded. The bullocks all got shot down one by one.
Here I stuck for ages blazing away chiefly into space. I should have
said that at about 2 p.m. 'H' Coy under Barnett came to reinforce
me. He sent a section to my left to engage the Boers on my flank and
with the other 3 sections continued my line on the right. It was at
this point that Seymour rejoined me with what he had of his ½ Coy
telling me of the rush at the point when Walnut, Jones &c were killed
and where I lost 1 killed and 1 wounded (Color Sgt). After a bit H
Coy's section on my left was withdrawn and rejoined the Coy as the
Boers on the flank ceased fire. At about 4.30 p.m. the most fearful
thunderstorm came on and in the middle the Boers attacked again
most pluckily. Those infernal flankers got at me again killing 1 and
wounding others. During this storm the Devons charged losing
heavily and never actually reached the Boers but cleared them off.
Then H Coy and myself charged but fortunately most Boers had left
and we got over the top and lined the crest and fired away. The noise

---

* The Gordon Highlanders.

was terrific, thunder, shells and a fearful fusilade. Ceased fire after a bit and when it began to get dark collected our Companies and began building Sangars. Very wet cheerless night on picket. Got a sandwich, some rum and blanket. Soaked through and through.

The supporting artillery fire was particularly effective. A further attack on the naval gun emplacement in the early afternoon was successfully driven off, and by 4 p.m. Hamilton correctly concluded that the Boers had had enough and were only waiting for darkness to allow them to withdraw; but White, risen from his bed of sickness, insisted that a further attack must be made to drive them back before then. Lieutenant-Colonel C. W. Park, with his 1st Devons, was given the task just as a thunderstorm drenched the ground with rain. They reached the crest, but the Boers fought on from positions beyond until darkness fell, the only officer of the Devons remaining alive or unwounded being Park himself. The Imperial Light Horse also played an important part in this counter-attack. British casualties totalled 424, 17 officers and 152 soldiers killed, 28 and 221 wounded, mostly of the Manchesters, the Imperial Light Horse and the Devons. Boer casualties are not known, but over 50 bodies were found on the battlefield. Sergeant Rumbold also took part in this action and describes it:

Jan. 6th.
The alarm was given this morning about 3 a.m. The enemy had made a combined attack on Ladysmith. We the 2nd Battalion Rifle Brigade, have been ordered to proceed to Caesar's Camp, about four miles march. We started about 3.30 a.m. light marching order, with 200 rounds of ammunition, and an emergency in our haversacks. When we were within two miles of Caesar's Camp, the Boers opened fire on us from Long Tom on Bulwain's Hill, and we had a very hot time of it (The Manchester Regiment were holding Caesar's Camp, and we were to reinforce them). We reached the Camp about 5.30 a.m. and rested for two hours. All this time firing has been going on all round us. At 7.30 one company go out to reinforce the firing line of the Manchesters. We open out to four paces interval, two sections in the firing line and two in the supports, and advance to the crest by the hill. Bullets were flying round in all directions. But we were not taking much notice of these as we were anxious to reach the firing line. We reached the crest of the hill and never shall I forget

the pleasant surprise that awaited us. Instead of the Manchesters being there we found Boers. We were then about 25 yards from them. The first thing I saw was our Captain throw up his arms and roll over on his back. As he fell he shouted to his company to drop down, and open fire to the front. The order was instantly obeyed but not before eight men had been shot dead and about twenty wounded. We had run into a trap. I got shot through the top of my helmet. A man called Gilbert on my right got a round of buck shot in the knee; he lay down and shouted and kicked. The Boers were all in hiding around us and could see Gilbert kicking and gave him another through his stomach. Then he got up and walked to where I was lying and begged of me to shoot him. It is needless for me to say how sorry I felt for him, but I could do nothing for him only to give him some water and get him to lay down. He was quiet for a time and then he got mad again with pain. He stood up bared his chest and challenged the Boers to shoot him, but he was not to get another that day altho' I don't know how he missed it. He afterwards had the pluck to try and walk back to the camp, but he did not get far.

On my left was a man named Northcot; he was shot through the liver. I crawled up to him and gave him a drink from my bottle, and gripped his hand for the last time, for by this time I had crawled back to my place he was dead.

The Battalion could not get stretcher bearers out to us or doctors, neither could they send us out supports, on account of the terrible fire they would have to face before they reached us. So we lay down and blazed away till the majority of our ammunition was gone expecting every minute to see the Boers rush on us and annihilate the remainder of us. But they had very bad hearts, and probably did not know our strength, for had they come they must have sent us under. To move was almost certain death. One of our signallers got behind a rock and started to signal for assistance, when instantly, he had seven bullets through his flag. Others were plucky enough to volunteer to crawl back for assistance, but out of the four that went, three were shot through the head, dead. Thus we had to lie all day in the scorching sun, not daring to move, and ever on the alert for the slightest sign from the front. We lay thus from the first thing in the morning till 6.30 p.m. The rain came down in torrents about 4 p.m. and soaked us all to the skin, but we had to lay in it like ducks, for the Boers had their eyes upon us. Then at 6.30, just as it was getting dark we fixed swords [bayonets] and rushed the position, driving the Boers down the hill and knocking them over like rabbits. Several got shot in crossing a stream. They would drop into the water, spin round a few times and then go floating merrily down. Thus my own little company helped to repulse the Boers on that bloody and memorable day at Ladysmith on 6th January, 1900. Others did equally well. The Devons did splendid work on Waggon Hill, and the Artillery were beyond all praise. The Doctors were able to get out to the wounded at night, and what a sight they saw; dead and dying on all sides, Briton and Boer lying side by side in death. In the Sangers where the Manchesters had been surprised, the dead were lying five and six together, and there was blood all over the rocks; we were also falling over dead men as we walked about in the dark. We had to remain on duty in the Sangers all night in our wet clothes, perished with cold and without a blanket or coat to put round us.

Sergeant David Maxwell described the part the Imperial Light Horse played in a letter to his parents, written on 10 January:

Here we still are waiting for Buller as patiently as we can. We had a very stiff fight on Ben's birthday (Many happy returns of day to him). I am still on sick list with dysentery & so missed the first part of it. Our Sqdrn & another were picketting Waggon Hill & the naval guns were being changed from their old place to this hill – when the Boers made a most determined attack about 2 a.m. – The hill is almost vertical & consists of big rocks & it is about 150 ft high. They got right up to the top – our 2 sqdrns being only 65 strong (reduced by sickness etc) & were shooting at 6–7 ft interval, we being severely handicapped by not being armed with magazine rifles. – Our chaps stuck to their place like men in spite of losing half their men. When the alarm came into camp Harbord & I went out with the Regt a fearful hot time we had – in ½ an hour we had 2 officers killed & 7 wounded & I don't know how many men – the Boers holding the crest of the hill all day. Gradually reinforcements came to us & we had an easier time – but the Boers (all Free-staters) were splendid brave fellows; – again & again charging up only to be shot down – It was a beastly time – seeing one's pals being knocked over right & left – all thro' the head nearly – They kept up the attack till dark & finished with another charge in the midst of a tremendous thunderstorm – they were met by the Devons with bayonet, who shoved them back over the Hill – the gallant K-R-Rifles refusing to charge. The Gordons lost heavily again owing to a panic when 60 of them cleared out of a Sanger – when rushed by only 4 Boers – they had no officer with them – which accounted for it – A Sergt of ours saved the sanger by sticking & shooting 2 of the 4 & the others cleared. He then managed to get the Gordons back – but only about ½ – the other ½ being killed & wounded. Poor old Coningham was killed by a stray bullet about 2½ miles from the fight – just outside the camp. We lost 2 officers & 27 men killed & 29 wounded (including 9 officers) all the men are severely wounded – one man in no less than 8 places – Our Colonel is amongst the wounded. Our total loss is about 150 killed & 160 wounded. So you see how hot it was. The Boers were splendid brave fellows & several of them were old greybearded chaps – They told us afterwards that their orders were to take the hill & stay their [sic] – There was a general attack all round by the Transvaal Boers – but only half-hearted – the Free staters expressed great disgust at their behaviour. Our fellows & the wounded had to lie out wet thro' & bitterly cold all night – Fortunately (in a way) our Dr saw Harbord & me & sent us home with a flea in our ears.

The Regt now instead of being 5 sqdns here of 87 each – is now formed into 2 sqdrns of about 60 men each – thro' sickness & casualties. There are something like 1400 patients in the Main Hospital (on neutral ground) & a good many in the camp. Everybody is looking thin & weak but still cheerful.

White heaved a sigh of relief, but, in reporting the success of his defence to Buller, stated that he was no longer able to make a sortie to help a further attempt by the latter to relieve the siege. Roberts arrived at Cape Town on 10 January and agreed to Buller's proposal to try again, reporting to Lansdowne that 'Buller does not conceal that the operation is risky, but says that it is the only possible chance for Ladysmith where there are over 2,000 sick and supplies running out'.

Buller realized that White could no longer help him and also that the other reasons why he had rejected his initial plan to cross the Tugela further upstream from Colenso no longer obtained. With the arrival of Warren's 5th Division to reinforce him, he decided to revert to that plan. While Lyttelton's 4th Brigade distracted Botha by a feint attack at Potgieter's Drift, Warren, with 10,600 infantry, 2,200 mounted troops

and 36 guns, would cross seven miles higher up at Trikhardt's Drift and
capture the hills a few miles beyond, which were thought to be held by
only about 600 Boers, his left flank protected by Dundonald's 3rd
Mounted Brigade. As he did so, Buller, with 7,200 infantry, 400 mounted
troops and 22 guns, would attack the hills beyond Potgieter's which were
more strongly defended. Once through the hills, fifteen miles of open
plain, offering no easily defended obstacles, would lie between them and
Ladysmith.

In spite of his previous message, White was anxious to cooperate by
making a sortie to the west towards Warren, with 7,000 men, leaving
only 3,600 to defend Ladysmith. The first step in this would be an attack
on Rifleman's Ridge. Rawlinson preferred an attack to the south-east on
Flag Hill and Lombard's Kop 'if Buller gets on well'. By 9 January, after
the battle on the Platrand, he was having doubts, as he records in his
diary:

> Our sick list this morning shows nearly 2000 in hospital and in
> Saturday's (6 January) fighting our losses were heavier than we
> thought. Our garrison is frightfully reduced in officers and if Buller
> cannot reach us this time we shall I fear have to give in.

In another entry he wrote:

> It is very disgusting and disheartening, everything we attempt to do
> seems for some unknown cause to turn against us and I do not
> believe now we should be able to take Rifleman's Ridge unless the
> spirit of the troops improves. There were a great many shirkers
> amongst the company of the Leicesters we had at Star Hill – half of
> them were not for it and I fear that the residence in holes and
> constant 'taking cover from the enemy's bullets and shells' has had a
> serious effect on men's nerves and I doubt if they would stand night
> work now they are too jumpy. We want some marked success to put
> the life into them again for they are much shaken and worst of all
> there is a feeling of want of confidence abroad – amongst other
> things last night deserters said that the Boers intended to attack us
> on Monday next. This is most improbable.
>
>   It is curious how in a siege like this the bad or moderate regts go
> to the wall and how a good regiment with a good CO comes to the
> front – Not only is it in smartness and appearance but also especially
> in the way of sickness. The Gordons are in the better fettle and in as

good health as when the siege began though they have have had one of the worst camps in the place. The Liverpools and Leicester are exactly the reverse with over 100 sick each and filthy dirty in every way. Of course Khaki is practically worn out. It is torn and patched in every direction and covered with grease and filth of all sorts. We have no further supply in store. The Boots too are in very bad order owing to the rough wear they have undergone on these stony rocky Kopjes. This is a serious matter for it makes it impossible for us to march any distance till we get fresh supplies. The men are however fairly cheery under the circumstances. The 60th [Rifles] are in a bad way. They were very roughly handled both at Talana and Lombard's Kop and Grimwood who commands the second Battn has quite gone to pieces and is unfit to command a Battn. When communications are opened he must be invalided.

Rawlinson himself took bombardment phlegmatically. He describes the occasion when a shell from a Long Tom landed on the headquarters:

Bang went a shell into my office and blew the little room clean out. Smashed the floor to pieces and blew out all four walls the two side walls going perfectly flat. If I had been in the office nothing could have saved me for the shell would have struck me on the right knee, as it was I was two rooms off so that beyond the concussion of the explosion which was not as severe as I expected I have only the discomfort of having all my books writing things letters &c blown to smithereens. The chief who is bad with fever this morning we induced to move and carried him up to Christopher's house in a dhoolie where he must remain for the present. I only just shifted the telephone in time – it is now safe in the splinter proof and I have had all the other telephones moved there so they at least are safe. It is marvellous that no one was touched by these shells. The stink of them is disgusting a sort of dull, sickly, heavy stench quite unlike anything else and it remains in a way which is most unpleasant. The Melinite charge is only about 5 pounds but it is quite enough to smash up everything that is really near, (within a yard), of the shell when it bursts, I have kept some pieces of the shell and also my chair which is a sight worth seeing – it has no legs and the seat is blown in half. It has damaged this book to a certain extent by spluttering it with ink [this can still be seen: it is red] & smashing the binding but the damage is not serious. My letters too I managed to save and though my box of drawing instruments was broken open and thrown all over the place I have been able to collect most of them [his diary is illustrated with beautiful neat ink sketches]. It was extraordinary shooting on the part of the Boers. They put 4 successive shells within a distance of 35 yards at a range of 9,000 yards.

There was nothing wrong with the concept of Buller's plan for his next attempt to relieve Ladysmith. The fatal flaw was to give the principal part to the newly arrived Warren, particularly as Buller had no confidence in him. Warren, having taken two days to march the five miles to Trikhardt's Drift from Spearman's Camp, took two more to cross the river and two more before launching his first attack, on 20 January, against the Rangeworthy Hills, his main objective, with Hildyard's 2nd and Hart's 5th Brigades, which succeeded in reaching the southern crest at no great cost – 31 killed and 300 wounded. Dundonald, with 1,200 mounted men, had reached Acton Homes at the western end of the hills the day before. Major William Birdwood of the XI Bengal Lancers, who was Dundonald's brigade major, wrote in his diary:

18 January.
We advanced ... by the pontoons to the W. to further outflank the enemy's position – we alone went out & occupied series of kopjes roughly parallel to the Tugela. I insisted on Lord D. allowing Graham to shove forward 2 of his squadrons. We sent on the I.L.H & N. [Natal] Carbiniers – occupied 2 hills through which the Acton Holmes–Ladysmith road ran, most successfully ambuscaded a party of about 200 Boers who were reconnoitring out from the enemy's position. We killed about 12 of them & took 30 prisoners – own casualties being 5. We occupied position for the night extending in a semi circle, round the enemy's position & joining on to our Infantry's left.

19 January.
We practically sat tight all day on the positions we had held last night, Sir C. Warren being furious at our having gone so far & saying he wanted us to cling to him, & even between him and the heights held by the enemy instead of rt. away to the flanks as we should have been. In fact he took away the TMI [? Thorneycroft's Mounted Infantry] – 2 Sqdns R. D. [Royal Dragoons] & 1 sqd. Hr [? Horse] to keep up on the hills. I said he didn't care what we did: will give us

no orders or ideas of his intentions. We only vaguely knew we had to cooperate on his left next day.

Lieutenant C. A. Calvert of the Royal Dragoons felt much the same. In a letter home he wrote:

Just about a fortnight ago we left Pretorious Camp and marched to Springfield Camp and remained there one night. Next morning I was told to take my troop as a covering party and guard the R.E. who were working on some road to which I would be taken. This job took me all day till dark. . . . The R.E. did not finish their work till it was quite dark. When we started off and to my surprise when I got over the hill not more than 1½ miles away I was challenged by a sentry and then came upon the whole army, all prepared to move in the night in order of march. I had some trouble to find the regiment which was saddled up, fed my troop, and then lay down in my macintosh and went to sleep. We mounted some time about three and marched to the position from which the attack was to commence, to make our passage over the Tugela. The guns opened fire on a farm, and the pontoons went down with the Devons. There were practically no Boers and the bridge was put across. While this was going on we had our breakfast, then crossed later in the day by a ford which was rather deep, but we had no one drowned, although the 15th did. Then our Generals made a real hash of it, as if they had gone on as everybody wanted to, we should have taken the positions and long before this should have been in Ladysmith. The Boers themselves say that our flank march had quite taken them by surprise.

One of those taking part in Warren's attack was Lieutenant Fred Raphael of the 1st South Lancashires. He started a letter to his mother on 17 January. In it he wrote:

We are in for it now, yesterday evening at 5 o'clock we started and marched all night till about 1.30 a.m. with the idea of turning the enemy's right flank, a front attack being made by another lot at the same time. When we arrived here, we deployed and lay down and woke about 4.30 a.m. soaked with heavy dew and shivering with cold; the guns have been going on our right, but ours have not started yet. It is now 7.30 a.m. We are supposed to be a surprise but I have no doubt the enemy know of our presence by now, or at any rate, part of us who have got across the river by a ford, they neglected to guard, this will probably develop into the real attack.

I can't say I feel any excitement yet, or that I am risking my life and limb, or that there is any danger, but I fancy when the bullets begin to fly, I shall feel a bit unpleasant at first, but excitement will soon drive all that away. We shall soon be on the move now, so I shall finish this letter later if I am able. If not, good-bye but I hope I shall not be bowled over.

He added next day:

The hill we have to take is very high and steep, I don't at all fancy climbing it and it is swarming with Boers ... I had an excellent breakfast yesterday made of tinned beef and biscuits which I made into soup with some potatoes and carrots I dug out of a garden which we passed in our attack yesterday. It was great luck we got across the river so easily, the enemy were evidently taken by surprise, as there was only a small outpost and we soon shelled them out. It is wonderful with what accuracy they fire. Our balloon has just gone up, causing great excitement to the Tommies. It will photograph the Boer position or at any rate sketch it so that we know where our [sic] guns and trenches and reserves are ... This is my last piece of paper so will send a line from my pocket-book after the fight. I shall have to carry this in my pocket on the chance of its being found and sent on if I am bowled over. However I hope I shall be able to post it myself.

He wrote again on the 22nd, addressing it 'Across Tugela River':

We made a forward movement in the direction of Van Reenen's Pass and firing went on all Friday afternoon. We formed the rear guard, but did not get any fighting. We were all asleep when we were told to get up quietly at 1.30 a.m. Saturday and take the enemy's outlying posts at the point of the bayonet. We went on expecting to be fired on every moment, but they bolted as we came up the hill, where we stayed till daybreak. Several batteries of Artillery came on then and we formed their escort, where we have been through the whole battle forming outposts at night, and keeping hid by day. For all that, on Saturday we got fairly hotted and lost nine men wounded. Since then, although our guns are still shelling, all, or nearly all, danger has left us and the battle is going on about two miles to our left front, this being the third day. If it goes on to-morrow, it will be the longest on record. I got a magnificent view of it all on Saturday, it was a grand and awful sight. About fifteen men were killed and wounded quite close to me, but only one in my Company got wounded. Our fellows have fought splendidly.

Private Harry Phipps was with the 1st Borders in the attack on the 20th. He described it in his diary for that day:

Started to attack the enemy about two miles from our camp on another hill & a series of kopjes. It was thought that the enemy were not in strong force but on commencing the attack we were soon undeceived. They were in exceptional number & also had splendid cover amongst the rock at the top of the hills. Their front extended for nearly eight miles. We commenced the attack with the artillery, who, for two hours, shelled the positions uncessantly. The Boers appeared to have no big guns, not a shot being answered to our gunners magnificent practice. We commenced advancing in extended order and on leaving the cover, we realized what a stiff job lay in front of us. The hills the enemy occupied were in a half circle. The valley we had to advance over was practically devoid of cover with the exception of a small hill about five hundred yds away. Our firing line consisted of the Lancashire Fusiliers & the York & Lancasters. The Dublin Fusiliers & the Border Regt. was supports, with the Inniskillings in reserve.

As soon as we started to advance the bullets began to fly, but we took no notice of this; when, imagine our surprise to see our firing line cuddled up in a heap behind the small hill I have mentioned. When we got to them we could plainly see they were in a state of blue funk, the officers were as bad or worse than the men. Our men indignantly told them what they thought about their action, & after a lot of persuasion (one way or another) they commenced to advance like a pack of frightened sheep. All of a sudden a automatic Maxim Nordenfeldt began to play upon us. That stopped the firing line, for flat on their faces they fell & devil of a move would they make at all. Then the effects of discipline was exhibited. Our officers equal to any emergency shouted, 'advance & leave the cowards there', and to a man the Dubs & Borders responded, walking along like men on parade. A cheer from our line was the only indication of feeling they gave, & that at a word of praise from the general. Our men began to fall rapidly now, being only eight hundred yards from the position. The Maxim Nordenfeldt was doing considerable damage too, but a moment later our artillery spotted it & three flashes immediately followed, then, exit maxim for that day at least. We commenced blazing away at the rocks we knew the Boers lay hidden behind. The General gave us orders to hold the place where we were; while another Brigade rolled back the left flank of the enemy. The fire now became furious, & we noticed that some appeared to be coming from behind. I said I would go back and let the second line know that their fire was dangerous to us, & proceeded to do so, with the permission of the officer. While going back I realised the meaning of having a place marked, for on my crossing a piece of ground which had a rock on it, the bullets fairly rained on me, but fortunately I did not get hit. I delivered my message all right & started to return when a bullet hit me in the leg, & now I am in the Field Hospital.

In his diary entry for 22 January, he wrote:

Transferred to Springfield Field Hospital. Never in my life shall I forget the ride. We were put on trek wagons, & had to come over very rough ground for five miles. The jolting of the wagon affected the wounds & half suppressed shrieks issued from our lips at every jolt. One poor fellow next to me had his leg splintered by a shell; big tears streamed down his face with the agony which he was undergoing, but never a word of complaint passed his lips, for he knew & we knew that the proper ambulances were needed for men hurt more badly than us. Everything the authorities could do, was done for us. At halfway we got some stimulants which we badly needed & when we arrived in Springfield a cup of Beef-tea was immediately given us.

Warren demanded more artillery before making a further attack, Buller sending him four howitzers. Meanwhile Botha was hastily transferring troops from elsewhere and established his headquarters only two miles north-east of Warren's. Buller was bursting with impatience. On 23 January he rode over to see Warren and insisted that he must attack, having considered dismissing him but rejecting such a drastic measure. Instead he urged a renewal of the attack on the Rangeworthy Hills; but Warren protested that he could not find suitable artillery positions from which to support one, and must first capture the conical hill of Spion Kop on his right flank. This was launched during the night of 23/24

January by Major-General E. R. P. Woodgate's 11th Lancashire Brigade reinforced with 200 men of the Natal Mounted Infantry and a company of the Royal Engineers. The hill was undefended, apart from a small picket, and well before dawn Woodgate's men were on the summit shrouded in mist, which did not clear until 8 a.m. Under its cover Botha had been concentrating every gun he could, while organizing 400 men of the Carolina and Pretoria Commandos to clamber up the rocky hillside. The mist had concealed from Woodgate that the ground his men had occupied was only the western end of the summit and that they were overlooked by two pieces of high ground at the eastern end, which they named Conical Hill and Aloe Knoll. By the time that this was realized, the Boers were already occupying them and beginning to fire down onto the British, crammed into their shallow and ill-prepared defences. As both sides fired artillery and rifles at each other, casualties mounted in the rising heat. One of the first was Woodgate himself, command devolving onto Colonel Blomfield of the 2nd Lancashire Fusiliers. He attempted to organize an attack to capture Aloe Knoll, but, when it failed and he himself was wounded, Colonel Malby Crofton of the 2nd (King's Own) Royal Lancaster Regiment called off further attacks and made a feeble attempt to request reinforcements before effectively abandoning command to the huge, energetic Lieutenant-Colonel A. Thorneycroft, the 'special officer' in command of the Natal Mounted Infantry. By 10 a.m. Warren had received an alarmist message from Crofton and ordered Major-General J. Talbot Coke, commander of the 10th Brigade (2nd Middlesex, 2nd Dorsets and the Imperial Light Infantry) to reinforce him and himself set in hand attempts to move guns up onto the hill. Meanwhile he asked Lyttelton to attack Boer positions from the east, but to stop shelling Aloe Knoll which he mistakenly believed Crofton to have occupied. He made no attempt to take advantage of Botha's preoccupation with Spion Kop to order Hildyard and Hart to renew their attack on the Rangeworthy Hills.

Buller had so far made no real contribution; but, shortly before midday, he signalled Warren: 'Unless you put some really good hard fighting man in command on the top you will lose the hill. I suggest Thorneycroft.' Warren complied, and Thorneycroft received a message to that effect about half an hour later, not long before he personally prevented some Lancashire Fusiliers from surrendering to a Boer attack.

Both sides on Spion Kop were now suffering heavy casualties and

1. Paul Kruger.

2. General Joubert
and staff, Newcastle,
17 October 1899.

3. Lieutenant-General Sir George White VC, in the uniform of the Gordon Highlanders.

4. Lieutenant-General Sir Redvers Buller, on board *Dunottar Castle*.

5. Major-General Lord Methuen and staff, Klerksdorp, 1901.

6. Colonel Ian Hamilton.

7. General Louis Botha.

8. General Piet Cronje and Colonel Schiel as prisoners of war.

9. Winburg Commando at Harrismith, October 1899.

10. Balloon Corps Transport.

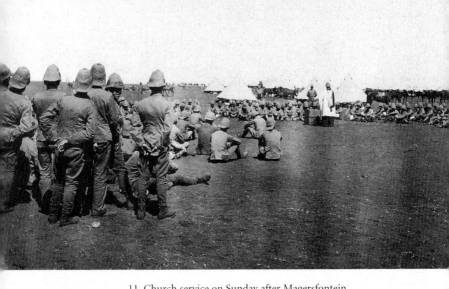

11. Church service on Sunday after Magersfontein.

12. Battle of Colenso: 4.7in gun firing.

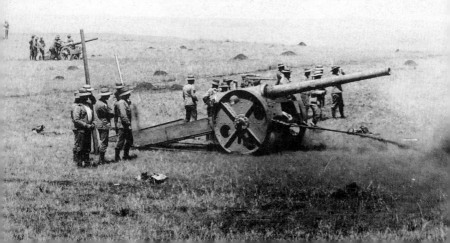

13. Lord Roberts with his Indian Army orderly.

14. Kimberley. George Labram's gun 'Long Cecil'.

15. Kimberley. Defences of Bishof. Top of West Kopje.

[*sic*] Kop which people thought were impossible & we somehow got
to the top & thereby attracted attention from others in bad case. You
will see all the news in the papers, as to the turning movement on
Warren's part & will know more than we can on the right. We
moved on the 24th from camp about 10 am fully convinced that the
Boers were on the run & that we were going to quicken the pace.
This was sort of confirmed when we got the orders to go up the
Spioen Kop. The Rt ½ Bn went up one spur & the left ½ the one on
the left & nearer the main hill. My company was in reserve & I
gradually closed as we got to the base of the hill. While lying here
I noticed the advance was slowing a bit & made up my mind to go
through with my lot. I found that Briscoe and Thistlethwaite were
both wounded & their men came on with me or at least some of
them. Reggie Cathcart who had the other leading Coy was a little in
front of me & on my left but I caught this lot ½ way up & then we
went on gradually getting men up & up. The place was precipitous
in parts & then has a grass slope & getting over there was jumpy
work as they were all covered with cross fire. Poor Frank Brewster
was killed about half way up & Robin Grant was first wounded in
the shoulder & started rolling down the hill when a brute shot him
again & killed him. There is no doubt they marked the officers &
both Reggie & I compared notes on the subject. It was a case of
hands & knees in a great many places & I shouted hunting calls to
the men & got them up by me guiding them as best I could across
places which I knew to be dangerous. Eventually about 5 pm we
reached the top of the hill (the Rt ½ got up theirs about 4.45) we
sent out scouts who got into a small work but were shot out of it at
once, & then we lay on the top just clear of one of their works
praying for darkness, as we only had about 100 men up actually at
the time. A lot more collected about 100 ft down & as Algie Copley
was not up I was practically in command & Reggie and I with
Hereward worked out what were to do on advancing as we had no
idea we were to be withdrawn. About 7 p m Algie came & told us to
retire. I had to make a speech to the men & we had a regular rough
& tumble back, leaving a few men at each point of vantage to cover
us. Most of the way we did sitting down & sliding & the distance
seemed endless. Taking the wounded down was a terrible business &
we had to leave several out as it was impossible to find them. Our
casualties 93, 3 off killed 4 wounded. People seem to think a good

deal of the affair. Bron Herbert told me he heard it was a most splendid bit of work. Personally I didn't feel as if I were doing anything enormous & I know I went to sleep for a short time. There is one thing however that, tho' we were practically a beaten army again, the Bn did what was wanted. I write this as we can't say where we shall be soon. Anyhow I hope we manage something soon & get a turn of luck.

The 60th Rifles' success in gaining the Twin Peaks caused near-panic among the Boers, who were already contemplating the abandonment of their positions on Spion Kop. When darkness fell, they abandoned the Twin Peaks and by 10 p.m. were in the process of doing the same from Spion Kop, when Botha tried in vain to send them back. Ignorant of this, Thorneycroft had decided to withdraw. All the battalions on the hill were mixed up together, several had suffered severe casualties, and all were hungry, thirsty and weary, some leaderless. His decision was challenged by the CO of the Middlesex, Lieutenant-Colonel Hill, who claimed seniority, and by Coke's staff officer, Captain Phillips, Coke himself having been summoned to see Warren. By 2 a.m. the hill had been abandoned with 243 British dead. It was not until daylight that a Boer patrol, returning to the summit, found the hill deserted to the dead of both sides. Riddell's men, whom Lyttelton had unfortunately tried to recall earlier, withdrew from the Twin Peaks after dark, and on the following night all Warren's and Lyttelton's men withdrew across the Tugela, having lost 1,500 killed, wounded or captured. The Boers lost 335 and were too exhausted to attempt any pursuit or even harassment.

One of those killed at Spion Kop was Fred Raphael. On 27 January, his commanding officer wrote to his father, announcing Fred's death and expressing his own sorrow and that of his brother officers. Having briefly described the action, stating that when his captain was killed he had assumed command of the company, and two hours later was killed himself by 'shell fire in the head', he went on to explain:

Most of our dead and wounded lay on the hillside and on the following morning, received burial or attention from our people and from the Boers. Your dear son, all of him that is mortal, lies decently and reverently buried on that ill-fated ridge surrounded by comrades and friends. Every effort was made by a surviving brother officer to find your son's body when the firing ceased after dark, but in the darkness and multitude of dead and dying, his could not then be found, but, as I have written, our burying party in the morning found it and aided by the Boers, gave it reverent burial. Of our four Officers engaged, two were killed outright, of the Battalion now [pre]sent [with] me as I write to you of 24 officers there remain eight fit for duty.

Raphael's cousin, Hugh Atlay, was serving in an RFA battery supporting the attack, and wrote to a mutual aunt a few days after the battle:

I am writing to tell you all I can about how Fred Raphael's death [*sic*]. On the early morning of the 24th a force consisting of the Lancashire Fusiliers, Middlesex Regiment, two companies of the South Lancashires and some of the local levies made an attack on a hill, called Spien Kopje which commanded part of the right of our position. My battery was sent to support it by shelling the ridges on its left. We got into position about daybreak having heard cheers on our way to it, showing that the hill or part of it had been taken. We shelled the ridges and cleared the Boers out on our side and thought everything was going on splendidly, when about 10 a.m. some of the enemy's guns, concealed on the higher ridges so well that noone could find out where they were, opened a terrible fire on our fellows on Spien Kopje. We were helpless; guns could not be got up the hill, we could see nothing to fire at, and had to stay doing nothing. The Boers whose rifle shoots accurately to 2000 yards were shooting down the men whenever they showed from behind cover. The morning had been so misty the men did not know in which direction to make their shelter trenches when they got to the top of the hill. The infantry fought magnificently and rushed several of the enemy's trenches, but they were exposed to a terrific fire the whole time. I gather that Raphael was shifting his position and showed for a moment from behind cover when he was shot through the head, so that death must have come very mercifully to him. He was lying where he fell for eight hours before they could get to him. The remainder of his Regiment were down below close to us. I heard early in the day he was wounded and that the two captains, both of whom I knew, were killed, and it was not till late that night I heard the truth that he and Captain Birch were killed and that Captain Lynch was untouched, the only one of the officers to escape, the other subalterns being wounded. In the afternoon reinforcements were sent up and they held their own till dark, the hill being evacuated that night. The losses were terrible. General Woodgate was shot through the head early in the day and noone seemed to know what to do; his brigade major assumed command and was very soon killed too. Colonel Thorneycroft, who was in command of a regiment of his own raising, saved us from absolute disaster by rallying the troops who were getting a little demoralised in a wonderful way. As night fell however his nerve failed him and he ordered a retirement which was a fatal mistake. A mountain battery was on its way up the hill and I was going to have tried to get my two guns up, in fact was ready to start my movement, only awaiting final orders which never came, as for some reason we don't know no attempt was made to reoccupy the hill. The Middlesex Regiment lost 9 officers and 95 men killed and wounded, while the Lancashire Fusiliers had only one unwounded officer. It has checked us completely and we have retired about three miles beyond the Tugela to give the troops a rest after their seven days continuous fighting. The infantry badly need rest, the whole of the work having been done by them, we having to be contented with shelling the ridges. We were only under fire twice and have had no losses, though the bullets were falling pretty thick among us on one ocasion. When if ever we shall get to Ladysmith we cannot imagine. The Boer positions are practically impregnable, but we all hope to have another shot at this very soon.

Lieutenant Calvert of the Royals felt that he was lucky to have survived. In his letter, already quoted, he wrote:

Thanks to the Colonel we are alive, but for him certainly at least the very half of us would be killed or wounded. After our infantry had retired from Spion Kop (which is an enormous hill) and the Boers had taken possession of it again, a staff officer came up to the Colonel and told him to take his regiment up the hill, find out if it was really occupied and if it was, retake it. The Colonel said to him 'Am I to take that as an order, listen carefully to what I say as I may be tried by Court Martial for it, but I refuse to take my regiment on only your order, but I will go up there myself and find out if the hill is occupied'. He then went to 'C' Squadron which was with him at the time, asked for 2 volunteers to go with him, and Arty Russell, and went up the hill. On his way up he met the stretcher bearers coming down the hill, who begged him not to go on as the Boers were swarming up there; when he saw they were, as we all knew of course the whole time, he came down again, and went straight to Sir Charles Warren and told him about it. Warren said he had never sent such an order and never heard of such a thing in his life and it would naturally have meant the whole regiment being practically wiped out.

Those sort of orders do not give one much confidence in the staff. Many Colonels would have taken their regiments up to save their own necks, but it was a real plucky performance on the Colonel's part.

From the time that Buller's attack had started, Rawlinson had spent most of every day on Observation Hill on the western edge of Ladysmith's defences. From there he could see the top of Spion Kop and the Rangeworthy Hills. On 21 January Buller had signalled, 'We are slowly fighting our way up the hill', but no further news came and on 25 January Rawlinson realized that the British troops that he had seen on the top of Spion Kop had been replaced by Boers. He wrote in his diary:

This state of uncertainty is very trying indeed and is having a bad effect on Sir George who rightly considers that Buller is not treating him with the frankness he has a right to expect. Personally I think that Buller received a check yesterday and does not like to confess it until he has made an attempt to retrieve it which I think he will do tonight or tomorrow.

But by 28 January it was clear that Buller had failed and given up the attempt to reach Ladysmith. An exchange of signals with Buller and Roberts confirmed this, and Rawlinson wrote in his diary:

We have now to stand or fall with Ladysmith. If Buller can, when he makes his next attempt, get within reasonable distance of us and if our sick have not very largely increased by then, we might send out a small force.

He had had to argue with White, who had conceived a plan to try and break out with most of the garrison in a forlorn hope of somehow joining up with Buller, on the grounds that this would be better than waiting until they had to surrender for lack of food. Rawlinson saw it as quite impracticable, and objectionable as abandoning their sick and wounded. He believed that an offensive by Roberts would soon have its effect and draw Boer strength away from Natal. Provided that they ate the horses, instead of hanging on to them for the purpose of effecting a break-out, they should be able to survive long enough for Roberts's offensive to save them. He won the argument, but White became more difficult to handle. He seldom visited the troops in their defences, and, when Major-General Hunter, his chief of staff, did so, accused him of trying to usurp his position. Rawlinson commented on this in his diary:

If I were Hunter I do not think I could take so unjust an accusation as quietly as he does for I should feel very much inclined to 'strike' or at any rate clear the air by having a row of sorts – Hunter has and has had to do everything whilst Sir George has practically done nothing, and if credit is due to anyone it is due to the former.

Reporting his failure to Roberts, Buller telegraphed:

I mean to have one more try at Ladysmith but fear that a great part of Warren's [? division] is not in good spirits. There are mutual recriminations but I blame myself most as I was very uneasy and ought to have interfered before.

Roberts replied:

Unless you feel fairly confident of being able to relieve Ladysmith from Potgieter's Drift, would it not be better to postpone the attempt until I am in the Orange Free State. I am hopeful of having sufficient [transport] to move on or about 5 February. If White can hold out and your position is secure, the presence of my force in the north of the Orange Free State should cause the enemy to lessen their hold upon Natal and thus make your task easier.

At the same time he cabled Lansdowne:

It was a great shock to me to learn that Buller had been compelled to relinquish his second attempt to reach Ladysmith, and I can understand how deeply the news must have been felt in England.
Buller's despondent telegrams from the very first made me fear the worst, and it is difficult to believe from the reports which have reached us that the enemy would not have given way if he had continued to press them – The mere fact of their having allowed him to carry out his retirement practically unopposed shows they had not much heart left in them, or they would undoubtedly have taken advantage of the retrograde movement of our troops to seriously

harass the retirement. The despondent tone of Buller's telegram regarding the possible attempt [*sic*] of a third attempt to relieve Ladysmith makes me think that it had better not be attempted until we have seen the result of my operations in the Orange Free State – My telegram of the 28th will enable me to learn what his intentions are, and unless I consider them sound and likely to be carried through I shall direct him to remain on the defensive.

His telegram to White had said:

Trust you will be able to hold out for longer than 15 February [as White had recently estimated]. Shall be greatly disappointed if by the end of February I have not been able to carry out such operations as will compel the enemy to materially reduce his strength in Natal.

White replied that by using his horses as food he could hold out for six weeks longer and still have his guns efficiently horsed and about 1,000 mounted men available. Rawlinson had considered sending the cavalry out instead of eating their horses. In his diary he wrote:

I think I would let them make a bolt for it to the North and then to the East into Zululand and so South to Maritzburg. They cannot go East of course – there is the alternative of our breaking out ourselves with our whole force and trying to force a passage south to join Buller. It would be a desperate undertaking, a regular forlorn hope and we should suffer very heavily for we could not make it in less than two days which would be heaps of time for every boer within a radius of 20 miles to collect and crush us in the bad country along the banks of the Tugela – So it is our duty I think to stick to Ladysmith until food is nearly finished – 6 weeks may make a great difference to the situation – Who knows – It will be time enough for forlorn hopes then.

Rawlinson took heart from Roberts's forecast of his progress towards Bloemfontein. He wrote:

The campaign must be won in the Free State not in Natal and I would hasten the movement North from the Orange River on Bloemfontein at all hazards. I would risk the fall of Ladysmith even, to get well north in the Free State and threaten Pretoria.

It is like kicking a man in the shins instead of going for his heart. By kicking his shins you may hurt him or break his leg by going for his heart you kill him though perhaps at the risk of getting hurt yourself.

Carry the war into the enemy's country at all costs – Strike for his vitals as rapidly as possible and the issue of the campaign is certain. To fight him in Natal is to fall in with his wishes and to loose [*sic*] certainly twice the numbers even if at the end you are successful – which is no certainty.

Buller, however, was determined to make another attempt, to which Roberts gave his reluctant agreement, reporting to Lansdowne that he hoped that Buller's new venture would be more successful than his last, but that, if it failed, 'We must rest content to defend the line of the Tugela until we know the result of the approaching operations at Kimberley and in the Orange Free State'.

Meanwhile the spirits of the garrison of Ladysmith were at a low ebb. David Maxwell wrote in his diary for 2 February:

Now we are beginning to realize that we are besieged, 2/3rds of the horses not being fed at all (except by grazing), the other 1/3 only getting 1 lb of corn a day. One horse killed daily from our Regt & given to us as an extra ration in shape of sausages or beef tea – & very excellent it is. Two days we go ½ ration of biscuit & 2 days ¾ ration of bread – ½ the meat ration is horse. We graze every day & in the same place – so the poor horses don't get very much. Biscuit days are very lean days as ½ lb only pans out at 2½ biscuits per man – & they are small to fill one's little tum-tum. This past week has been delightfully cool & cloudy – regular English weather with a Scotch mist every morning. Tobacco is very scarce. I still have a smoke or two of terrible stuff left which I managed to buy off a coolie. Yesterday I heard of a pound of cake Tobacco being obtained for £2 – but I couldn't raise the money – though I tried everybody I could think of.

On 5 February Buller renewed his attempt to break through Botha's lines at Vaal Krantz, three miles east of the Twin Peaks. Captain Edward Burrows was with the Chestnut Troop of the Royal Horse Artillery in Dundonald's brigade. He described his experience of the battle in a letter to his wife on 7 February:

Just a scrawl from the actual battle field. This is the third day of this protracted engagement which we hope is going to end all right, but which is a little slow in working itself out. The first day was a success which wd have been complete had daylight lasted a few hours more – the 2nd day we got on a little & inflicted I believe heavy loss by our big guns & today we still hope we may finish it off – but the time it takes is perhaps slightly in the Boers favour as they seem 'cute' at moving their guns about at night – Our performance so far has not been glorious for we are part of the Cavalry B'de & cant do anything till the way has been cleared for us – I just got the troop into action on Monday night & fired a few rounds at some Boers & then was ordered to move to a second position, limbered up & gave our people a show at how the Chestnuts can move at the galop [*sic*] but also dear old Maud put her foot in a hole (of which there are many tho' blind) & over she went & knocked me perfectly senseless – somehow or other the gun didn't go over me & Trump'r Tucker (my pet boy as you know) was off his horse & pulled me out of the way like a shot so I only got a tumble & came to in an ambulance cart & spent the night in Hospital but was on parade again yesterday & perfectly right again now. I hear they may have reported me wounded by mistake and also because Tullibardine was more or less instrumental in picking me up or coming to the rescue & the reporters I fear will make me pay for being picked up by a Marquis by making copy of my misfortunes. Mr Burnett Durley (? spelling) I know put the whole thing down in his notebook, Yesterday we never fired a shot & I was in no danger at all except when they accidentally dropped a shell near the hospital just as I was getting up on Maud's back to get away again to the Troop, & today at present we are again far out of it and I dont fancy shall do anything. We are all perfectly well & happy & only want to distinguish ourselves.

Major G. F. Ellison* of the Royal Warwickshire Regiment was Assistant Provost Marshal of Clery's 2nd Division and described events in his diary:

> *Monday 5th. [February 1900]*
> Demonstration against Drakfontein by 11th B'de & guns from 7 am

---

* He was to play a key role in the reorganization of the army after the war as secretary of the Elgin Commission and the Esher Committee and as staff officer to Lord Haldane, when the latter was Secretary of State for War, holding the post of Director of Organization at the War Office. He finished his career as Lieutenant-General Sir Gerald Ellison.

till about 11. 2nd Div'n with 4th B'de (Lyttelton) began flank march across enemy's front soon after 7. Pontoon bridge over Tugela beyond enemy's left finished 11.30, but batteries not up & crossing not begun until nearly 1 pm. Buller took command about noon, and nothing more done all day but to send a batt'n supported by two more against Munger's Farm & Vaal Krantz, under a heavy art'y fire – about 70 pieces – which literally blew enemy off hill. Green hill E of Vaal Krantz ought to have been attacked simultaneously &, in original plan, was to have been, but for some absolutely inexplicable reason Buller stopped the attack. Position in evening, E end of Vaal Krantz, held by Lyttelton, with Devons at Munger's Farm.

Tuesday 6th.
Fatal results of not taking Green Hill yesterday are visible. Enemy pounded Vaal Krantz from that direction & from Brakfontein all day fire getting hotter towards evening. 6 pm went over with Hildyard's B'de to superintend relief of garrison. 4th B'de a good deal shaken by shell fire – about 70 casualties during day. Feeling bitter in camp at nothing being done. General Clery down all day with bad leg.

Wed. 7th.
Exact repetition of yesterday. Shell fire against Vaal Krantz hotter than ever, & our art'y unable to keep it down owing to long range. Losses in Vaal Krantz not great as cover much improved during night. 11th B'de brought up to Swartz Kop bivouac in morning, otherwise absolutely nothing done. Everyone in despair about Buller. Council of war in afternoon in Clery's camp as he is still unable to move. 7 pm – midnight out superintending withdrawal of Hildyard's B'de & breaking up of two pontoon bridges.

On 5 February Roberts cabled to Lansdowne:

The position we shall be in at the end of the month will depend on the result of operations to be begun today by Buller for the Relief of Ladysmith, and how I succeed in the Relief of Kimberley. If Buller is successful and I am able to hit the Boers hard, we ought not to experience much trouble in the Orange Free State, and I should hope that I ought to get some assistance from Buller in the way of troops, but I am not very sanguine about this. White's men will require rest and feeding up, and I will need a good sized force either to push through Reemen's Pass or to hold the enemy in check near Newcastle while I work round him.

I hate even to think of the possibility of White's force not being relieved. It is too dreadful to contemplate. If, however, he has to surrender, I shall advise him to destroy all his guns, ammunition and saddlery.

Buller's attack failed at a cost of 333 casualties, and led to an acrimonious exchange with Roberts, in which Buller requested reinforcement. He went on to state:

It is right you should know that, in my opinion, the fate of Ladysmith is only a question of days unless I am very considerably reinforced. Wherever I go the enemy can anticipate me in superior force. I turned yesterday from Vaal Krantz and am moving towards Colenso. The enemy have left Vaal Krantz and are now at Colenso. They do in six hours and seven miles what takes me three days and 26 miles. When I said I would try and save Ladysmith the fifth division had arrived at Cape, and the sixth and seventh were shortly to be at my disposal, but two days afterwards you were appointed and directed that all troops arriving after that date were to be kept at the Cape. I understand from you that you expect to occupy Bloemfontein by end of February and so relieve pressure on Ladysmith. I hope the forecast will prove correct but I cannot help feeling that to leave Ladysmith as it is for such a chance is a great risk and it is right I should say so. As for myself I am doing all I can and certainly have reason to think that I retain the confidence of this force who know my difficulties but if it is thought anyone else can do better I would far rather be sacrificed than run the risk of losing Ladysmith. I should like you to forward this to Secretary of State.

This brought a sharp rejoinder from Roberts, in which he stated:

By the middle of January you were acquainted with White's position, resources and inability to afford you material assistance, and that on 26th January I gave you specific information of my intentions which involved the employment on offensive field operations of every soldier in Cape Colony that could be spared from defensive duties within the colony. It will also be seen that from the date of my assumption of the chief command until yesterday I have had no reason to suppose that you considered reinforcements necessary for the relief of Ladysmith. To send you large reinforcements now would entail the abandonment of a plan of operations the object of which was explained to you on 26th January, and in the prosecution of which, I am convinced, lies our best chance of success both in Natal and on the north of Cape Colony. Such a course would involve endless confusion and protracted delay and as Cape Colony is weakly held might not improbably lead to a rising of the disaffected Dutch population. I must therefore request that, while maintaining a bold front, you will act strictly on the defensive until I have time to see whether the operations I am undertaking will produce the effect I hope from them. The repeated loss of men on the Tugela line without satisfactory results is what our small army cannot afford. I will gladly meet your wishes as regards the remaining battery of five inch guns but can do nothing more. Your two telegrams under reply and my answers to them are being repeated to the Secretary of State for War.

4

THE TIDE TURNS

February 1900

Roberts had originally intended to leave the relief of Kimberley until after he had captured Bloemfontein, which might by itself achieve that; but threats from Rhodes that if Roberts did not come straight to Kimberley he would surrender it to the Boers, and the fears of Milner about the security of Cape Colony, caused him to change his mind and decide to give priority to the relief of Kimberley and advance to Bloemfontein from that direction. In an attempt to free his forces from close dependence on the railway, he attempted to build up a centralized transport force, removing control of their transport wagons, drawn by mules and oxen, from lower formations and units in the infantry divisions, and handing it over to the Army Service Corps, formed in 1888. Roberts however was critical of the Corps. In a letter to Lansdowne after the Battle of Paardeberg, he compared the supply and transport system unfavourably with that in India, placing much of the blame on Wolseley's reforms, which had downgraded the Quartermaster-General's Department. He wrote:

> The Army Service Corps officers carry out their duties of supply and transport well enough in peace time, but they are quite unable to grapple with the heavy transport demands which a large army in the field makes upon them. The whole matter was in such inextricable confusion when I arrived in South Africa that I had to organize a special transport department at the head of which I placed Major General Sir William Nicholson, an officer of considerable experience in this particular kind of work, and I have no hesitation in saying that, had I not taken this step, this force would still be immobile and confined to the line of the railway, an arrangement which would have effectively prevented my carrying the war into the enemy's country.
>
> As regards 'supply' too, there are a good many shortcomings.

Bread is quite an exceptional issue. The ovens are so clumsy that they cannot be carried on the line of march, so that throughout the campaign we shall have to depend mainly on biscuits – not so good for, or so much liked by, soldiers as bread. On the march from Kabul to Kandahar, I don't think there was a day when the men were without bread.

Our water supply arrangements are quite inadequate for an army operating in a barren dry country, such as this; and, as you know, we have had to apply to India to send us bhisties and puckals* for bullocks.

Our signalling arrangements are very faulty, and the necessity for their being capable of expansion in time of war was evidently overlooked at Aldershot. This country is admirably adapted for heliograph and flag signalling, but we cannot take full advantage of it for want of a sufficient number of heliographs and properly trained men. Signalling is essentially a duty which belongs to the Q.M.G.'s Department.

I feel sure you would wish to have the benefit of my experiences, and will not think I have any desire to draw invidious comparisons between the home and Indian arrangements.

The centralization of transport was unpopular and was criticized as having seriously adverse effects on the mobility and flexibility of the infantry, of which Roberts had five divisions, Methuen's original two having been reinforced by the 6th (Lieutenant-General Thomas Kelly-Kenny) and the 7th (Major-General Charles Tucker), both recently arrived from Britain, and a newly formed 9th Division (Major-General Sir Henry Colvile) of two brigades, one of which was the Highland Brigade which had been at Magersfontein. French's cavalry division of 5,000 cavalry and mounted infantry, including six regular cavalry regiments, kept control of its own mule-drawn transport. The whole force, including that of Methuen still manning the Modder, totalled 40,000 white troops and 4,000 native drivers.

Roberts now thought it prudent to consider who should take command, if anything happened to him. In a letter to Lansdowne, he wrote:

---

* OED: 'Bheesty, bheestie. In India, the servant who supplies an establishment with water, which he carries in a skin slung on his back.' A puckal was a canvas bag for carrying water, which kept the water cool by evaporation.

Kitchener is the only man able to manage this business, and I trust that he will be appointed. I cannot recommend any of those senior to him. Buller is evidently wanting in self reliance, and the reverses he has met with must have shaken the confidence of the troops in his power to lead them to victory. Warren I hardly know, but he has the credit of being a bad tempered, wanting-in-tact sort of man, and it is evident that something went wrong between him and his officers during the attack on the Spion Kop, by Buller using the expression 'mutual recriminations' and finding it necessary to take over the command of the operation himself. Methuen is out of the question [Roberts had been scheming with Lansdowne for some time to get rid of him; but he appears to have been protected by Wolseley and perhaps because he was in the Guards] – Clery does not strike me as being a man of any great ability – Forestier Walker would never do, and then comes Kitchener. It is unfortunate that there are no men of military genius amongst our senior officers, but I believe this has always been the case – Napoleon experienced this, and Wellington too always said that he had not a single General he could trust to act alone. The only possible conclusion is that very few men are fit to be commanders of armies, and the stake is far too serious for any untried man to be appointed when a tried man is available.

The force had assembled round Ramdam, ten miles east of the railway at Graspan and twenty from the Modder, by 11 February, from where Roberts, using Kitchener more as a deputy commander than a chief of staff, planned to outflank Cronje to the east, directing French to thrust rapidly to Kimberley.

French set off before dawn on 12 February and crossed the Riet River by three fords almost without opposition, but halted on the far side waiting for his mule wagons to catch up. However they had got stuck behind Tucker's oxen-drawn ones and did not leave Ramdam until 5 p.m. They then got mixed up with Tucker's at the fords, and it was not until 15 February that French was at last free to start his advance beyond the Modder. His leading troops contacted two Boer positions, held by about 2,000 men, at Abon's Dam, four miles on; and French ordered his men to charge through the gap between them.

Captain R. W. D. Bellew was with the 16th Lancers and recorded in his diary:

Up at daylight again, and moved N of Kimberley no water or feed horses in desperate state were sent out as advanced squadron and came under the hottest fire we've yet had while cutting wire had to retire fortunately only 4 horses hit Got back after dark

Rhodes's threat to surrender, signalled to Roberts on 9 February, was provoked by a new threat to Kimberley, which seriously affected the morale of its population, who, although on short rations, particularly the Africans, had remained on the whole phlegmatically calm. They had been sporadically shelled by Boer 9- and 15-pounders, but those had caused little damage and few casualties. The garrison's own 7-pounders lacked the range to answer back. This prompted Rhodes's enterprising American mining engineer, George Labram, to construct a 4-inch gun out of steel piping, to fire a 28lb shell. He named it Long Cecil, and it fired first on 19 January. The Boer response came on 7 February when the Long Tom, which had been damaged in the raid on Gun Hill at Ladysmith on 8 December and since repaired in the Pretoria railway workshops, came into action, firing twenty-two of its 94lb shells into the centre of Kimberley. Next day it was thirty shells, and then, on 9 February, seventy-four, one of the four people killed being George Labram, while dressing for dinner in the Grand Hotel. Relations between Rhodes and the garrison commander, Lieutenant-Colonel Kekewich, had never been good. Now they became openly hostile, as Rhodes summoned a public protest meeting and instigated a leader in the *Diamond Fields Advertiser* which ended with the words: 'Is it unreasonable, when our women and children are being slaughtered, and our buildings fired, to expect something better than that a large British army should remain inactive in the presence of eight or ten thousand peasants?'

When Kekewich reported this to Roberts, the latter replied on 10 February:

I beg you will represent to the Mayor and Mr Rhodes as strongly as you possibly can the disastrous and humiliating effect of surrendering after so prolonged and glorious a defence. Many days cannot possibly pass before Kimberley will be relieved as we commence active operations tomorrow. Our future military operations depend in a large degree on your maintaining your position a very short time longer, and our prestige would suffer severely if Kimberley were to fall into hands of enemy. Those therefore who counsel surrender should carefully consider the very serious responsibility they incur from a national point of view.

In a separate message Roberts told Kekewich:

As I understand that Kimberley is under martial law, you have full power to prohibit, by force if necessary, any public meeting you consider undesirable under present circumstances and also to arrest any individual, no matter what his position may be, who may act in a manner prejudicial to national interests. I desire you to exercise to the full, if necessary, your powers defined above; you will have my full support in so doing. You can assure all who are now apprehensive that we shall strain every nerve to relieve you, which will I hope be in a few days' time.

Kekewich passed the first message on to Rhodes on the latter's assurance that the timing of Roberts's move was kept secret; but Rhodes immediately broke his promise by announcing the news from the steps of the Kimberley Club. Kekewich, understandably, made no attempt to implement the directive in the second message.

True to their principles, the Boers silenced Long Tom on Sunday 11 February, while the inhabitants improved their shelters and Rhodes, without consulting Kekewich, announced that the mineshafts would be available overnight for those who wished to shelter there. 2,500 women and children did so, finding that no sanitary arrangements had been provided. It was therefore with enormous relief and excitement that French's vanguard, Rimington's 'Tigers', a rough-riding outfit raised in Cape Colony, and the Royal Scots Greys, was welcomed as it rode into the town at 6 p.m. on 15 February after a gallop across the veld that tested the unacclimatized horses to the limit. 500 had died or collapsed even before the division reached the Modder. Rhodes prepared his own welcome to French with care. Champagne and locally grown fruit, with other delicacies that others had not seen for many months, were produced for a splendid meal at the Sanatorium Hotel, to which Kekewich had difficulty in gaining access in order to report to French, with whom he appears to have had a frosty interview. Two days later his place as garrison commander was taken by Colonel T. C. Porter, commander of the 1st Cavalry Brigade.

Captain Foster was with one of the Royal Horse Artillery batteries accompanying the relief force and wrote in his diary for the day:

Feb 15th.

An eventful day in the history of this war, as to-day the relief of Kimberley was effected with comparatively very slight loss. The cavalry division left Klip Drift at 9 a.m. & soon 5 Boer guns commenced shelling some of our cavalry who appeared on a ridge North of the Klip Drift. Q, T & U batteries RHA were taken up on to this ridge to shell the Boer guns. Naturally they came under a very hot shrapnel fire as they came into action, as the Burghers had already found the range very accurately & the huge target they presented as they came on to the crest of the hill showed the Boers exactly where our guns were situated. Q & U batteries lost rather badly. Carbutt in U was killed & Barnes & Humphreys in Q wounded, also about 19 N.C.O.'s & men killed & wounded & many horses placed hors-de-combat. G & P were ordered up at one time to reinforce these 3 batteries on the left, but their movements were altered just as they were coming up into action thank goodness & they moved behind Q, T & U & forwards towards the North coming into action against Boers in Kopjes on our right front. At this time Gen French decided to risk a bit & make a dash up a plain about 2 miles broad with all his cavalry & thus turn the enemy's left flank. The move was entirely successful and it was a grand sight to see line after line of cavalry galoping as hard as they could for 5 miles up the plain. Kopjes lined both sides of the plain & the Boers blazed away from either side but we soon cleared them out. The 7 batteries RHA followed the Cavalry as fast as they could & the whole force halted for ½ an hour at the top of the plain, where we collected our own wounded and the Boer wounded & prisoners. The Lancers had managed to spear some twenty odd Boers. On resuming our march the three Brigades marched separately, Broadwood's on the left. About 3 pm we sighted Kimberley in the distance across a huge plain & also saw two Boer guns firing at the town. The Division moved across the plain Broadwood's Bde halted for the night at a farm called Wimbledon Common or rather Bernhardhuitsfontein on the outskirts of & about 5 miles from the centre of the town. The other two Bdes moved round by the East towards the north of Kimberley shelling two Boer laagers on their way. The Boers got the guns that we had seen firing away before our stone cold & exhausted cavalry horses could reach them. Two or three of the defenders rode out to meet us as we approached & they appeared indeed delighted to see us. We eat a good meal & then lay down, tired but glad indeed that we had at last relieved Kimberley after 2½ months of delay. Gen French & some of his staff dined with Cecil Rhodes.

Mrs Haddock was the wife of William Haddock, a doctor in Kimberley. On 2 March she wrote a long letter to her sister about her experience. After expressing her great annoyance that people like her had had no opportunity to see or hear Roberts and Kitchener, who spent all their time with Rhodes, when they visited Kimberley on the previous day, she started her account:

The first day Martial Law was proclaimed 15th [December] – All water cut off, All lights out & everyone must be in their own houses by 9 p.m. seemed to be terrible at the time – the boys each ran off to their Forts, also Willie to his naturally. We did not know what was going to happen – but everyone expected something terrible – trains & waggons flew in every direction as nearly all the women were expecting to be called into laager – Sunday tho' it was – I felt it surely couldn't be so bad as that – & went down to see Lora – she was sitting in her bathroom arranging roses for her dinner table in little vases!! I stayed for a while and came back to my Chickens here – we *did* have some dinner & looked out see the poor fathers and mothers wandering about that had come in from the outskirts of the town – I truly never realised there were so many children in Kimberley – however things settled down – but if we had thought then that we had to wait for *124* days before relief came – and that the men & boys would be at their forts all that long time we would not have felt even as brave as we did – Dick and Lance have never [? been] home for a single night yet. One of my great anxieties at first was the way some of the merchants ran up the price of household necessaries – and I had not been able to lay in any stock at all, lots of people had laid in a six months store – parafin 60/- to 80/- a case tin milk 1/6 a tin candles 12/- a packet & so on – but thanks to Lieut. Col'nl Kekewich he soon put stop to all that – he was very angry – so he made a limit to prices and any one who charged more was liable to have all his or her goods confiscated and to be imprisoned – I did glory in that as all the rest of us who had no store room filled with goods – it really was a regular business after the first few weeks to tramp all over the town in search of something to eat: or what could be got to put on our bread – we found a little *chutney* not too bad at last – in fact we really lived on dry bread very often – black tea & coffee without sugar – the latter from choice – at first we were allowed half a lb of meat per adult per day – but my dear the struggle to get it – it had to be *gone* for & it was no use sending a colored servant & I did not like the girls to go alone – so it was a case of getting up about five o'clock, leaving your house as soon as you could then going down to wait in the fearful crowd I used to say of the 'great unwashed' sometimes it would mean standing three hours then the best left would be [illegible] soup meat. I used to come home often not able to get anything & then I would say 'Oh I wont try any more'. but duty used to come and say – the Children must have something to keep up their strength, so I would make other attempts. The Military then put police to regulate the crowd & you had to stand in line as you got up – but I far more often came away with nothing as I would be nearing my turn to be served I would hear the announcement *No more meat today!* Afterwards we had to do with ½ lb for two days – then we came to 1/3 horse flesh – then all horse flesh or mule or you could get your meat rations in one pint of Siege soup in place of your ¼ lb of horse flesh – it was not nice, but still we made the best of it – I certainly do not like horse flesh Ugh! some of it was fearful – the mule if in good condition is not bad – then of course such a thing as a vegetable was not to be got – excepting dry beans for a while – dry [illegible] soup (crushed mealies), rice was able to be had until the second week in January, after that if you had none, you could only beg it from the Military store, with a doctor's permit. When it came to the end of the second 6 months – we were all rationed; you could only buy a certain amount of meal or flour, if you baked at home, if so you could not buy a loaf of bread; on the other hand if you used your bread permit you could not buy an oz of flour or meal. I used to exchange sugar for meal – as we use so little of the former & the Colonials as a rule are 'sweettooths' – that we have always had plenty of bread. Of course I could not draw any rations for Dick or Lance as theirs were drawn for at their camps; you could not buy any milk without a doctor's certificate – unless you could find a friend with a cow – I used to think it a sin for healthy people to take milk simply as a luxury while so many babies & delicate people died for want of milk diet. It was almost impossible to get such a thing as a bit of fat of any kind after the first month or two, then it was found that Cocoa

or Salad oil was a good substitute so there was a run on oils!! Until
there was none left – then many turned their attention to 'Russian
tallow' & I used to make some quite nice biscuits of mealie meal with
oil and a little flour, – of course you could not buy any. & eggs were
and still are 20/- to 30/- a doz: we often had mealie meal porridge
twice *even three* times a day; we often had great jokes on what we
had been able to buy – & where we got it – in fact you felt quite
proud to carry a bunch of carrots or *even more so* if you had been
fortunate to get a pumpkin or vegetable marrow to bring home; the
trades people were nearly all short of hands as nearly every man was
engaged on the Town Guard – they all wore 'Khaki' which gave quite
a Military appearance to the whole town – Lora's husband was
member of the Buffs fort – so of course was never at home at nights
– so one of the girls always slept at their house with her – it used to
be our nightly job to back down and leave one – then it used to be
such a hurry scurry to get back by nine o'clock – that I got a permit
from Capt'n McInnes (it reads like the permit of a rake) it simply
said 'pass Mrs Haddock and daughters from nine o'clock until twelve
o'clock' with his signature. After that we were never in a hurry – at
last we were so well known to all the guard we never had a 'halt who
goes there'.

Euphoria at the successful relief of Kimberley was dampened by a
setback which had befallen the transport of the infantry on the same
day. There had been long delays at Waterval Drift over the Riet, near
which Roberts had set up his field headquarters. Steeply sloping banks
and a muddy bottom had imposed considerable strain on the 3,000 oxen
as they hauled their 200 wagons across. It was therefore decided to allow
them to rest and graze on the far bank, but no measures were taken to
protect them there. De Wet, whose Commando was hiding not far away,
seized the opportunity to attack them, scattering the oxen and seizing
the contents, on which Roberts's infantry were relying for their supply
on the way to Bloemfontein. Impatient to embark on his march to the
Free State capital, Roberts decided to abandon the wagons, although they
constituted a third of the transport on which he was relying for his
supply. In ordering Tucker to deal with the situation there, he said:

If Cape boys have run away, and you don't see your way to bringing
the wagons here during the night, leave them, destroying them as

well as you may be able and driving out the bullocks. I want you and all the troops to be here before daybreak and am anxious there should be no further loss of life – even leave the bullocks if necessary.

Percy Sunderland, an NCO of the Lincolns, was in this force and wrote about it, a considerable time afterwards, in an account of the campaign:

When day broke about 5 a.m. we found a large force bivouacking there, the bivouac resting on the Riet River, which ran immediately to the S. of it. The new arrivals were the Highland Brigade and Gen'l Smith-Dorrien's Brigade. The camp was in an awful state, littered with the paunches of slaughtered sheep and oxen, there being no time for clearing up. Lord Roberts and his Staff were in a dirty, squalid little farmhouse in the middle of it all. We breakfasted, and were then allowed to rest after our night march, for a few hours. About the middle of the morning we heard the sound of firing from the W. and shortly afterwards an order came for the King's Own Borderers, a company of Mounted Infantry, and a Field Battery, to go back to Waterval Drift, where a large Convoy of ours had been attacked. At the same time, the 15th Brigade under General Wavell, half a company R. Engineers, and a Battery, were sent to take the town of Jacobsdaal, about 5 miles off. Soon after we heard gun-fire from both the Waterval and Jacobsdaal directions. About 4 p.m. the rest of the Division, i.e. our Brigade, were ordered to march to Waterval in support of the force sent in the morning, which had failed to extricate the Convoy.

We marched for about an hour and arrived at the Drift just at dusk; after being arranged in fighting order, ready to attack at daybreak, we lay out on the rocks all night, and very cold it was, wondering what would happen in the morning.

However this was not to be our baptism of fire, after all, as about 3 a.m. orders arrived to retire again, leave the Convoy to its fate, and resume the march, Lord Roberts evidently thinking the loss not so important as the loss of life and time involved in fighting for it, but the men were angry and disappointed and there were many who disagreed with him over this affair, even at the risk of some loss of life, as there were about 200 wagons full of rations and forage, and one of the first fruits of this was cutting down of our rations of bully & biscuit from 5 to 1½ per day – quarter rations, and on this starvation allowance we had to march and fight. This weakened the men, so that thousands afterwards fell victim to dysentery and enteric on the way to Bloemfontein.

At one moment Roberts contemplated abandoning his plan to deal with Cronje and to withdraw to the railway, but one of his transport officers persuaded him that the use of French's mule transport and some wagons that Cronje had abandoned could meet his needs. In reporting this to Lansdowne, he wrote:

Yesterday, as I wired to you, French got through to Kimberley and found the garrison cheery and well. I was sorry that a force of Boers was able to harass yesterday a convoy of provisions at Warteval [sic] drift, on which we greatly depended for food, and before I could send back reinforcements to the escort, they had so damaged the oxen and carts with their guns, that they could not be removed without a risk of the force becoming involved in an attempt to dislodge the Boers from the strong position they had taken up which would probably have resulted in an unnecessary loss of life. I therefore ordered the Officer Commanding to leave the convoy and withdraw his force during the night, which he did unopposed. This loss of provisions and transport has of course been very inconvenient, but we have been able to replace deficiencies by having opened up communications with the Modder River.

While Roberts was facing this crisis and French was enjoying Rhodes's hospitality, Cronje decided to abandon his position at Magersfontein and trek eastward up the Modder towards Bloemfontein. He set off by moonlight that night and passed undetected north of Kelly-Kenny's 6th Division at Klip Drift, twenty miles upstream from the Modder bridge, his bullock-drawn wagons plodding along at the rate of ten miles a day. Next day, the 16th, Kelly-Kenny's vanguard caught up with him, but he shook them off. On the 17th 1,500 cavalrymen, all that were fit from French's cavalry division, were guided by Captain Chester Master of the 'Tigers' to find Cronje near Paardeberg Drift, thirty miles upstream from Modder River Station and twenty miles north-east of Ramdam. There Cronje, with some 5,000 men, formed a laager of covered wagons on the north bank of the river, protected by positions dug into both banks of the river on the pattern that Methuen had met lower down at the end of November. Captain Foster's diary describes this:

Feb 17th

A very different day to what we expected. Were suddenly ordered at 2 a.m. to saddle up; the Brigade left camp at 3 a.m. We heard that Kitchener had said that if we could head Cronje off a certain drift, that we ought to smash him. Away we went South East at a very fair pace, in fact as much as our horses could do. About 11.30 a.m. we seized 12 Boers in a farm, 12 others soon afterwards came & gave themselves up. We then heard that the guns were badly wanted. Off we went again; & this time not further than 1½ miles when we suddenly appeared in full view of Cronje's huge laager at a range of 3,400. The wagons were in the act of crossing the drift. Off we loosed our guns; whizz-bang came the Boer shells in return, but altho' they burst all round us they luckily did no harm. Some of the 12th Lancers seized a drift on our left but had to retire as the Boers turned up in strong force. On the right the Boers came out & tried to encircle us, but the Tins* raced for a Kopje's got there first & held the Boers in check on our right flank for the rest of the day. After being in action for about 1½ hours, I was sent up to the Tins with my two guns. On coming into action the first trumpeter was hit by a bullet in the knee, but we chased some Boers out of a range of Kopje's where they had become annoying. There we remained from 1 o'clock on Saturday till 9 a.m. on Sunday, when we moved down into the plain & got some distance nearer to the Boer trenches. During the Saturday afternoon we kept on plugging away at the Boers, and at one time a squadron of 10th Hussars was sent forwards from our Kopje's to see if another certain Kopje's was held; but they came under such a heavy cross fire that they had to come back with 7 or 8 empty saddles & many men walking & about six horses carrying two men each. About 4 p.m. we began to look rather anxiously for Kitchener & our Infantry which were marching up the further side of the river. Kitchener had promised that they should be up by 10 a.m. About 6 p.m. we saw some M.I. which we made out to be the advance troops of Kitchener's two divisions under Tucker & Kelly-Kenny. They appeared to come under a very hot Boer fire & retired into some scrub from which they kept up a desultory fire. Just before dark in the far distance we made out the head of two longer columns approaching on the further side of the river. We remained in action

* The Life Guards.

all night with Boers all round us & fired our guns at hourly intervals at the Boer laager just to keep them awake and busy. Our men & horses had had no food all day & except a little tea in the evening had to lie down hungry. The horses had to go 3½ miles to get water in the evening.

While Captain Foster was thus engaged, the seventeen-year-old Midshipman James Menzies, with the Naval Brigade's guns, was writing his Sunday letter home:

Jacobsdaal, Orange Free State, Sunday Aft. Feb 18th 1900
Dear Mother, You see Jacobsdaal has fallen to us. Cronje is flying from Magersfontein with Kitchener in chase & we are cutting him off. Its Sunday aft & so I am writing to you. I can see you at home writing your sunday aft. letters with a roaring fire. Can you picture me writing my sunday aft letter in camp, a roaring sun overhead.

Well we left Enslin on Tuesday morning last at 4 o'clock with the Canadians, Highland Brigade & Gordons under General Macdonald (Sir Hector). We marched to Ramdam (in the O.F.S. 10 miles) & then to Waterfall on the Riet River. There we had a sharp engagement whilst crossing. The Naval Brigade had no casualties, though for 6 hours we were under a hot fire (the 6 hours passed like 5 minutes). Here I must relate a little incident. You have doubtlessly heard of the 'Pom-Pom' if you have not, it is a maxim throwing a 1 lb bursting shell at the rate of 10 per second. Two years ago & it was refused by the English government and so the Boers bought it. Well ever since the war began every one was quacking about this 'terrible weapon', they attribute the loss of the 10 guns at Colenso, to it, but it is harmless absolutely harmless as I will show. The Boers had two of these guns in the hills by the Riet River & were using them on us. I was standing by the Commander near the guns, when four of these shells hit the sand, one after the other, about 6 inches from my foot. They every one burst & threw up a little sand but the explosion was no worse than a squib, did no harm, at all. It is the noise that damages. Well we crossed the Riet River all night & went on to Waydraw [?] drift where we arrived at 5.30 am on Thursday morning [15 February]. From there we marched to Jacobsdaal had a sharp engagement outside & took the town. Here we are paying 3/6 a bottle for beer, we are awfully badly off we feed on biscuit & tinned beef nothing else. We are waiting here for Cronje to be smashed & then we are off to Pretoria. It is very strange being under fire. You can see the enemy's positions plainly always but they are always behind a big rock.

It is a beastly country here. The Boers are quite welcome to it all as far as its value is concerned.

Jacobsdaal is full of the wounded Boers. We are nursing them back to life, it is also crammed with German doctors.

One of the English soldiers was hanged this morning for looting gear out of a house in the town, the troops had all been warned about it & the penalty, as soon as we got here so it was the fellows own fault.

P. S. Please send a bottle of 'Thirst Tabloids' Borroughes & Wellcome.

Lieutenant Edward Manisty of the City Imperial Volunteers was also involved in the attack on Jacobsdaal and described it in a letter to his mother:

About a mile from Jacobsdaal the 1st & 2nd lines were dismounted & advanced in skirmishing order. I had no idea that we should have a fight as the place had been passed through a day before by our cavalry. Soon after the firing line had dismounted the Colonel ordered me up & to close my men up to 2 horses length interval, & advance. He advanced us through the firing line at the trot which I could not understand, & we rode up to the point C. on the plan, coming up with us himself, which I could not again understand the necessity for. He halted & dismounted us, when immediately bullets came whizzing at us from three sides. He immediately gave us the order to mount & retire. I ran to my horse but it would not stand so I dodged behind a dead horse & lay down. When I looked round I only saw 3 or 4 mounted retiring, & thought all the others had gone. I then found the horse I was behind was a dark one so wriggled back on my stomach about 10 yards away from it & lay still. I then found that there were some men behind me unhurt, & who were also lying low, Stallard amongst them. Out of my 15 men none were hurt except two of those who had mounted. It appeared that the others had not heard the order to retire.

Sergeant Major Rouse bullet through thigh –

Private Edwards, my groom, bullet through seat: neither serious.

I must own that I was in a blue funk at first.

The main attack was then directed to the left flank of the village – so we were practically left alone for about ½ an hour. Then the guns began to play behind us & they shelled the kraal on our left, also parts of the village. A battalion of Infantry came across the plain behind. As soon as they came up we joined them & advanced.

It was awfully pretty the way the shells burst just at the right moment.

As soon as our main body got to the village on left flank the Boers scooted across the hills behind on horseback, being followed by shells.

It was rather a rum experience, having bullets whizzing over one's head from 4 different quarters (3 Boer & 1 English) a few feet above one's head.

Buckets of water were drunk when we got in.

We were formed up in market square, & ordered to take up outpost position on North side, but only a few horses had been brought in. I took the first that came which was a brute, but just as we were moving off my own was brought in. We were on outpost until 10 P.M. when I made my supper off a slice of bread & a biscuit, & slept in the street.

I now find that we were sent forward to draw the enemy's fire & so unmask their position. We have stayed here since.

Roberts was suffering from a chill and deputed Kitchener to exercise command, telling Kelly-Kenny to his annoyance, aggravated by his seniority to Kitchener, to regard the latter's orders as his own. Kelly-Kenny's plan was to surround Cronje, cutting him off from any help, and bombard him into surrender; but Kitchener was impatient. He decided to attack him before he could move or any help could reach him. His plan for the 18th, a Sunday, was for the 6th Division to attack frontally across the river from the south, while Colvile's 9th Division on the left would attack upstream, Major-General Hector Macdonald's Highland Brigade on the south bank and Major-General Horace Smith-Dorrien's 19th Brigade, having forded the river at Paardeberg Drift, on the north. On Kelly-Kenny's right, Colonel O. C. Hannay's Mounted Infantry and two battalions of Brigadier-General T. E. Stephenson's 18th Brigade from 6th Division would also ford the river and attack down-stream on the north bank. This involved 6th Division in an attack almost identical to that which Colvile had experienced when commanding the

Guards Brigade's attack on the Modder, and the result was much the same. It was not long before the leading battalions were pinned down by fire from the river bank and forced to lie in the open in the blazing sun as casualties mounted.

The 2nd Buffs were in the 6th Division and their second-in-command, Major J. B. Backhouse, wrote in his diary:

> *Sun. 18th. 3 am.*
> Marched off, changed direction, retired, & finally turned squarely about. 6 am: after we had gone a little way, I was detached with 4 companies as a Baggage Guard, at the same time a fight began, which eventually became a big one in [*sic*] our front: the enemy held a strong position in the bend of the Modder River, we occupying the ridge above it: about 2 p.m. my 4 companies were ordered to join in in support of the attack, & were now under a hot fire, until 7 p.m. when we retired, & took up a position as outposts. The fight resembled, in many ways, the attack on the Modder River in November last, attempts were made by us to get over the river, & ended in, at one point, our men being on one side, & the Boers on the other: our loss has, I am afraid, been severe, about 800 casualties: Generals Knox & McDonald wounded: Buffs loss Captain Geddes wounded, 2 men killed, 14 wounded, & 2 missing. The chaos at the end of the fight was unique, the Staff helpless, Regiments mixed up, no one to give any definite directions, & the whole day's operations, to my mind, a blunder: no attempt should have been made to get over the river. All tired & done up at night, nothing to eat all day.

> *Mon. 19th. 4 am.*
> After an awfully cold night, not having any greatcoats, we had to walk about all night to keep ourselves warm. About 6 am, we took up a position on the ridge, overlooking the river, as a containing force, as although some of the Boers have gone, a good many remain. Cronje unconditionally surrendered during the afternoon, and we all gave three cheers but it was premature, he changed his mind, & we began bombarding him with about 40 guns until evening. General French co-operating on the other side of the river, so we must capture them eventually. We did outpost duty at night on the right of the positions. The Oxford L.I. & Gloucesters attacked a Kopje on our right, which they did with some casualties: the night passed quietly as far as we were concerned: the Artillery firing shell

occasionally at the Boer Laager, which was set on fire to-day, as it also was yesterday. Lord Roberts visited our Brigade in the afternoon, & was loudly cheered, he rode from Jacobsdaal, 32 miles, with the Foreign Attaches to-day. We are getting filthy, & have not washed our faces for 3 days.

Lieutenant Charles Veal of the Welch Regiment also took part in this attack and wrote in his diary:

About 2 am on the 18th Feb'y 1900, we were ordered to fall in, and, as we had laid down as we were in the ranks, this did not take long. I overheard part of a whispered conversation between the staff officers (I think it was Kelly-Kenny & his staff) to the effect that he had better send the first regiment he could find on as advance guard in the new direction. The Welch was the regiment fallen upon & off we stumbled in the dark not knowing in the least where we were going. Dawn broke about 3.30 am & then we got a little clearer as to passing events. We now formed three extended lines of double companies with two companies in support and advanced along the plane [*sic*]. About 5 am we topped the edge of the plateau and saw before us the Modder River running right across our front and the long slope of the other side up to the hills about 10 miles away where French's heliograph flashed in the morning sun. We continued to advance down towards the river and I took the opportunity of Totfords coming up to shift onto him the burden of some of my kit. I handed him to a drummer and that was the last I saw of him.

About 1000 yards from the river banks, which were thickly shaded by Mimosa trees & small bushes, we came under a very heavy fire which the concealed Boers opened upon us. Hunger & want of sleep did not make us, or me at any rate, feel particularly brave but we continued our advance in alternate rushes of three lines. I was in the third line under Maj. Ball, who presently came along to me. We lay down for a little in a shallow dip in the ground & discussed the situation until we came to the conclusion that one particular Boer was making remarkably good but unpleasant shooting at us. We hunted for him in the bushes through our glasses, and at last I thought I saw a suspicious object up a tree. As the officers were armed with a carbine, I luckily turned to borrow a rifle from Sergt. Phelps or some other man near, when I received my quietus in the shape of a bullet through the head. Major Ball came to the rescue at

and advance across an open plain and attack with the Highland Brigade under Hector McDonald, which we did and soon found ourselves in for a big fight as the Boers were in great numbers on the opposite side of the river. The bullets & Shells soon began to fly thick and fast and our poor comrades began to topple over. The enemy's fire got so heavy that we had to lay down and advance by rushes. It soon appeared to me that (as usual) I was in the thick of it, for as we advanced my poor old section went down like *ninepins*. Poor old Dave McHay was the first man hit, and shortly after poor old Forbes was killed oh 'my God' it was awful poor fellow to see him in his last struggle. I shall never forget this and none of us could help him for if we moved an inch, we got such a shower of bullets after us that it was certain death. However we presently got the order to advance again and rushed on and I saw some more of the section topple over but kept rushing until we got the order to lay down again and the only one of the section I could see was Sgt Pirie, and we stuck together for the remainder of the day. We made one more rush after that and everyone seeing it would be madness to go any further in the face of such a fire we got as good cover as was possible and remained there for the remainder of the day. Our fellows soon ran short of ammunition and some more was sent to us on a mule but both mule and man were shot attempting to reach us. Pirie and I reserved our ammunition and only fired when we saw anyone to fire at. About 1 o'clock one of the Enemy's Batterys of artillery about 5 or 6 guns came and formed themselves up right in front of where we were laying. Well I thought we should all have been blown to atoms for there was not a single big gun of ours anywhere near, and their shells were soon flying all around us doing some terrible work. They kept this up for about 3 hours shells all the time dropping in front to the right and left and behind me. At last this Battery moved a little further on, and I can tell you we were all very glad of it. After that the firing was not so heavy for a time and I managed to get a 'smoke'. About 4 o'clock a mixed party of Canadians and Seaforths got round the left flank of the Enemy and tried to charge them. Alas it was a fatal charge for many, for poor chaps they were met with terrible fire and fell in dozens. However it had the desired effect for shortly after I saw the Boers retiring their Artillery. Soon after it got dark and the firing ceased altogether, and never I think in my whole life was I so glad to see the darkness come. I asked one officer whether we were to go back to camp and he said there were no orders but to remain where we were. I felt a bit queer I can tell you as we had none of us had a bit[e] nor drop this day. Pirie and I with one or two more lay there for a long time, hearing poor fellows moaning all around us, till we could stick it no longer and agreed to carry one of the poor fellows into camp without asking permission from anyone.

In commenting on the battle, Roberts wrote to Lansdowne:

Another point which affects military operations nowadays is the long range of modern weapons which necessitates such a large area of ground being taken up that troops are exhausted before they reach a point where a supreme effort is required of them and this is accentuated by the great heat and the impossibility of providing an ample supply of drinking water to troops on the march.

As the battle started, he signalled to Buller:

The present appears a favourable time for the attempt [to afford assistance to White, if only such as will occupy the enemy sufficiently to prevent them from attacking him] to be made if you feel fairly confident of success. Cronje is now almost surrounded by our troops ... If we are successful during the next few days, the Boers are bound to be greatly discouraged, and if Ladysmith is ever to be relieved now would seem to be the time.

This was reinforced by a signal two days later saying that there was information that the Boers were hurrying troops to oppose Roberts and ending: 'Do all that is possible to effect the relief of White's garrison.'

By midday on the 18th the attack at Paardeberg had petered out. Kitchener now told Colvile that Smith-Dorrien should start his attack on the north bank and ordered Kelly-Kenny to renew his, the latter, in order to do so, removing the troops at Stinkfontein Farm who occupied an important kopje (later known as Kitchener's Kopje) which dominated the right flank. Hannay also was to start his attack from the right downstream on the north bank. In the event Kelly-Kenny did not renew his attack. Hannay led his mounted infantry in a charge which petered out 200 yards from the Boer defences, Hannay himself being killed. Smith-Dorrien's attack was no more successful, having been prematurely launched by one of his battalions before a proper fire-plan had been made.

While these attacks were going on, De Wet, who had been hiding his Commando of 300 men thirty miles away to the south-east, rode to the rescue and, appearing out of the blue at about 5 p.m., seized Kitchener's Kopje, posing a significant threat to the right flank, which could not be ignored, and offering a possible escape route to Cronje, although it would have involved him in crossing the river. As the evening shadows lengthened, Kitchener had to admit failure, reporting to Roberts:

> We did not succeed in getting into the enemy's convoy, though we drove the Boers back a considerable distance along the river bed. The troops are maintaining their position and I hope tomorrow we shall be able to do something more definite . . .

Nevertheless the British artillery had done its work. Cronje's wagons had been smashed and casualties to men, and even more so to horses, had been heavy. Morale was low and on the 19th Cronje asked for a truce in which to bury his dead and for help from British doctors to tend his wounded. This was refused by Roberts, his reason being that he suspected it as designed to gain time for Boer reinforcements to arrive. Cronje replied: 'If you are so uncharitable as to refuse me a truce as requested, then you may do as you please. I shall not surrender alive. Therefore bombard me as you please.'

Roberts, who had recovered from his chill, prompted by Kitchener, at first wanted to renew the attack on the 20th, but was dissuaded from it by all the other generals. He then swung to the other extreme and suggested a withdrawal to Klip Kraal Drift. Kelly-Kenny opposed that, but Roberts was still intending it when De Wet withdrew from his position on Kitchener's Kopje just as it was being attacked by Tucker's 7th Division, in which Percy Sunderland's Lincolns took part. He described the action:

> *Wednesday Feb. 21st.*
> About 5 a.m. while it was still dark, the officers came round waking us in whispers, and presently my Colour Sergeant gave me an order to take 3 men, roll up the company's blankets, and pack them on the wagons, but to make no noise. This occupied about 10 minutes, when we had done, we were surprised to find that the Battalion had formed up and marched off. It was just getting light now, and we could see them in extended order moving towards Kitchener's Hill. I remarked, as we shouldered our rifles and started off after them

'Take it easy, chaps, we shall be in at the death', quite thinking they were making an attack on the hill. Just then the wagons behind us started to move off, the Kaffir drivers making the usual hideous cries to start the oxen, when to our great surprise, from *behind* us came a tremendous rifle fire, the bullets fairly whistling about our ears, – and looking ahead, we saw the Battalion open out into wider interval and commence to double. We were retiring, under fire! As afterwards transpired, the guide had led us wrong, (either accidentally or purposely, for they were all Africanders, and many of them spies) nearly into the Boer trenches, and we had laid all night within 300 yards of them. As soon as day broke, however, and they could see us, they opened fire. It would have meant annihilation for us to have attacked just then, so [*sic*] they had the advantage of cover, so we got the order to retire.

The morning was thick and foggy, and this was our salvation, as they could not very well distinguish us in our khaki uniforms from the veldt, but here and there would come a cry or a grunt, and a man would drop, killed or wounded. I ran across a Corporal of E Company and kept with them. The very air seemed to be alive with the bullets, which hummed past us like angry wasps, and raised little spurts of dust around us. We lay down behind an ant-hill to get our breath for a minute, as I did so a bullet cut right through my water bottle strap.

Now the rifle fire seemed to slacken, so we again rose and retired; we were getting out of range. Presently '*BONG!*' came out of the mist, and a screaming noise overhead told us they had commenced to shell us with one of their Krupp guns; '*BANG*' – and it had burst about 100 yards in front of us! scattering its deadly fragments in all directions.

They fired about 6 shells at us and then ceased evidently coming to the conclusion they were wasting ammunition, which was true, for no one was killed by the shell fire, but one fell among the wagons and blew several oxen to pieces. By this time we were now close under Kitchener's Hill, but rather scattered and disorganised, and we now got a second surprise. We had forgotten the Boers still held it, and a hot fire was opened on us from the top. We were now between the fires, so the order 'Left Wheel' was given, and we swung round and gained the shelter of some trees by the river-bank where we formed up into Companies, and the roll was called to see who was missing.

Officers and men alike were shaking with excitement and anger –

It had been a rude baptism of fire, (and to retire under heavy fire is one of the hardest tests, without being able to return it) and on empty stomachs too. They found 15 missing, of which 6 had been killed and 9 wounded. The teams of 2 of our wagons had also been killed, and various stores had to be left on the plain till after the surrender. A party at once went out under the white flag and brought in our dead and wounded. Among the former was the pioneer sergeant before mentioned who had been talking to me the previous morning. He was a fine figure of a man, bearded and 6 feet in height, and one of the best shots in the battalion. Our regimental doctor, Major Sutton, had been shot through both legs, but insisted on attending to the other wounded before seeing to himself.

We had breakfast and rested a while, and then about 11 a.m. moved out in open order to attack Kitchener's Hill, co-operating with the rest of the Brigade. The enemy opened a somewhat heavy fire on us, but we gradually advanced and nearly surrounded them, until at the last moment, they bolted, got on their ponies, and tried to escape. But before they had got very far they were caught up by our Cavalry, who rode right through them, killed a great many and took 50 prisoners. We advanced up the hill and found 40 prisoners, 2 wagons and a water-cart, and 30 horses. We had about 10 casualties, all wounded. After this the hill remained in our possession until the end. So the day began badly for us, it ended well and we returned to our camp in good spirits (and carrying curios in the shape of Boer bandoliers, cartridge clips, rifles, and many explosive bullets that we had taken from the prisoners) about 2 p.m.

My Company was on Outpost Duty that night facing South, and we had to lay down most of the night, as the air was alive with bullets from the laager. This kind of thing is called 'Sniping' they couldn't see us in the dark, but had a good idea where we were. A few men were hit in this way, but only slightly wounded.

It became known in the morning that for some reason or other some of the regiments in the most advanced trenches on the N. side of the river had been without food for 24 hours. So every man of ours at once offered half his scanty allowance of biscuit, and it was collected and sent to the Essex Regiment. Years afterwards in India, I met men of that battalion, who told me they should always remember with gratitude how the Lincolns sent them half their rations when they were starving.

De Wet's departure, when Cronje showed no sign of being prepared to break out, saved Roberts from a crass blunder.

On 26 February Midshipman Menzies wrote his dutiful weekly letter to his mother:

We left Jacobsdaal at 9.0 pm on Sunday night last & marched without a halt through the night until 6.30 am on Monday morning. At 7.0 Lord Roberts came up & asked us if we would proceed the same afternoon (We were at Klip drift) to where Kitchener had bottled Cronje. Although we were all fagged out we agreed to try & at 1.0 pm on Monday last we started again & marched till 8.0 pm when we bivouaced for the night. at 5 am on Tuesday we started again and at 11.0 am we arrived here at Paardeberg at 2.0 we were hard at work fighting. All this time we had nothing to eat but some putrid water & hard biscuit. marching in the heat & dust the dry thirst which overtakes one is shocking ... Our troops have surrounded Cronje who has an island & a bit of the north bank. We have placed our guns on top of a hill which is 3000 yards from their laager last tuesday afternoon we shelled them for 6 hours and must have killed hundreds there are 7000 of them altogether but they are in a splendid position. The worst of it is that we have to get our water from the river below them & they the dirty beasts throw all their refuse dead cattle & offal in the river which of course comes down to us. Every day we pull out horses & oxen in a state of decay. The water stinks and of course every drop has to be boiled before it can be used for anything. We cannot get water from above them. What we shall have to do is to starve them out, they have about 500 oxen on the island. The cold here at night is something awful the night before last I was from 8 pm to 4 am in a beastly trench on outpost duty. We lay in the trench without any shelter whatever and it rained & hailed the whole time the worst is when you come back to the bivouac in the morning like that you have no change of clothes to put on & you have to go about in wet clothes it is the rainy season here in March so it is just commencing before we arrived in this place we had not seen rain for weeks & were complaining of the dryness now it is the wet & cold, at least it is only cold at night. When we settle Cronje we shall start for Bloemfontein. Cronje will have to surrender soon they must be an awfully plucky set those Boers the way they ignore our bombardment is wonderful they take absolutely no notice of our shells. but they pay dearly for it. I suppose we kill about 200 every day. Whenever any of them show themselves we pot them. They have found out that the English are not quite the 'Verdommed Rooineks' they at first thought us although they still think us damn fools. Cronje has no doctors with him here & the other day Roberts sent in to offer him medical assistance but he said he would only except [*sic*] it on certain conditions & so of course we dried up.

The other day he sent in to say he would surrender uncon-ditionally & when Kitchener marched in to bag them he said he would not surrender & fired on our men. That is what they call playing the game.

Sniping is real sport. You get a rifle & a couple of packets of ammunition & grovel on your stomach until about 2,000 yds from the Boer lines. Then you get behind the biggest rock you see rest your rifle on it & snipe at the enemy it is rare sport. They some times fire back but never do any harm except to the rock.... I am in perfect health.*

On 27 February, the nineteenth anniversary of Majuba, Cronje surrendered with 4,019 men, 150 of whom were wounded, and 50 women. Roberts's casualties on 18 February had totalled 1,270: 24 officers and 279 men killed, 59 and 847 wounded, and 2 and 59 missing, the highest casualty figure of any one day in the war. Most of them could have been avoided if Kelly-Kenny's plan had been adopted.

*

On the following day the siege of Ladysmith was at last raised. Buller had had no intention of acceding to Roberts's 'request' that he should 'act strictly on the defensive'. He appreciated that to do so would have a serious affect on the morale of his men, who, in spite of a string of failures and casualties, were still keen to 'have a go', and, of course, on that of the garrison of Ladysmith itself. He also guessed that the threat which Roberts now posed to the Free State would draw away at least Free State troops, if not others, from Natal. Morale in Ladysmith had certainly sunk to a low level: the siege had now lasted for 100 days: in order to preserve the possibility of making some use of his cavalry, White had kept fodder for them in the form of 'mealies', which could

* He was to die of enteric the following year.

have been used for human consumption, and rations were therefore meagre: sickness was rife, including an epidemic of typhoid, and the medical arrangements were unsatisfactory under the incompetent direction of Colonel Exham. 563 soldiers died of sickness in the siege, 393 from typhoid. From Ladysmith observation posts had been able to see Spion Kop, and spirits had fallen low when it was seen to have been abandoned. A temporary lift to morale ensued as a result of White's decision on 30 January that hopes of using his cavalry had vanished and that both the mealies and the horses themselves could now be eaten; but spirits sank again after the failure at Vaal Krantz on 7 February when White decided that he had to face the possibility of an even longer siege and rations were cut again.

Buller realized that he must try not only another direction but also different tactics. Instead of attempting to gain victory in one day by employing all his forces at the same time, he must try a gradual and methodical advance, step by step, each step being supported by the largest number of guns that could be brought to bear, his superiority over the Boers in that arm being significant – fifty guns to their eight. The terrain north-east of Colenso lent itself to this method, being dominated by a series of hills leading up to the southern bank of the Tugela. Buller began his operation on 12 February with the temporary occupation of Hussar Hill four miles east of Colenso, from which Buller could observe the Boer positions on Hlangwane and Green Hill, two miles to the north. From there he could also see Cingolo Hill, four miles to the east of Green Hill, and the highest, Monte Cristo, running north-west from Cingolo three miles to the river. Those were to provide the ladder which would lead him to a position from which he could tackle the formidable barrier of the gorge through which the railway ran on the north bank of the river to Ladysmith. On 14 February Hussar Hill was reoccupied by Dundonald's brigade, which included Lieutenant-Colonel Sir Julian Byng's South African Light Horse in which Winston Churchill, having escaped from Pretoria, was combining service as a lieutenant with journalism as war correspondent of the *Morning Post*. His younger brother John, who had only arrived that morning to join him, was slightly wounded in the foot, and was fortunate to be evacuated by rail to the hospital ship, *Maine*, financed by generous Americans, which their mother had just accompanied to Durban. Next day Barton's 6th (Fusilier) Brigade took Green Hill, and by the end of Saturday 17 February

the 2nd Division, now commanded by Lyttelton, had also secured
Cingolo, so that Hildyard's 2nd Brigade on the 18th could attack and
capture Monte Cristo. Hlangwane was the next to fall, as the Boers
abandoned all their positions south and east of the river, and Colenso
village was reoccupied. From the summit of Monte Cristo, Buller could
now see the outskirts of Ladysmith. He had hoped to be able to cross
the river there and outflank Botha from the east, but reconnaissance
showed this to be impracticable. He therefore decided to push Lyttelton's
men across the river north of Colenso and erect his pontoon bridge
there, below Hlangwane. Thorneycroft's Mounted Infantry were sent
across to occupy Fort Wylie, and, when the bridge had been erected on
the 21st, Major-General C. O. Wynne's 11th (Lancashire) Brigade crossed
and captured two hills on the far side, named Wynne's and Horseshoe
Hill on the following day.

On the 21st Private Greening of the Cameronians, who was a clerk
on Buller's intelligence staff, happened to be near Buller himself. He
wrote in his diary for the day:

Wet morning and cool. Was not required to day, so went on top of
Hlangwani and watched our artillery shelling the hills across the
river. The Boer fire was very feeble and they seemed to be in great
trouble as we had received news that Kimberley was relieved and that
a large body of the Boers had gone from here to the Free State to try
and get Cronje out of his fix. 3 prisoners brought in to day, one was
a young boy only 16 years of age, he told me his brother 13 years old
was killed by one of our shells. Some of the Devons dug up a box of
women's clothes, curtains &c looted from a farm somewhere in the
neighbourhood. At 2.30 p.m. we inspanned again and moved to the
north of Hlangwani, waited there on the road for the troops to pass
us on their way down to the river. I got on top of a kopje close by
and watched the battle in full swing. Down on the plain below were
batteries of field artillery dotted about, cavalry and infantry were
pushing across the pontoon bridge at full speed, over against us were
the heights of Grobler's Kloof, from whence every now and then a
big shell came roaring across over our heads to burst with a great
crash behind us on the rocks. Buller sat on a rock near where I was,
looking through his telescope and sending messages by a signaller
who was standing by him, to the troops down by the river. The rifle
fire was incessant and made a great rattle among the hills. It was a

cloudy day and cool, and the scene was something like the fight at Vaal Krantz last week. At this height, about 800 feet, the view is grand, we could see Colenso village, the river winding in and out, the ruins of the big iron bridge, and the railway running in among the rocks below Grobler's Kloof, which loomed high up above it, covered with green trees and thick bushes, from among which came every now and then a puff of white smoke and then a dull roar, as a shell from Long Tom came across to us, or fell among the troops down at the river with a mighty bang. Across to my right in the distance was Umbulwana, a long flat mountain, grim and stern in the light, and we could see the puff of smoke from the Long Tom on the top, as it fired into the town of Ladysmith. About 5 p.m. I moved on down to the river and outspanned my wagon by the pontoon bridge. The scene here was a busy one and the troops were all in good spirits, as they moved across to the attack on Green and Railway hills. By dusk the fight slackened down, and about 9 p.m. the firing ceased for the night. All round were little twinkling points of light where our men were in position on the same place as they had captured during the day. The country is so hard and difficult and the hills so many, that progress is very slow and we have to hold on to our positions once we capture them from the enemy.

22nd Feb.

Woke at daybreak to the tune of our big guns firing on Grobler's Kloof. Hot day and the sun was very powerful. After a hasty breakfast, prepared to move, but got word to remain where I was until the railway line had been captured. About 8 a.m. the Boers began throwing 7 lb shells into our laager and it became very hot among the wagons, we gave them a good mark to aim at, as there was about 30 wagons of the Head Quarters Staff all clustered in a lump down by the pontoon bridge. Several times a shell fell into the soft ground close to my wagon with a big squash, and one I had dug up went about 10 feet into the earth. 2 fell among the Irish Fusiliers who were our escort and upset a small card party, causing some strong language. As we could not move off until the evening, I spent my time in sitting on top of my wagon and watching a battery of howitzers across the river to my left, they were busy shelling the woods on the top of Grobler's Kloof trying to get at the gun which had been shelling our wagons. It was curious to see the little squat guns sitting like a row of frogs behind a small hill, throwing shells up in the air and dropping them with a big splash of red flame and yellow smoke among the trees, and soon the gun up there was shut up for the day. Our infantry were still hard at it among the hills by the railway, driving the Boers out of one position after another only to find more waiting behind another hill. It is a wonderful place this part of the country, wave after wave of hills all reaching back towards the plain outside Ladysmith, a distance of 15 miles. Now and then could be seen a thin line of men in khaki going over the top of a hill, and disappearing below on the other side, and then a scattered mob of Boers could be seen getting across the other hill behind it and trying to make a stand there, only to be driven back on to another hill by our slowly advancing infantry. All day long the guns roared and threw shells on to the Boer positions and the air was filled with the throbbing and bursting of lyddite shells. Shrapnel shells burst in all directions and the smoke drifted across the river in little woolly lumps. From letters found in the Boer trenches it appears that they are to make one last big fight here and then retreat on to the Biggarsberg, where they have made some almost impregnable defences. Our scouts were on the top of Monte Cristo all day and could see the movements of the Boers quite plainly. The evening closed in with a heavy thunderstorm which drenched us all to the skin.

It was now the turn of Hart's 5th (Irish) Brigade to pass behind Wynne and attack the hill to his right, named Hart's Hill, on the 23rd. Some of the guns east of the river which had supported Wynne were out of range and Hart's three battalions, the Inniskillings, the Connaught Rangers and the Dublin Fusiliers, had to follow each other along the narrow gorge, crossing a long railway bridge under Boer observation and fire. Hart, as impatient and hot-headed as he had been at the loop in the first Colenso battle, ordered the Inniskillings to start their attack up the steep rocky hillside and then sent the others up, company by company, as they arrived. The outcome was nearly disastrous, resulting in 500 casualties, the majority in the Inniskillings – 72 per cent of their officers, including the commanding officer, and 27 per cent of their men. The commanding officer of the Dublins was also killed. Captain Jourdain of the Connaught Rangers recorded their experience in his diary:

23rd Feb. Friday.
I was just in time to march off with the Battalion at 5.15 am. I had

no breakfast, but managed to snatch a biscuit from the Scotch cart. We marched north, not knowing what we were going to do. When we had marched about a mile, we got under some guns of the enemy who had got our range to a nicety. We were marched in column of route along a beaten road of which the Boers had got the range. The first shell burst near the Company in front of me, and made the men duck. The second burst just in front of me, and knocked out seven men. I was covered with dust and dirt from this one. The next shell did not burst and went slightly wide. A shrapnel next scattered me and Payne over with dust, but wonderful to relate did no one any harm. We got under cover when we had sampled two more shells, and I was only too glad to avail myself of a hole in the ground with a Colour Sergeant in the West Yorks named Kingsley. He gave me half a cup of tea which was grand. The Boers sent any amount of shells here, but they all went over us, and only killed a few mules. About eleven am we were informed that we had to advance on our right by the River and take a hill called Railway Hill. The howitzer battery came up and shelled this hill till about 12.30 when we were ordered to advance. The Inniskilling Fusiliers went first, then us, and then the Dublin Fusiliers and Imperial Light Infantry. We started down the Railway line, and before long had to face a good amount of sniping from the Kopjes on our left. The adjacent hills were held by our troops for about a mile but we had at times to run the gauntlet for some yards in an awful fire. There was one spot by the river, in which were six dead Inniskilling Fusiliers, and we had to trudge knee deep in the mud with the white faces of these men staring at you, while the bullets whistled over your head, and many a man was wounded here. A few yards further on was an iron bridge over which we had to double one by one exposed to a very severe cross fire from two kopjes. We lost one man killed & 3 men wounded here. Wratislaw was hit near this bridge through the leg, his wound is not dangerous. He had only joined us about three weeks from England. G. H. F. and E. Companies were to form our firing line and D. C B and A our supports & reserves. The former went on in front of the right half Battalion. We had marched for nearly two miles when we moved up a small kopje overlooking the river, and studded with trees in which the Boer laager had been situated. We passed two waggons loaded and ready to move, which had been abandoned by the Boers. There were any amount of provisions, and tweed trousers

from dysentery all night, so passed a wretched time behind a big stone.

24th Feb. Saturday 4 am.

Just before dawn we were ordered to throw up stone sangars to enable us to hold the hill. We had about three quarters of an hour's work at this, making small traverses. The fire slackened on both sides just after dawn, and we saw the Boers come out of their trenches and give the wounded water, at the same time collecting any rifle and useful kit they could lay their hands on. This was about 5.15 am. After this we lined the sangars and awaited events. We saw some Boers creeping up the donga on our left rear, and taking shots at us. Their fire was returned but it did not keep down their fire. After a while they began to draw closer and the bullets came with greater frequency, striking the stones round us. A few of my men were hit, one wretched man was hit in the chest, he got up ran about 100 yards screaming and then fell dead. Not contented with the movement the Boers began to advance from their trenches and then we were attacked in front, on our left and in rear. This went on for about half an hour, bullets flying all round, and even coming through the crevices in our sangar. I saw one man shot clean through the sangar. Some of the men began to feel unsteady and to run down the hill. I made the rest get down and lie close. The company of the Inniskilling Fusiliers on my left, had retired to the Railway line unknown to me. The word now came (9.15 am) that all our men were retiring down the hill. I was lying with Capt Woulfe Flanagan of our 6th Battalion (attached) behind the sangar at the time. He started off at a run, and not many minutes afterwards I followed him. All my men had gone some few minutes. I reached the bottom of the slope, and jumped down on the Railway line. The Imperial Light Infantry who had been told off to protect our left, and to advance up the Railway line, had failed to do so, and we were being enfiladed on the line, so I ordered all the men to retire behind the Railway Bridge. I followed myself and found Hag there who told me to take a few men, and take up a position on our left rear to cover the retreat. I went back about 50 yards and got behind a small kopje, but found some men of the Dublins in front of me. Soon after the Durham Light Infantry began to advance through us to cover our retreat. I lay down here thoroughly exhausted, and after drinking some water I felt rather worse than better. Some of my men carried me down to the Tugela, and put me under a tree and bathed my face with water. The firing gradually became rather quieter.

Suddenly there was passed back word to signal, shout, or communicate in any way with our guns on Monte Christo to cease firing, as they were firing at our own men retiring. The distance was great, and round after round from our own guns was hurled at our own men before the mistake was remedied. I remember being told here that our men were coming down to the river to get some rations, and that Colonel Brooke was safe. Harling was hit in both hands and the leg, but got across all right. Wise was hit in the thigh the previous afternoon. Hutchinson was hit in 5 places, the most dangerous being one in the groin. Lambert was hit in the wrist, Flanagan was hit in the hand, and got a splinter on his forehead.

Two reinforcing battalions, the Durham Light Infantry and the Rifle Brigade from the 4th Brigade, succeeded in stabilizing the situation on the 24th, digging in on the lower slopes, while the wounded Irish were left on the summit.

Private R. H. Gavgan was with the Rifle Brigade and wrote in his diary:

> 23 Feb. 1900.
> Crossed the river about 1 a.m. this morning we are in support of the Irish Brigade. 8 p.m. this has been a terrible hard day and I fear our losses are large we had to give three cheers every hour, the reason of cheering was to give the Irish Bdge confidence. 12. we are still fighting and it is still raining.

> 24th.
> Irish Bdge retire they have had fearful losses, we get the news of Cronje's capture fighting all day long still raining we have no overcoats not had any since we left Chievely 5 p.m. we retire about 100 yards for the night light fires to try and get warm and to get some food. 8 p.m. the Boers have opened fire and we soon get arms.

> 25th.
> Bombard the position for about 2 hours when it suddenly ceases this quietness seems very strange after the continued rattle of guns. 8 p.m. outpost we start wall building we can hear the boers singing about a mile away and we remember it is another Sunday night they

have women with them the voices can be distinguished quite well. 8.30 Singing ceases and in its place we get a very hot rifle fire for about half an hour we laid flat with fixed swords [bayonets] but never fired a shot then we finish building we are getting use[d] to this at night luckily it does very little damage or their sniping either.

26th. [omitted]

27th.

Today is Majuba day if we don't get our own back today, I want no more our artillery and Naval guns is bombarding heavily we shall soon be stuck into it again we got the order to advance we had proper running fight the boers wont stand like men, Majuba day was in every man's mind as we dashed The Lancashire Bdge took the hill on our right we took the railway hill and Kopjes leading to the hill trench after trench was taken and finally we got the sword to work with but they never waited for that only those that held their hands up we captured a large number of prisoners the fight finished about 8 p.m. I hear that 104 guns was used in this day. Our Coy and C. has to occupy a trench to the right, 8.30 p.m. We find a trench full of dead men just behind us one of our chaps is dressing the wound of a boer woman this one also some killed our losses are 7 killed 49 wounded. I think we will relieve Ladysmith this journey.

28th.

Having a well earned rest and buried our dead comrades.

Fortunately 25 February was a Sunday, which made it easier for Buller to arrange a six-hour truce during which the wounded could be removed and the dead buried while the troops on both sides fraternized with each other, the Boers being particularly grateful for cigarettes.

Buller now made a significant change to his plan. Reconnaissance had detected a favourable alternative site for the pontoon bridge further downstream below Hart's Hill, and it was transferred there. Warren's 5th Division was to cross it and attack the three hills astride the railway as it led away from the river towards Ladysmith, Pieter's Hill to the east of it, Railway and Hart's Hill to the west, from right to left, supported by all the artillery from east of the river, which could support all three attacks without redeploying. Confident in his plan, Buller signalled White on the 26th, 'I hope to be with you to-morrow night'. Tuesday 27 February, the nineteenth anniversary of Majuba, saw, first, Barton's 6th

Brigade attacking Pieter's Hill, which was finally cleared by 2.30 p.m.
5th Brigade, now commanded by Kitchener's brother Walter, followed
with a successful attack on Railway Hill, and finally Major-General C. O.
Norcott's 4th Brigade drove the Boers off Hart's Hill.

28 February, the 118th day of the siege, dawned cloudy over Ladysmith and strangely silent after the distant rumble of artillery fire of the
last few days. The first sign that the siege might actually be ending was
the sight of a long Boer column trekking away to the north-west. It was
not until 1 p.m. that White received a message from Buller saying: 'I
beat the enemy thoroughly yesterday and am sending my cavalry . . . to
ascertain where they have gone to. I believe the enemy to be in full
retreat'; and 5 p.m. when the first of Buller's relieving troops were seen,
two squadrons of cavalry, one of the Imperial Light Horse and one of
the Natal Carbineers, under the command of Lieutenant-Colonel Hubert
Gough of the 16th Lancers. They reached the centre of Ladysmith an
hour later amid scenes of great emotion and jubilation. Major Birdwood
describes this final advance in his diary:

> *28 February.*
> Ash Wednesday. We crossed Tugela in early morning & marched
> through foremost line of Infantry, & began reconnoitring across
> Peters plain to rt, seven [? some] kopjes & hills to left – our men
> were opposed at Peters & when we advanced in force TMI [?
> Thorneycroft's Mounted Infantry] were heavily fired on, their led
> horses stampeding & 5 being killed – We gradually pushed along
> kopjes & got a position overlooking deep valley in which enemy
> laagers were, & as a body of about 100 Boers marched unsuspiciously
> down the valley we got into them with 5 machine guns, & they broke
> up all over the place – we then advanced further, but were shelled
> from Umbulwana. However we got behind kopjes to left – Gough
> with I.L.H & N-C scouted towards Ladysmith & reported all clear.
> Lord D – self – Winston Churchill & Saint Clowes rode on sending
> back SALH [South African Light Horse] & TMI – we had a never to
> be forgotten mad gallop *into Ladysmith* coming first to Intombi
> neutral camp, where the hospital people cheered madly, then across
> Klip river, where Brocklehurst met us, soon to Sir G. White's Hd.
> Qts, where the Duff, Ian Hamilton, Sir G. Col Ward ASC who put
> us up. Ladysmith looked very clean, & showed no signs of bombard-
> ment. troops very much done up & of the 15,000 only a few hundred

being fit for duty. 6000 civilians to be fed: excellent chevril-jelly etc made by Col Ward only horses and mules. All quite delighted to see us.

Rawlinson recorded in his diary:

We first saw the cavalry of Buller's force on the ridge above Intembi about 5 p.m. and sent out Royston's men to meet them – and by 6 p.m. the two squadrons were in. Sir George went down to meet them. The cheering was immense. Sir G. on his way back was surrounded by a mob of civilians and soldiers opposite the gaol who cheered him to the echo and obliged him to say a few words. This was very appropriate and quite a scene to be present at.

G. S. Preller was a Boer artillery officer. His account of these two days, not surprisingly, struck a different note:

A Majuba day (not to be forgotten) this day will always be to every true Afrikander. In the morning everything was fixed between the guns. In the afternoon we heard musketry fire and hurried forward. The enemy was on the kopjes already and our left wing already beaten back when we arrived on our last station. Lood brought a gr. Maxim into position against this kopje and opened fire. Later on the Howitzer arrived from the neck and opened fire also, then a French gun also, all in the neck over which the road passes. The Howitzer was directed on the kop behind (obliquely) the Krugersdorp position, and the French gun the ridges in front of us. The maxim first these ridges and then the kop. It did not last long or they were on us with another Lyddite where our pieces were so exposed. The conduct of the gunners was exemplary. They took no notice. One Lyddite shell burst about 4 yards from where we sat. All the best efforts did not avail, we had lost the battle – hopelessly lost – we had to retire. The Standertonians retired first, then the Johannesburgers, the Krugersdorpers followed, (nearly all captured and killed) and Pretorians. The enemy was now obliquely behind the Middelburgers and they had to retire also. The order (unavoidable) was given to withdraw all pieces. This was done when it began to grow dusk and all went up the kloof in the direction of our little camp where they spanned out late that evening, in the neck. The enemy were master of the bloody battlefield and we had to flee. O terrible word:– God, how I have prayed never to see this. All was lost here. Back for home. The people are tired, it is said they have had to endure a Lyddite bombardment for 14 days and are fagged. They appear to have no idea that with returning home they are also selling everything, everything that is dear to them. We slept very little that night. At 12 o'clock we arose and began to fix everything straight for departing. A lot had to be left behind, 7 tents not even opened were burnt, and clothes were left lying. Terrible it was, enough to make one gray. It was dark yet when we departed back through the kloof. At 2 o'clock we breakfasted. About 10 o'clock we had crossed the Klip river bridge and chose position in the ridges behind Bulwana. From here we saw cavalry of the enemy coming across. Later on it commenced raining. Cavalry were fired upon with French guns, but when I ascended Bulwana with Lood to bring down Long Tom, we saw the advance guard of the enemy already entering Ladysmith. Near Long Tom there were no oxen, it rained and enemy fired wildly from the troubled town, whose saving was so near. Finally mules arrived. We returned and lay down under some old trees worn out and despondent. It rained and we were drenched. Long Tom did not arrive. Finally (about 11 o'clock) Lood told me to proceed with the guns which were there (3 French) Maxim 2 caissons, to Modderspruit and truck. It was a bitter and regrettable journey drenched to the skin, through mud and rain, all our positions already deserted. At 12 o'clock we passed through the deserted Head laager – everything as quiet as the grave, only yesterday it was activity generally. At 1.30 we reached Modderspruit but discovered no provision had been made here for the loading of the guns. Everything was topsy-turvy here and then stood ready to clear. General J. telegraphed that the guns had to come to Elandslaagte, after having outspanned for fifteen minutes we departed again through dark mud and slush. This little distance was if possible still heavier than the former was, besides this way was blocked with wagons, cannons etc. When the day broke we arrived at Elandslaagte. Here was a terrible sight, wagons arrived in hundreds from all sides in streams, there were thousands already.

Christopher Balfour's diary entry for the day gave a laconic account:

> *Feb. 28th.*
> Rations down to starvation point 4 oz biscuit 3 oz mealie meal. Everyone very depressed fearing Buller has had another knock. Lot of wagons moving N.W. over great plain all day, Boers in thousands

and hundreds of wagons. Very big trek. Wire about 5 p.m. from
Buller of his victory. Great rejoicings. Some S.A. Horse got in just
before dusk, great cheering in town. Very heavy thunderstorm at 4
p.m. Paid 30/- for 1/4lb Boer tobacco (worth 3d) on the day we are
relieved. Pathos! Fearful wet night got wet through. Man in my Coy
buried under a wall which was struck by lightning (not badly hurt!)
So cheered up that I didn't give a damn for the rain. Our guns fired
all night to try to prevent Boers from taking theirs away but I think
they had already gone! Volunteers were called for to walk 6–12 miles
with a fight at the end. About 20 of coy and all officers responded.

Buller arrived on 1 March and was entertained to lunch by White, at
which Buller was said to have made tactless comments about the
abundance of food. He was reluctantly persuaded two days later to lead
a grand parade through the town, which caused some embarrassment to
participants and onlookers alike.

Frank Rhodes describes the scene:

Troops marched in at 11 a.m. through streets of Ladysmith – it took
about 2 hours – it was a magnificent sight it is a grand force and the
men looked fit to do anything. Winston Churchill was in great form
and most interesting. Winston stood by me most of the time troops
marched and was quite overcome – could not speak and had tears in
his eyes, did not think he could show so much feeling. They say
meeting between White and Buller was far from cordial, Buller
almost ignored him. They met near the prison and a lot of the
inhabitants standing about noticed it, Winston says.

The Royal Dragoons from Dundonald's brigade took part in this
parade, and an unnamed sergeant describes the experience in his diary:

We marched through Ladysmith on the 3rd. As we approached those
of the garrison in the trenches ran out to meet us and we gave them
the ration of meat and biscuit, & also all the tobacco we had. The
garrison lined the streets; they had donned their best uniforms &
looked painfully clean compared to our ragged army. We expected
to find them looking bad on 3oz mealie meal, a biscuit and a little
horse flesh per diem, but were shocked to see how attenuated & weak
they really were; some of them like shadows, their drawn faces, &
sunken eyes, hardly strong enough to stand; in fact some dropped to
the ground as we were passing, but still raised a feeble cheer. The

garrison must have been hoarse that night, each regiment as it came along being hailed by name followed by volleys of cheers. The town itself did not show many signs of the shelling it had been subjected to for one hundred days, owing to the majority of houses being of corrugated iron. The town hall, one of the few masonry buildings, had evidently suffered the most, part of the clock turret being shot away, a hole in the [?] iron marked the passage of a big shell while many of the buildings in 'Tin Town' where we were quartered were literally riddled with shot holes.

In the evening we met old & new friends of the 5th Dragoon Guards, 5th Lancers, & 18th & 19th Hussars & heard all about the attack on Ladysmith on January 6th.

While there was general rejoicing everywhere that Ladysmith had at last been relieved, and its defenders, even White himself, were hailed as heroes, feelings were mixed among both the relievers and the relieved. Many of those who had been besieged were bitter about the length of time it had taken for Buller and his troops to reach them and at the hardships and disappointments they had suffered as a result; while many in the relieving force accused the garrison of having done little to help and of exaggerating their hardship. Foremost among the critics of Buller was Ian Hamilton, who, with Rawlinson, left to join Roberts's staff. He exercised no restraint in spreading harsh criticism of Buller far and wide, notably to Leo Amery on Milner's staff, who was to edit the *Times* history of the campaign. Roberts initially offered White the command of a corps of two divisions, the 6th in the north-east of Cape Colony and the 5th, which he intended that Buller should send there, shipping it to East London; but that plan was changed and Roberts thought of making him military governor of the Orange Free State, when that had been occupied, but changed his mind. White was in any case in poor health and there was general relief when he was allowed to go home on medical grounds.

5

CLEARING ORANGE FREE STATE

March to May 1900

After Paardeberg Roberts could at last start his advance to Bloemfontein. Kruger and Steyn realized that if they were to achieve a negotiated peace which would preserve the independence of their states, they must prevent the occupation of their capitals. Kruger therefore hurried down to join Steyn and, together, they assembled what forces they could to try and hold Roberts before he could reach the Free State capital. By 7 March they had mustered 8,000 men to join De Wet, who was holding some kopjes on either side of the Modder at Poplar Grove, fifteen miles east of Paardeberg and fifty from Bloemfontein. Roberts's plan was for French to outflank this position by a wide seventeen-mile move and then attack from the north, while Kelly-Kenny and Tucker attacked from the south and Colvile's 9th Division crossed the river and attacked upstream, as at Paardeberg. But a combination of Boer irresolution and British sluggishness defeated him. French thought that his weary cavalry were being made to go too far too fast, and his leading troops were continually held up by De Wet's delaying tactics: Kelly-Kenny moved slowly, blaming his difficulties on transport problems stemming from the Waterval Drift affair. The result was that the Boer force, including the Presidents, got away almost unscathed.

Captain Bellew's account of the part his squadron of the 16th Lancers played illustrates why Roberts felt that the cavalry had been unenterprising:

> 7 March.
> Heard guns early and saw main body disappearing over horizon turning position on enemy's left. Saw them leave kopje hill and finally they left Table kopje to our front without firing a shot as infantry threatened their right. We at once advanced and occupied

Table kopje from which we had glorious view for a long time of the whole movement. Enemy retired as fast as they could get their waggons away while cavalry swept round on the right and infantry pressed them back on the left. Towards evening bivouacked beyond Boers' furthest position.

8th.

Halted all day to rest horses and get up forage. Heard that one of our shells had knocked over the waggon in which the Russian and Dutch attachés were travelling – This was too much for them and they came in to us – Told us that both Kruger and Steyn were in the Boer position and prayed them to hang on, but the Boers weren't for fighting and would have nothing to do with them. Pity we hadn't known about this sooner, might have had a try to catch them – Yesterday was completely successful though there was not much firing and very few casualties on either side.

De Wet made another stand three days later at Driefontein, fifteen miles further on, from which, after losing 100 men, he was evicted by Stephenson's 18th Brigade, which lost 87 killed and 438 wounded in the attack. On 13 March Roberts entered Bloemfontein unopposed, preceded by members of the press and a detachment of Royal Engineer signallers, rolling out their line. His men received a surprisingly warm welcome, described by Lieutenant Ronald Charles, who was in command of a Field Troop of the Royal Engineers with the Cavalry Division, in a letter to his mother:

The town council came out in all their glory of white top hats &c about 10.30 am on the 13th & solemnly handed over the keys of the capital to Lord Roberts, who promised to respect life & property & all the rest of it & the Advanced guard of the British Army marched into Bloemfontein in rather scattered detachments to the accompaniment of the ringing cheers of the inhabitants, black & white. I never heard such cheering, though doubtless many of them were cheering the Boers a week before we arrived – everyone was wearing tricolor favours, brand new Union Jacks were being flown, people were singing 'God Save the Queen', 'Rule Britannia' & other patriotic & marshal [*sic*] airs. I don't suppose we could be given a more hearty reception even on returning home; & mind you we were entering the enemies' capital as victors, not as a relieving force.

In the early hours of that morning, Ronald Charles had been involved in blowing up the railway to the north of the town, presumably to prevent the Boers taking things away with them. His letter described the venture:

I was woken up by Hunter-Weston, (the Major who is supposed to command this unit, but who is usually to be found on Gen. French's staff) who told me to get up & choose half a dozen men with fit horses & accompany him to destroy the Railway north of Bloemfontein. It took some time making necessary arrangements as regards explosives &c, & we finally started at 1.0 am on the 13th – There were eleven of us all told, viz the Major, 4 sappers, 3 Cavalry pioneers, 2 local guides & myself, & all our horses had already done over twenty-five miles that day – we made a wide detour to the east of the town, & then worked north & west till we found the railway about two miles north of the town about 4.0 a.m. We had fortunately up till then met no one to interfere with us, though the moon insisted on shining brightly most of the time. The only occasion when I have objected to light during a night march. As soon as we got to the railway I sent a Corporal towards the town along the line with orders to go a hundred yards in that direction to see if he could find a culvert, while I did the same thing in the other direction; meantime, the other climbed up the telegraph poles & cut the wires; the Corporal & I came back simultaneously, he having found nothing (though I saw next day a platelayers cottage not 40 yds off which he had not seen, which shows what a jumpy soldiers idea of 100 yards is in the night); I had been more lucky & had discovered a large culvert of two spans of 9 feet each, so we carried our guncotton down to it & fixed 10 lbs of that explosive at each end of one of the girders; in spite of the dark, I saw some niggers dwellings 20 yds from the far side of the line, so we had to work pretty quietly, as I thought there was probably a farm there; anyway we were ready by half past four, & set light to our fuzes, which I had made short on purpose; when we were about forty yards off, my Charge exploded & three seconds after the one that the Major had fixed went off – the air was full of fragments of iron hurtling round over our heads, so we did not go back to ascertain the damage done, but mounted at once, the rest of the party having already done so – One of the guides – a gentleman who was commandeered to fight for the Boers, but escaped & was rather naturally a little bit nervous of being caught, remarked 'Now we shall have to gallop like Hell', to which the Major answered 'Not at all, we will trot on slowly', which we did for a quarter of an hour – we thought we were well clear of the town to the northeast, but had reckoned without our host, as we suddenly came on a spruit, a sort of nullah, full of a picket of Boers, whom we at first took to be natives in charge of oxen: it was just getting light, so we made a bold front, & the gentleman guide in fluent Dutch enquired what Commando they belonged to, & then peremptorily ordered them out of the spruit & told them to stand upon the far bank – by this time we had dismounted & drawn our carbines, & I for the first time in this campaign got hold of my revolver – the Boers obeyed like lambs, mounting their horses & riding up the side of the nullah – I thought the stream of men was never going to stop, till finally about thirty of them stood mounted on the opposite bank not ten yards from us, we promptly got down with our horses into the nullah & started to climb the other side, my pony of course chose this as an opportunity for refusing to move complaining he was tired, so one of the men beat him smartly over the quarters with a carbine & he followed me to nearly the top, when he slipped back the whole way, pulling me after him; the walls of the nullah were nearly perpendicular & nearly twenty feet high; by this time I was beginning to think we were in a tight hole, however, with another sound beating with a carbine I pulled him up to the top & found that our thirty Boers had taken to flight in the face of the 'Verdommdt rooinecks'; So we mounted again & rode on another 30 yards when we came to another beastly spruit, where we heard some more Boers talking, they never challenged us & so we rode past them, *literally*, within four yards of them, down into the spruit & up the other side – most of the party came up with me & we walked on, the major stopping to see that no one was left behind in the second spruit. while we were in this formation, the Boers fired again at us; the major swears the shell burst forty yards behind me, but though I was looking out for it, I confess I never saw it – he & his two men caught us up in a couple of minutes, & then we trotted on – they fired another shell after us, but the light was so feeble that they recognised it was no good – so we pushed on without further interference till we were well out of range, by which time it was quite daylight, we were then about three miles east of the town right out in the open, so we pulled up to a walk & went slowly back the way we came till we struck our outposts about 6.30 a.m.; it was with a sigh of relief that we walked past them as we had done our job without losing a man or a horse & had undoubtedly given the Boers a good fright. It was a most fortunate thing that none of our men lost their heads at the critical time, as if one shot had been fired by us, the whole Boer Camp would have been alarmed & started firing madly in our direction.

Roberts entered Bloemfontein in style, riding in with a cavalry escort at midday on 13 March to the cheers of the British members of the population, who flourished red, white and blue rosettes and sang patriotic songs. After a Union Jack, personally embroidered by Lady Roberts, had been hoisted at the Presidency, a satisfying lunch was eaten at the English Club, where in the evening a celebratory dinner was held, at which mutually congratulatory speeches were made, while the band of the Highland Brigade played outside. This complacent air of relaxation continued for some time, but was not shared by the Africans, who waited in vain for release from the harsh restrictions imposed on them by the Boers; nor was it shared by the majority of Roberts's soldiers.

Some may have shared the views of Ronald Charles, who described Bloemfontein as 'quite the brightest spot I have seen in this apparently desert country – it was quite refreshing to suddenly reach the top of the low hills which surround the place, & look down on a large green basin', but they were in a generally poor state. Their clothes and boots were in tatters and many were sick with typhoid, probably caused by using water from the Modder River for drinking. Roberts's Surgeon Major-General, W. D. Wilson, was as incompetent as had been Colonel Exham in Ladysmith. Buller sacked the latter, who was promptly transferred to Bloemfontein; but Roberts, although admitting in a letter to Lansdowne that Wilson was ' a poor creature and does not seem to have any idea of what is required', did nothing about getting him replaced. Lansdowne had shown some anxiety on this score soon after Roberts's arrival in South Africa, perhaps anxious that there should be no repetition of the scandals of the Crimea, and had especially enquired about whether there were enough nurses. Roberts had reassured him, but mentioned that 'The Surgeon-General with the force is not very responsive or sympathetic on the question of receiving an ample supply of lady nurses', adding, 'but I think you will not be far wrong if you send us out 40 or 50 instead of the 20 we asked for'. A week later he reported that forty-six local nurses had been recruited and that a reinforcement of ten per month would suffice. By June 1900 there were ninety-nine nurses with the army in South Africa, nine from the regular Army Nursing Service and fifty-seven from its reserve: the remainder were recruited from South Africa itself or other colonies. Roberts was to be largely responsible for the formation of Queen Alexandra's Imperial Military Nursing Service after he returned to England and became Commander-in-Chief in 1901. On 4 February of that year, soon after Queen Victoria's funeral, he wrote the following letter to the new Queen:

Miss Knollys gave me Your Majesty's message about the nurses for Military hospitals, and I understood from her that Your Majesty wished me to submit my ideas as to the manner in which Your Majesty's desire might be carried into effect.

Nursing in the Army is not altogether satisfactory, and the means by which it could be improved has long been a subject of anxious thought to me. If, however, Your Majesty will take the matter up, and give it Your Royal name and support, I have little doubt but that an organization could be devised which would be productive of good and important results.

In the first place I think it would have the best possible effect if Your Majesty would consent to allow the Army Nursing Service to be called 'Queen Alexandra's Military Nursing Service for the United Kingdom, India and the Colonies.' I am anxious that the Indian Nursing Service should be amalgamated with the Home Service, in order that the same care may be taken in choosing the nurses for India as I hope, under a new system, will be given to those for the Home Service, and also because we undoubtedly lose the services of a very valuable and experienced class of nurses for whom, after 5 or 10 years work in the plains of India, it may not be advisable to remain in that trying climate, but whose services in a military hospital at home would be invaluable. – And who, after a year or two's change, would be quite ready to either return to India, or to go to South Africa or elsewhere.

The Secretary of State for India would have to be approached as to this part of the scheme, but I have little doubt, if Your Majesty approves of it, the expression of your wishes would be sufficient to gain his consent.

I would suggest that, subject to Your Majesty's approval, a small committee of experienced ladies should be formed, who would work under Your Majesty as President, and discuss before laying them to you, Ma'am, the rules for, and the conditions of the service.

Some of the causes of the shortcomings of the present Nursing Service are:-

A great number of the Nurses are too young which leads to their being somewhat frivolous, and also renders them more liable to fall victims to enteric, climate, &c.

Sufficient care has not been taken to get the opinions of the Matrons of hospitals where the nurses have been trained, as well as certificates from the Doctors as to their skill and general fitness – sometimes the most attractive and not most suitable for work in military hospitals have, I am afraid, been preferred.

And finally a great number of the nurses are not of sufficiently good class.

There should be on the Committee an experienced nurse from one of the great London hospitals – for preference a lady who has gained experience during the war in South Africa.

I thought, and Lady Roberts (who saw more of them than I did) tells me that the nurses Your Majesty sent out to South Africa were all excellent. You will therefore understand Ma'am the kind of nurse we think it would be desirable to have in 'Queen Alexandra's Military Nursing Service'.

He followed this up in April 1901 with a letter to the new Secretary of State for War, the Hon. St John Brodrick, accompanying a copy of the scheme which Queen Alexandra had asked him to prepare, in which he wrote:

There is no doubt improvement in the Nursing Service is needed, and in the Nurses being placed in a position to enable them to carry out their work in a proper manner. The Nurses are not as a rule in favour with Army Doctors, the good ones value them, but the others find they see too much of what is going on – then again the relations between the Nurses and Orderlies are not satisfactory. . . . The Queen is pressing for the scheme.

Miss D. L. Harris was a nurse with the New Zealand contingent in South Africa. When she arrived at Cape Town in April 1900, she was

posted to the military hospital at Wynberg, but was moved on to
Bloemfontein, where she arrived on 7 May, as she records in her diary:

> We reached Bloemfontein about midnight, so stayed in the train, it
> was very noisy on the platform. We got up early, left our luggage and
> found our way to Langman's Hospital and were told where to find
> the sisters. They lived in a cottage close by and were awfully surprised
> to see us. We had breakfast with them, and then reported ourselves
> to the P.M.O.* and then to Col. Williams. He sent us out to No. 8
> Gen. Hospital. It is all canvas – right out on the veldt, no trees except
> a few in a clump a little way off. We arrived about 12, and found
> Sisters Warmington and Stevens from N.Z. had come out just before
> us. We did not go on duty till about 6. I helped Sister Walker and
> am to have 4 of her tents, they are all enteric. There are over 1400
> patients here, and things are not very nice.

> *May 8th.*
> Went on duty after breakfast, it is certainly working under difficulties.
> Dr. May is my Dr. and is nice enough. Nothing special. After tea Mr
> Shand (a N.Z. war correspondent) came out and brought some
> letters from Australia. We had a long talk and I liked him. It is very
> warm here through the day, but bitterly cold at night. There are 5 of
> us in our tent. Some of them are nice girls – all Army reserve nurses.
> I have 4 tents with 8 men in each, nearly all enteric cases.

Another nurse was Katherine Nisbet. She joined the Imperial Yeomanry Hospital in Pretoria in January 1901, where she met a Major
Watson of the Yeomanry, with whom she began a correspondence and
to whom she became engaged and, after the war, married. In her letter
of 9 March 1901, she wrote:

> *2 a.m. March 9.*
> What do you think of being written to at 2 a.m.? It should surprise
> you & it should also surprise you that, having had a sound talk with
> you yesterday afternoon I think of writing before some weeks have
> elapsed. This is not a letter. It's another talk & I will explain how it
> comes about. As I handed your man my mail Dr Washbourne came
> to tell me S. O'Neill (the sick Sister you thought me rather heartless
> about yesterday afternoon) was worse, dying in fact & knowing I

---

* Principal Medical Officer.

wished to be with her he had come over to the night house to let me know. I came to the day house at once & am spending the night here watching & waiting. At the present moment I am sitting behind a screen in the room writing by the light of a dim lantern. I think she will certainly live through the night. Dr Washbourne says decidedly not. We shall see. Doctors don't know as we nurses do the minute signs that tell us how long. They never sit hour by hour beside the patient [words cut out of the paper] varying expression is imprinted on their minds & can be read like a book. That is our work & alas! we get enough practice to make us perfect.

In a letter of 30 April, by which time 'Dear Major Watson' has become 'My Dear Little Chap' and most of the letter is taken up with expressions of affection, she wrote:

The days go on much the same as when you were here. Work all the morning, some days worse than others, exercise in the afternoon as much as possible, reading, writing (not arithmetic unless accounts!) odds & ends in the evening. The hospital is full and fairly busy – much dysentery of a bad type & a good deal of enteric. The people are behaving wonderfully well on the whole & the Sister I had to admonish so severely is quiet & I think really trying to do better & the Med: officers are lying low & polite. They are soon leaving thank Goodness & the relief of having this place without them I can hardly imagine. One Sister, a terror, has elected to go too – the best thing she has done [in] the hospital since it existed so we hope for some peace in the future. I hear we have a good deal of money over & am afraid that may mean a still further extension of work but it is not suggested yet. If so it would probably mean getting home at Christmas – another 3 months – it wouldn't really matter only it is such a long weary time to keep our affairs dark. This is not more than an idea, but seeing the thousands of Yeoman [sic] now newly out & coming out it is not beyond reason.

These new Yeomen are for the most part under sized, pale, seedy looking youths of 18 & 19 yrs old. This hospital is already full of them & they come up from Elandsfontein in almost daily batches of 20 or 30. Many are being returned home as unfit & they say quite openly, almost braggingly, that they came out for the trip for their health. Many have heart disease, some pthisis [sic], some no teeth, others are surgically unfit & won't be operated on for fear they become fit. It really is a scandle [*sic*] & *ought* to make bother at home.

Ld Chesham & Capt Darley were here a few days ago & they say the same thing, but they say there is one brilliant exception & that is the Sharpshooters – I felt so glad because that is what Robin is in, they say they are a very fine, picked set of men, almost exceptionally fine & Ld K. went specially to see them the other day. There are 600 of them, 2 companies. They had only seen one Company, the 22nd, not the one Robin is in but they thought it unlikely the other Company the 23rd would be less good. I should feel quite ashamed to have him in one of those dreadful sets we see specimens of.

French's horses were in as bad a state as the men. Roberts wrote about this to Lansdowne from Poplar Grove on 9 March:

I am anxious to bring to your notice the urgent necessity for a constant supply of horses being sent to South Africa. Owing to absence of forage and hard work a good many have been lost during the past month. Five hundred and fifty-eight were either killed, died or missing during the relief of Kimberley, and on the 7th instant 54 were killed, 47 wounded, 62 died from exhaustion, and 116 others were reported unfit for work. It must be remembered too that the sickly season is approaching when large numbers of horses are sometimes carried off. The artillery and Household Cavalry consider that English horses suit them best, but the Artillery would gladly take well bred Walers such as are in use by batteries in India. The rest of the Cavalry prefer Indian Country breds, Argentines, or any good stamp of small horse – Large numbers of smaller horses, such as have already been sent from India or even smaller ones and Burma ponies are required for Mounted Infantry. The success of the campaign depends so materially on the mounted troops being efficient that I trust there will be no lack of good serviceable horses.

Unsuitable horses were still being sent in January 1902, when Kitchener, in a letter to Roberts, complained about the ones that the Bays (2nd Dragoon Guards) had brought from England: 'These big-framed rather coarsely bred dragoon horses will I feel never stand unless they are constantly nursed, and we cannot continuously do that, and obtain any results. I hear the 7th horses are better and that the 20th and 3rd [all Hussars] are very good.'

Roberts was far from feeling that French's cavalry were efficient after their disappointing performance at Poplar Grove, and was planning an increase in the number of mounted infantry, in spite of the shortage of horses. The favourable view he had taken of French at the beginning of the campaign had now faded. In a letter to Lansdowne at the end of the month, in which he estimated that the number of Boers in the field opposing him had been reduced to about 30,000, he wrote:

One would think there ought to be no difficulty in bringing this number to terms with our large force, and there probably would not be if we could only come across them, but they slip away in the most extraordinary manner. At the same time I think we might have done better on more than one occasion if our Cavalry had been judiciously handled. French will never make a great cavalry leader, he is wanting in initiation and has no idea how to take care of his horses. He carried out the Relief of Kimberley in a satisfactory manner because he acted exactly in accordance with the instructions I gave him. But the following day, instead of giving his horses a much needed rest, he worked them from daylight till dark without any injury to the enemy or advantage to ourselves. I have never been able to get a complete return of the horse casualties on that occasion, but a large number of men had to be left at Kimberley as they had no horses to ride.

At Poplar Grove French started late and allowed himself to be beguiled by the enemy into fighting a series of rear guard actions, instead of giving them a wide berth and placing himself in the Boers' line of retreat. They were thus enabled to carry off their guns, and Kruger and Steyn effected their escape!

It was much the same at Driefontein, and at Dewetsdorp a day or two ago the enemy ought to have caught it, if our Cavalry had shown a little intelligent activity.

Our Mounted Infantry has much improved of late, and I intend to see whether their employment in large bodies will not bring about more satisfactory results.

Captain Laurence Maxwell of the 2nd Bengal Lancers, some close relation of David Maxwell, had brought remounts from India and describes moving them up by train in a letter to his sister, dated 2 March 1900:

[At Stellenbosch] I received orders to accompany a horse train to Modder River next day. So next day I said goodbye to the comfy little farm & found myself at the Ry Stn. The horses are shoved into trucks just like cattle & with room enough to turn round & get mixed up higgledy-piggledy & kick & do all sorts of mischief. Watering feeding clothing or unclothing them are almost impossibilities. They are much better done in India. The Kafir boys who accompanied the train in order to look after the horses & my two syces, bearer & baggage, were all piled onto a half loaded open truck, very dangerous. Next morning we were travelling thro' the Karoo, or desert, rushing down hills or climbing up: not much of a desert as such things go – green & always in sight of low barren hills, some like Indian Frontier ones. My companions were a gentleman private in the Imp Yeomanry & an Australian war correspondent – the former going up to buy horses for his company – & the latter going up for the Daily Chronicle. Occasionally we passed dreary tin roofed places & are fed at these very good meals, – perhaps a little expensive, 2/6 breakfast or lunch & 3/- dinner – This train was the first train going thro' to Kimberley & was full of people going to resume business there. Our long compartment contained a great mixture & very exposed to the elements. It rained & thunderstormed most of the 3 nights they were on the train. The only place for me was the Guards van, a smelly little place shared by two warrant officers & the guard. [page missing] So away we rattled & in two hours came to Wellington where the Stn Mr apologised for not having 1st Class carriage. I had wired to be attached & I settled to leave the train & await the mail.

This place was garrisoned by Cape Town Highldrs under a very surly Captain, They were very fine soldierly fellows, in the Gordon Tartan, & occupied the platform in great force – It is a most disloyal place I was told, most of the folk wearing the colours which I enclose – & which the gallant Captn gave me. He gave me his room in the hotel, as I had some hours to wait for the express. After dinner the news of Cronje's surrrender arrived on Majuba day & all & there was a rumour of Ladysmith being relieved. I went and had a look at the Ambulance Train full of our wounded coming down from the Front – They looked very comfortable – with doctors, nurses & everything with them – Despite the disloyalty of the inhabitants, there were a number of young women on the platform, handing out milk, eggs & fruit to the sick men.

16. Kelly-Kenny's infantry at Driefontein.

17. A pom-pom in action.

18. A naval 12-pounder being hauled up Schwarz Kop.

19. Colonels Rawlinson and Thorneycroft.

20. Infantry climbing the Tugela heights near Colenso.

21. Relief force entering Ladysmith, 3 March 1900.

22. 2nd Mounted Infantry crossing the Vaal River, 26 May 1900.

23. Major Ford's field hospital during operations.

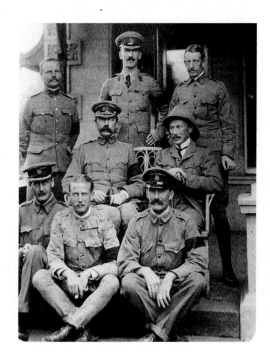

24. Lord Kitchener and staff.

25. Colonel Baden-Powell.

26. Artillery at Mafeking.

27. Annexation ceremony, Pretoria. Chestnut Troop marching past.

28. Commandant Jan Smuts.

29. General De la Rey
and his secretary.

30. General Christiaan De Wet and staff.

31. Boer burghers.

32. Transport, Frere, Natal, 1900.

At last the mail came in & I substituted my guards van for lying down accomodation in a Pullman car – Cape Town Highdrs bundling my servant into a 3rd Class & my kit into the van.

After further incidents, including the engine breaking down, he reached his destination, Modder River Station. Having handed over the horses, he did not return to Stellenbosch, as ordered, but managed to get himself attached to the Kimberley Mounted Corps.

*

On arrival at Bloemfontein, the army was dependent for supply on a single-track railway line, which split near the Orange River into separate tracks to the Cape Colony ports. The two bridges over the river had been blown up by the Boers and were not repaired until 19 March.

Major F. A. Molony of the Royal Engineers describes the construction of a pontoon bridge in his diary of 15 March:

Coxley (C.S.O.* to Clements) having asked me to report in the morning if the river was still falling, I started from my bivouac under the bush about 2.30 A M to try the ford again, but the current swept me off my legs & I had to swim back & report the ford difficult even for mounted men.

On getting back to the pontoons before dawn the infantry were assembling in dark masses, and the sappers putting the last touches to the launching places by cutting away the crest of the bank which was 25 feet high and sloped 30°. However with the aid of a 'preventer' rope passed round a tree I got my right & centre pontoons successfully down the bank and in the water. I was just going to see to the launching of my own pontoon when I saw Col Rochford Boyd & asked him what was to be the signal for starting: as the only order till then was that the right (that is Maj Burn Murdoch's) pontoons were to lead. He said 'are you ready'? I replied 'I have 2 ready!' & he said 'Start away then': so I gave the order & ran to my own pontoon (the left one), but we were a little behind the other two, though we lost no time. It was soon evident that the first part of the crossing was to be unopposed, as my right & centre pontoons were half way across the river & yet not a shot had been fired – Luckily for me probably,

* Chief Staff Officer.

as the night before I had taken the Khaki cover off my brilliant red & blue puggaree* so as to be known & forgotten to put it on again.

We should certainly have lost heavily in the crowded pontoons (15 in each) if even a few sharpshooters had been on the opposite bank, but the men who shot us down would never have escaped the heavy fire from our bank maintained all day, and Boers dont fight under such conditions. Still the idea of half sinking pontoons full of wounded carried over the rapids below was not very pleasant to contemplate. As it was the crossing was a beautiful sight. It was a very rosy dawn, & the party on the General's hill said it looked like a regatta. The river is very pretty here, the banks being high & well wooded, & the mountains near Vorval's post forming a fine background. On landing I hurried up the bank with the 10 infantry brought in my pontoon, and posted them where they had a fair view of the front, and then went back to business. First I had to choose & mark by a flag the best place for the end of the bridge, & then plant other flags 40 yards up and down stream, as guides for dropping the pontoon anchors. But before this was done the second trip of pontoons began arriving, and, there being a swirl near some rocks just there, those landing near me got into considerable trouble, tho' the men were all supposed to be expert boatmen.

After having had to whisper orders for so long, it was quite a relief to be able to shout at them!

Then I had to go and lay out the road leading up the far bank with tent pegs, and I flatter myself that my railway experience came in handy there, for a team of 10 mules will get into trouble if put round a sharp curve.

Presently the tools arrived, and then a party of 50 of the R. Irish who were soon started at work on the road, some cutting trees, others shovelling in the soft sand of which the banks hereabouts consist.

Meanwhile the 'C' Pontoon troop were getting to work at the bridge, bringing their materials out of the deep nullah. About midday the bridge was nearly across, and Col R. Boyd came & stood at the end and read us out a telegram just received announcing the capture of Bloemfontein. We gave 3 hearty cheers for the Queen, felt very happy & went to work again with a will.

---

* The band round a sun helmet, which was usually in corps or regimental colours, those of the Royal Engineers being red and blue.

But the day was very hot & the men had little water. I had brought over my Berkefelt filter to try and cleanse the pea-soup like river water, but at the 15th cleansing the man told off to the job broke it. However we discovered at tea-time that boiling precipitated most of the mud to the bottom – for we did not starve by any means on this busy day. A cavalry canteen is light to carry, but it will hold and do a lot, if properly packed. However about 2 PM the Royal Irish were fairly worked out, and as they had done the road, and the bridge (owing to leaking pontoons having to be replaced with casks) would clearly not be ready for some time, I started down river to see the site for the proposed suspension bridge from the far bank.

About ½ mile down I came on a deep donga in which was a man lighting a fire, who wore no article of uniform. As he was out of range of my small revolver, & would probably hear me if I got closer, I went back for 6 men of the R.I. and we came up to the nullah in line, but the bird had flown! There was his fire, put out with some of the water which stood in pools in the bottom, and the stone sniping place under a tree from which he had worried the General. The bridge covering party had evidently got behind him before he woke in the morning, but how he finally got away I cannot guess. The R.I. made a pretence of hunting him for a long time, but I went to see the bridge site.

About 5, the pontoon bridge was done and the troops began crossing – mounted infantry first. They promised me a 10 minutes interval between them and the guns in order that we might lay branches (which we had already cut) on the soft sand slope – but the guns followed close, & we had to get on the branches between them. That – the drivers whipping up their horses, and the column crossing the long bridge behind, made a scene of rare animation & go. But when the guns were up, and heavily laden ammunition and other waggons arrived, they would not go; and we had to have ropes ready to clap on behind & haul them up. Luckily all were over in time to let me get back to camp for 7.30 dinner – for which I was more than ready. But it was a grand day!

Roberts's logistic problems were formidable and forced him to pause before resuming his advance up the railway to Pretoria. Nevertheless he could have been more active than he was. The Free State General J. H. Olivier, who had blown up the railway bridges, was somewhere between him and the Orange River with 6,000 Boers. On 15 March Roberts learned that he was moving north close to the border of Basutoland, but did nothing for five days and then told French to send one of his cavalry brigades to Thabanchu, fifteen miles east of Bloemfontein on the Modder to intercept him.

Roberts's lack of urgency stemmed from his mistaken appreciation of the situation. The rapid withdrawal of the Free State forces, giving him unopposed entry to their capital, caused him to believe that once he occupied it and treated the inhabitants with clemency they would lay down their arms and accept a return to British sovereignty. He therefore, with Milner's approval, offered an amnesty to all burghers of the Free State, except their leaders, who agreed to return home, surrender their arms and take an oath of allegiance to Queen Victoria. He genuinely believed that many would do so, as he made clear in a letter to the Queen on 15 March:

> The Orange Free State south of this is rapidly settling down. The proclamations [of an amnesty] I have issued are having the desired effect, and men are daily laying down their arms and returning to their usual occupations. It seems unlikely that this State will give much more trouble. The Transvaalers will probably hold out, but their numbers must be greatly reduced, and I trust it will not be very long before the war will have been brought to a satisfactory conclusion.
>
> We are obliged to rest here for a short time to let men and animals recover, and provide the former with new boots and clothes.

Buller, with previous experience of South Africa, took a different view. He realized that occupation of the capitals of either Boer state would not bring about a rapid collapse of their resistance. It was defeat of their armed forces that mattered. He protested strongly against Roberts's proposal of 6 March that, although he could reoccupy Dundee and Newcastle, no attempt should be made to force the passes of the Drakensberg Mountains on the border between Natal and the Transvaal.

While Roberts's Irish troops were celebrating St Patrick's Day, 17 March, in Bloemfontein,* Kruger and Steyn held a council of war at

---

* Wearing shamrock on the personal order of Queen Victoria, as Rudyard Kipling, who visited them a few days later, recorded in an execrable piece of verse.

Kroonstad, 130 miles to the north. They decided to continue the war 'more energetically than ever' and do all they could to counter Roberts's offer of amnesty; but the problem was how. The answer was provided by Christiaan De Wet, who had recently replaced J. S. Ferreira as Free State Commandant-General, when the latter was accidentally shot by one of his own sentries. De Wet proposed abandonment of conventional defence and adoption of aggressive action by smaller fully mobile commandos, independent of bullock transport, against Roberts's long, vulnerable lines of communication and any detachments separated from the main body of his troops. The Transvaal General De la Rey supported him, and together they persuaded the hesitant Presidents that the first step was to let the burghers go home for a rest and then summon the best of them to form commandos for this purpose. Their offensive activity over a wide area would also discourage others from accepting Roberts's amnesty or otherwise cooperating with the British.

De Wet decided that his first action would be an attack on Bloemfontein's water supply, which relied on a pumping station at Sannah's Post on the west bank of the Modder twenty miles east of the city, defended by only 200 mounted infantry, and he assembled a commando of 1,500 men for the operation. In fact Brigadier-General Robert Broadwood's 2nd Cavalry Brigade was not far away, at Thabanchu, acting as a general flank guard to Bloemfontein and meanwhile posting up amnesty notices in the area. His force totalled 1,700, some 'Tigers', two regular cavalry regiments, the Household Cavalry* and the 10th Hussars, with only 332 horses between them, Lieutenant-Colonel Edwin Alderson's 830 strong Mounted Infantry Regiment and two six-gun batteries of horse artillery, and was burdened with a convoy of ninety-two wagons, many of them carrying civilian refugees and their belongings. As Olivier's commando approached him on 30 March, Broadwood decided to withdraw to join the garrison of the pumping station, which his force reached a few hours before dawn on the 31st, throwing themselves down to sleep, believing that the only enemy was Olivier's commando, still some way away.

They were rudely awakened at dawn by rifle and artillery fire from across the Modder to the north-east. Broadwood decided to withdraw westwards to Bushman's Kop, a few miles to the west of the Korn Spruit,

---

* A composite regiment was formed for service in South Africa drawn from all three regiments of the Household Cavalry.

a stream which joined the Modder two miles below Sannah's Post. Unknown to him, De Wet had concealed 500 of his men on the west bank of the Spruit, and, as Broadwood's column began to cross, they quietly ambushed them, immediately taking 200 men prisoner, including Major Taylor's 'U' Battery RHA. The other battery (Major Phipps-Hornby's 'Q'), alerted just in time, managed to get five of its guns into action and prevented the rest of the column from entering the ambush. They were soon under heavy fire from the Boers and only with the gallant help of ten men of the Essex Regiment were they able to extricate four guns and cross the Spruit by another ford. Broadwood had dispatched an officer on horseback to Roberts to ask for help and sent a helio message when he reached Bushman's Kop. These reached Roberts in mid-morning, two hours after being told by Rawlinson, returning from his morning ride, that he had heard artillery fire from that direction. Neither of them took any action until Broadwood's messages arrived. French was then told to send patrols to search for Boers in the eastern outskirts of the town, while Colvile's 9th Division set off to march towards Broadwood.

The 16th Lancers were involved in this reinforcement, and Captain Bellew recounts what happened:

> *31 March.*
> At 1130 orders came to turn out at once and repulse attack by somebody somewhere. All horses were out grazing and the men scattered about washing etc. After some confusion the regiment managed to produce 4 full troops. F then had a great scheme of forming a troop of officers and armed all present with lance and carbine, most fortunately some officers were away and it fell through or we should have had to carry the damned things for days. As we proceeded we met 18th H[ussars] and compos and learnt that Broadwood had had to retire before a largely superior force. When his horses were beat he camped near the waterworks, but during the night another force of Boers had come from Brandfoot and surrounded him, in getting out he lost 7 guns and convoy had several casualties, numbers stated from 100 to 300. Boers now hold waterworks.

By then De Wet had made off with seven guns, 117 captured wagons and 428 prisoners. Three days later he attacked the garrison of Reddersberg, thirty miles to the south, manned by 600 men of the Royal Irish Regiment with no artillery. Having held out for twenty-four hours, during which they suffered 45 casualties, 546 surrendered.

A month later, on 3 May, Roberts started his advance to Pretoria, at the same time sending Colonel Bryan Mahon from Kimberley with 1,100 men to ride to the relief of Colonel Robert Baden-Powell at Mafeking. Earlier on, immediately after the Battle of Paardeberg, Roberts had suggested to Rhodes that he should undertake this, signalling on 27 February:

> I am considering what measures are possible for relief of Mafeking and I should be glad of your advice and assistance in matter. Could you organize a force at Kimberley of Colonials for the purpose. I can send you several thousand mausers with large supply of ammunition and could strengthen the force with some maxims and (perhaps) some field guns. It would be difficult to send you Imperial officers but I believe it would have an excellent effect politically if relief of Mafeking were carried out by purely local instead of by Imperial troops. Kindly let me know your views fully and frankly as soon as you can.

Nothing came of that: if it had, its political effect might not have been 'excellent', at least not in Britain.

Mahon's main body consisted of three squadrons of the Imperial Light Horse, the two that had been in Ladysmith, in which David Maxwell was serving, and the one that had led the relief, in which his brother Patrick was, with a squadron of Rhodes's Kimberley Mounted Corps, which their relative Laurence had joined. They were supported by a battery of the Royal Horse Artillery and an ad hoc company of infantry composed of soldiers from England, Scotland, Wales and Ireland. With them were Frank Rhodes and Sir John Willoughby, making a nostalgic return to the starting place of the Jameson Raid.

The original intention had been that the siege should be raised by Lieutenant-Colonel Herbert Plumer with a 700-strong column of mounted infantry, recruited in Rhodesia; but, when the latter failed, although he got within five miles on 31 March, Roberts decided that he would have to send Mahon.

Mafeking was a very small town at a railway siding two hundred and fifty miles north of Kimberley, close to the junction of the borders of the

Transvaal, Cape Colony, Rhodesia and the Bechuanaland Protectorate, and it was from there that Jameson had embarked on his ill-fated raid. When hostilities against Kruger had appeared likely, Colonel Baden-Powell, who had taken part in the Matabeleland campaign, had been sent to raise a regiment of mounted infantry in Rhodesia, while Plumer, subordinate to him, raised one in Bechuanaland. Baden-Powell's secret orders were that, if hostilities erupted, he should move to Tuli near the Rhodesian border, and from there 'endeavour to demonstrate with the largest force at your disposal in a southerly direction from Tuli, as if making towards Pretoria'. It was hoped that this threat would draw Boer forces towards them, away from Cape Colony. By September 1899 it had been decided that the raid should be abandoned, but that Baden-Powell, with the Bechuanaland regiment, should garrison Mafeking, leaving Plumer at Kanya in Rhodesia, seventy miles to the north, as a back-up force. This deployment had the desired effect. Cronje, with some 7,700 men, moved up into that area of the Transvaal, surrounding Mafeking on 13 October 1899, and stayed there until Methuen's advance from the Orange River towards Kimberley in November caused him to move most of his force south to the Modder, leaving General Snyman with 1,500 men to keep an eye on Baden-Powell, who was more active than either of them, although he had only 771 men, of whom 20 were regular army officers, from the Bechuanaland Protectorate Regiment and the British South Africa Police, the majority in the first named. In addition 300 able-bodied white men were enrolled as a Town Guard and 300 natives as cattle guards, watchmen and police. The civilian population consisted of 1,074 white men and 229 white women, with 405 children, and 7,500 natives, most of them the local Baralong and some labourers from elsewhere. Half were armed with Lee-Metford and half with Martini-Henry rifles, with 600 rounds per man. His artillery consisted of four muzzle-loading 7-pounders, to which were later added two home-made muzzle-loaders, one an ancient (1770) ship's gun that had been used as a gatepost, firing a 6lb solid shot, and one made in the railway workshops, which fired a 16lb shell up to 4,000 yards. He also had an old Hotchkiss 1-pounder, a 2in. Nordenfeldt and seven .303 Maxim machine-guns. An armoured railway engine arrived from Kimberley shortly before the garrison was surrounded.

While Cronje was still besieging Mafeking, he had one Long Tom, nine modern 75mm field guns and the two 7-pounders which had been captured from Jameson. On seven occasions in the first two months of the war, Baden-Powell had sent out raiding parties to attack their positions, but, after 163 casualties, he decided that they were too expensive to continue. Cronje showed no inclination to do more than shell the town, causing remarkably few casualties. Baden-Powell's defences had to cover not just the small town where the white population lived, which formed a square of thousand-yard sides, but also three native locations, the largest of which, populated by the Baralong, lay astride the Milopo River three-quarters of a mile to the south-west. To help defend the latter, Baden-Powell, contrary to the convention observed by both sides, armed 300 of them. The Africans were also employed in digging defences. Baden-Powell, with his boyish enthusiasm, was the life and soul of the place, constantly thinking up ways of raising the spirits of the garrison and keeping them on their toes; but the exhilaration of Christmas festivities led him to overreach himself on Boxing Day by dispatching two of the four squadrons of the regiment to attack Game Tree Fort, two miles north of the town, which the Boers were strengthening. With no artillery support, it was a forlorn hope and cost him 24 dead, 23 wounded and 3 missing.

Sergeant Francis of the Bechuanaland Protectorate Regiment described the action:

But now I come to the saddest day of the siege Boxing Day 1899; Xmas night C Squadron under the direction of Major Godley with our 2 7 Pounders & quick-firing machine guns were sent out under cover of the darkness to take up positions for an attack at dawn on Game Tree fort held by the Boers in some force, you will see it marked N of the defences. A Squadron were also sent to the Northern forts to support if required and ordered to do so, of course I went with them. By some error of judgement or misunderstanding the sun was rising before any movement was made or a gun fired; we had been on the alert & standing to arms at 4 a.m. The first gun, fired about 5.15 which put the Boers thoroughly on the qui vive, our guns did little or no damage, and then we saw C Squadron advancing splendidly in open order against the enemy's position, very few fell in the advance; and at 500 yards they tried to rush the fort at the point of the bayonet. They actually got right up to & fired through the loopholes with rifle & revolver but the place was impregnable. It was about 80 yards square roofed in with iron sand bags and earth,

the walls being quite 9 feet high & only one narrow entrance at the
back. It was not to be & orders to retire were given which was carried
out and in good order & with no panic, but the losses were terrible
men fell on all sides & the marvel is how any returned alive. When
firing ceased & our ambulance wagons went out with an Armoured
train on the line, the former were soon filled & had to return twice
to the scene of battle; the Dutch crowding round them and robbing
the dead and wounded of articles of value and all their weapons. Our
losses were 26 killed and 3 taken prisoners. It terribly upset us all
and made us all very indignant at somebody's blunder. Capt Vernon
K.R.R. the captain of C Squadron, Capt Sandford & Lieut Paton were
all popular officers the former especially so & much respected
throughout the Regiment, the Squadron Sgt Major Paget & several
N.C.Os were killed or died of wounds, one a Sgt Barry a fine manly
young fellow only 22 I personally much regretted, but there I cannot
write more on this sad topic the whole Squadron was one recruited
from good class of men mostly in Cape Town; and the loss of so
many brave men was a serious weakening of our little garrison. I
have had poor Barry's Irish terrier bitch in my care ever since and
I can assure you she is well looked after & a great pet amongst all at
our fort.

From then on, Baden-Powell's main concern was food. Initially a
bonus had been provided by the discovery that a contractor, Weil and
Co., had stockpiled considerable quantities of flour, meal and grain there
in anticipation of changes in Rhodesian customs dues, but those supplies
were falling low and Baden-Powell imposed rationing on everyone, at
the same time as compulsory acquisition of the natives' own store of
grain, which he then rationed severely while making them buy it back.
By February he was contemplating a forcible reduction in the native
ration, which would persuade a significant number of them to leave and
move to Kanya, where Plumer was accumulating stocks of food. As the
months passed, he employed other ruses to eke out the dwindling
supplies, the burden of almost all of which fell on the African population;
but by the end of March only 500 had left. In his final report Baden-
Powell gave some examples of how he made ends meet. One was the
production of oat bread. He wrote:

Mr Ellitson, our master-baker, made up our forage-oats into a good
form of bread. The oats were winnowed, cleaned, kiln dried, ground,

steam sieved (twice) and made into bread in the usual way, with a small admixture of Boer Meal.

Another recipe was for sausages:

The horses which we used for meat were as a rule so poor in condition that we found it best to cut off the flesh from the bones and mince it for issue as a ration. The remainder of the carcass then went into the soup-kitchen. The mince was mixed with spice and saltpetre, and made up into sausages, the intestines of the same animal being used for sausage-skins. The meat thus treated lasted longer and was more palatable.

When Plumer's attempt at relief failed at the end of that month and it appeared that he could not expect relief before the end of May, further attempts to force the Africans to leave were made, which led to an unfortunate incident in which 700 women attempted the journey and were harshly treated by the Boers, who forced them back. On 20 April Baden-Powell wrote in his diary:

Meat and meal stocks at present will last to June 12. But by forcing natives away from Mafeking we can get their share of horseflesh for whites and their *sowen** which would improve the [white] ration in size.

Serving in Snyman's commando was a grandson of Kruger, Sarel Eloff. On 30 April he sent a facetious message to Baden-Powell, suggesting that some of his men should join the Mafeking garrison on a Sunday for cricket and an evening's entertainment, to which Baden-Powell replied:

Sir, I beg to thank you for your letter of yesterday . . . I should like nothing better – after the match in which we are at present engaged is over. But just now we are having our innings and have so far scored 200 days, not out, against the bowling of Cronje, Snyman, Botha . . . and we are having a very enjoyable game.
     I remain, yours truly,
          R. S. S. Baden-Powell

---

* A form of porridge made of oat husks, left after grinding.

When Eloff learned that Mahon had set off from Kimberley, he persuaded Snyman to let him make an attempt to seize Mafeking before he arrived. While others made a feint attack on the British positions east of the town, Eloff would lead 700 men, including some French and Germans, to attack through the Baralong location to the station, guided by some Africans and a British deserter, who knew the area. The operation was launched in the early hours of the morning of 12 May, after the moon had set and before the sun rose; but Eloff had only been able to raise 240 volunteers. He reached the location without difficulty and set fire to the Baralong huts before pushing on to the old Chartered Company barracks, between the location and the town, where he captured the 30-strong headquarters of the regiment, including its commanding officer, Colonel Hore, of whom Baden-Powell had no high opinion. But the blaze had alerted Baden-Powell himself, who, through the extensive telephone network which he had established, quickly arranged a counter-attack, led by the regiment's adjutant, Major Alexander Godley. This was successful, the infuriated Baralong barring Eloff's withdrawal. He surrendered as Godley's men attacked the barracks, having suffered 60 casualties; 108 of his men were taken prisoner. The garrison's casualties were 12 dead and 8 wounded, most of them Baralong. Five days later, on 17 May, Mahon's force, having joined hands with Plumer advancing from the north, approached the town as Snyman withdrew, and at 7 p.m. Major Karri Davies, whose Imperial Light Horse squadron had been first into Ladysmith, trotted in with an escort of 8, followed in the dark by the main body accompanying a food convoy. Both David and Patrick Maxwell wrote letters to their sister describing their ride to the relief. David, after mentioning their concentration at Dronfield on 3 May, wrote:

Next day 4th we left at 8 a m met L [Laurence] on march & he gave me last mail which I passed on to Pat – We only marched 9 miles – any amount of game – thick Bush. Next (15th) morning marched at 2 a m. Offsaddled at 9 a m on Karts River. Boers seen & caused much excitement & galloping – doubling up Kopjies etc. eventually resumed the march about 3 p m & bivouacked for night on same river at 7 p.m. having done 34 miles – no fires or lights allowed. Next day started at 6 a.m. marched (6th) 24 miles & was on picket all night – Very cold.

Left next day 7th at 6 a.m. & only did 18 miles – the nice open country full of small game, very loyal natives who sold & gave fowls & eggs readily.

Next day marched at 3 a.m. & got 10 prisoners as many horses & rifles.

On the 9th left at 6.30 & arrived at Vryburg at 3.30 being received with open arms & much show of Red, White & Blue rosettes & ribbons. Remained there for 24 hrs & marched about 5 p.m. on 10th till 2 a.m. next morning. Marched again at 6 o'clock till 8 for water, which was brackish. L's fever rather worse. Marched again at 5 p.m. till 11 o'clock which was mighty cold

On the 12th we started again at 5 a.m. took any amount of prisoners (rebels) arms – carts & horses. One of the carts & 2 horses we got for ourselves to carry our kit & saved the pack horse also buckets etc – as we always halted about ½ mile away from water & in the evening we struck [illegible] police station – Hotel & a J.P. The most loyal old Brit owned the hotel & refused to fight for the Boers telling them they might cut his throat first – this from the Kaffirs – the old gent & his wife not mentioning this little affair – They refused payment for everything – giving us eggs – fowls – butter & an excellent dinner to the Officers. 7 months since they saw an Englishman – it is to this place I think that L has been sent back. On picket again all night.

Marched at 6 a.m. on 13th to Brodie's farm where another loyal man entertained us royally – Here we had to leave our chariot as we had bush in front of us & heavy roads & the column had to be shortened as much as possible as the Boers were waiting for us.

Marched from here at 1 p.m. & met the Boers about 4.30 & after a miserable short little fight of an hour drove them off & found that our loss had been very heavy – 6 killed – 27 wounded – all the killed & most wounded of our regt. Mr L left his ambulance van at the 1st shot & joined his C.O., & got shot in the fleshy part of his leg for his pains – 4 neat little holes – I found him about 8 o'clock, very chirpy – haven't seen him since. Stood to without offsaddling all night & marched to water at sunrise (14th) about 5 miles & which we had to dig for in the sandy bed of a river – Marched again at 3 p.m. till 1 a.m. (15th) Very heavy sand & up hill. Marched again at 1.30 a.m. & met Plumer's force at 6.30 on the Molopo river – about 850 strong & 4 Canadian guns. Marched at 6 a.m. on 16th sighted Mafeking at

10.30 a.m. watered at midday when we found Boers – trying to get round us – had a good fight till about 4 p.m. mostly artillery & then advanced on foot till dark. When a patrol was sent in to see if the road was clear they reported all right at midnight & we marched in – our Sqdn being rearguard, Got in at 4.30 a.m. Dead cold & tired. Had to saddle up again at 9 a.m. & galloped out after Boers – but were stopped about 2 miles out & after wasting 2 hrs were marched in in state – passed B.P. we then came to this camp & no sooner let the horses out to graze (the grain being all finished) than we had to rush off again & catch them, & gallop out 3 miles – to another false alarm. However this time we got into the Boer camp & got plenty of loot in the food line for man & beast – which was welcome as we are on ½ rations. Since then we have done nothing but routine work. Today Sunday we had Service for the Relieving Force & a nice-short-sensible address from a young parson. I shall be out all night to-night on a patrol – the days are hot – but the nights are bitter. Tommy Cream, a huge Irish giant & I always share our blankets & as he is a restless person I usually wake up to find his enormous mass of flesh weighing about 18 stone lying over me – uncomfortable but warm. I am just going over to see L's C.O. as I hear that his corps is being disbanded – also I want one of his horses.

Patrick's letter was less informative. In it he wrote:

Every day we captured a few Boers, principally rebels found on their farms with arms in their possession and in nearly all cases their houses were burnt – At one place where we halted for a few hours in the afternoon we had a great time: at a farm which had been fired by the advanced guard, the place was swarming with pigs & fowls & in no time these were butchered & being roasted in the burning house; potatoes, onions & mealies galore were to be had from the garden & with any amount of oats, these for the horses we had a grand time. Poor Laurie was laid up with fever on the 3rd day out & had to do the march in the ambulance wagon which was the very height of bad luck & if the juggins had only obeyed the doctor he would have been with us again now instead of being compelled to lie on the front of his back with a mauser bullet thro' his person which will prevent his sitting down for some time.

His description of Mafeking was:

A miserable hole of a town & its few buildings have been tremendously knocked about by shells, far worse than Ladysmith: as far as rations were concerned they were doing much better than Ladysmith, were getting 6 ozs of bread every day & there is tobacco galore in the town. We are practically living on siege rations ourselves at present 6 ozs of bread, a little piece of fresh meat & a spoonful of tea & sugar per man being our allowance today, though hitherto we have always had biscuit instead of bread. I had some flour given me yesterday as compensation for not being able to go into the Boer laager & today Bramwell and I made our first attempt at baking & an immense success it was, 2 great heavy scone-like things turning out of the dish which proved most satisfying. We had a church parade this morning as a thanksgiving for the relief of this place. Baden-Powell was there & looks just the smart little man one would expect him to be.

On the day after the relief, which took place a week before Queen Victoria's eighty-first birthday, Mahon's and Plumer's men paraded past Baden-Powell, who was overcome with emotion, as London exploded with patriotic fervour which was to coin the word 'mafficking'. The total casualties from action during the siege had been: whites, 71 killed and 123 wounded; coloureds, 25 and 68; natives, 65 and 117; Baralong, 264 killed. 53 whites had died from various other causes. On 27 May Baden-Powell received the news that he had been promoted to Major-General and a telegram from the Queen, saying:

I and my whole Empire greatly rejoice at the relief of Mafeking after the splendid defence made by you through all these months. I heartily congratulate you and all under you, military and civil, British and Native, for the heroism and devotion you have shown.

*

That Mahon had been able to avoid serious Boer resistance on his way from Kimberley was due to their preoccupation with Roberts's advance towards Pretoria. Leaving 20,000 men to guard the Free State and his communications, and detaching Lieutenant-General Sir Archibald Hunter's 8,000 strong 10th Division to guard his left flank in the lower valley of the Vaal, Roberts began his advance on 3 May up the railway line with 30,000 men, Tucker's 7th and Pole-Carew's 11th Divisions and, on his right flank, Ian Hamilton with a new division consisting of

Broadwood's Cavalry and Colonel C. P. Ridley's Mounted Infantry Brigades, and Smith-Dorrien's 19th and Major-General Bruce Hamilton's 21st Infantry Brigades. The whole force, with 11,000 horses, 120 guns and 14 Maxim pom-poms, was accompanied by 22,000 mules drawing 5,500 carts and 40,000 oxen pulling 2,500 wagons. As Roberts advanced, the Boers defended each successive river line, but withdrew before they could be attacked, destroying the bridges as they did so with the help of John MacBride's Irish Brigade.

Squadron Sergeant-Major F. Cobb was with the 7th Dragoon Guards in Broadwood's brigade. They had been in action before the main advance started, as he told his wife in a letter, dated 2 May:

I could not write by the last mail, as we have been on the column from Bloemfontein, we left Donkerhook last Friday week; only had ½ hour to get ready. We have had a stiff ten days fighting all the time, I know now what fighting, and being under fire means, am glad to say, we have been very fortunate up to the present, we are the luckiest regiment in the Brigade, and have been under fire most of any, we had our first taste Sunday [Saturday] April 21st, we had 4 horses killed during the morning fight, in the afternoon Mr Jenkins took a patrol out, 2 got captured, Cpl Taylor and Pvt Cook, we had heard since that Taylor was killed, the remainder of the patrol had a narrow squeak, had to gallop for their lives. Broadly was the Sergeant, he says there was at least 150 Boers after them. From what I had seen of the Boers shooting, it is all a fable about them being such sure shots, but they are very good with their 'long toms'. We have had quite a busy time yesterday. The Boers got the range of our camp, and dropped shell after shell amongst us, not one of them burst, one shell hit a convoy wagon and killed 2 natives, & 2 mules, & one of our men wounded, Lieut Vaughan was wounded last Saturday. None of us have had our clothes off since we started, have been on duty myself for the last three nights. You wouldn't know the regiment now if you saw it, the men have grown beards, and are as dirty as niggers. I had a wash this morning, the first for five days, so you can guess what we are like, both men and horses are on ½ rations, so unless we can commandeer something we go short. We have been working between Bloemfontein and Waperneh, all hill fighting. Am sending this letter in with convoy, carrying sick and wounded to Bloemfontein. The artillery of both sides are having a duel at the present moment, don't know what damage each are doing, we are out of range, but can see the explosions, as I said before the Boers cannot use their rifles so well as we thought, we must hope for the best, and trust to Providence is the soldier's motto out here.

Ian Hamilton lost 59 men of his rearguard in a brief encounter with the De Wet brothers near Lindley, where Steyn had set up his provisional capital. Piet De Wet had earlier offered to surrender, with his commando, if he could be guaranteed immunity, but Roberts vetoed it. The latter's problems arose not from Boer resistance, but from logistic and medical deficiencies. The sick state reported to Roberts on 29 April, shortly before he began his advance, was:

	Officers	Other Ranks
Enteric fever	33	1123
Gun Shot Wounds	4	68
Other fevers	17	872
Other diseases	63	1123
Total	117	3,186
Deaths	3	41

By the time he reached Kroonstad Roberts had lost patience with his Surgeon-General, who had remained at Bloemfontein. On 21 May he sent him the following signal:

Hospital arrangements here are most unsatisfactory and I trust you to come here and superintend them. You need not wait until railway is open and you should bring as many surgeons and medical subordinates with you as possible – some hundred mattresses are urgently needed these you must order from Capetown or wherever they can be procured and have them sent up in charge of some responsible person who can see that they are not left on the road. The requirements for Kroonstad should have been foreseen and spare surgeons should have been on the spot they could have travelled in carts from railhead as many sick and wounded men have to do. There is ample accomodation for 20 or 30 nurses and these should be despatched on Wednesday next by which time the railway trains will reach this [place]. As soon as Kroonstad has been put in order, you should arrange for hospital accomodation [*sic*] being provided in the Transvaal where medical men, subordinates, nurses, and all necessary appliances will be required very shortly.

6

FALSE DAWN

May to October 1900

During this period Buller blew hot and cold on the subject of his advance from Natal. When Roberts first reached Bloemfontein, he had expected his advance towards Pretoria to make it unnecessary for Buller to attack the passes through the Drakensberg Mountains which formed the border between Natal and the Transvaal, as the Boers would be forced to withdraw. Buller had resented this restriction and had been keen that his force should play its part. However, as Roberts found himself delayed, he turned more in favour of Buller advancing, while the latter appeared hesitant about moving north from Newcastle. Nevertheless, when Roberts started off at last, he wrote to Lansdowne on 4 May:

> It is too late now for Buller to afford me any assistance by operating through the passes of the Drakensberg, and as the enemy cannot act against him from that direction in any force, and are almost certain to withdraw numbers of their men from the Biggarsberg as we advance North, I have suggested to Buller that he should work up the line of the railway and endeavour to help us when we enter the Transvaal. I fear, however, from his reply, that we shall have to depend mainly on ourselves.

On 17 May Roberts suggested to Buller that instead of attempting to force the pass at Laing's Nek on the line of the railway he should send a division from Newcastle by Botha's Pass to the west to Vrede and thence to Standerton on the railway about seventy miles north of Laing's Nek. In his signal he said:

> I am inclined to think this would cause the enemy to leave Laing's Nek and thus enable another of your divisions to move up the railway line without opposition. They will certainly leave Laing's Nek when we reach Johannesburg which we ought to do early in June.

Buller replied:

> I believe it will be easier for me to force Laing's Nek than to send a
> detached force by Botha's Pass, a troublesome route.

Four days later Buller reported Laing's Nek strongly held, and Roberts
signalled on 23 May:

> I think it would be better to defer attacking it until the effect is
> known of our appearance on the Vaal River, and, I hope a few days
> later, at Johannesburg. Laing's Nek is a pass which, if well defended,
> could not be taken without great loss, a loss which it is not worth
> incurring as your occupation of it would not now materially assist in
> our advance, and a few days in the repair of the railway will not
> signify.

He again pressed Buller to send a division to Vrede. Buller replied that
that would be too risky, as it would make his line of communications
vulnerable, to which Roberts's answer, on 26 May, was:

> It is quite unnecessary that you should run any undue risk with your
> force either in the Laing's Nek or Drakensberg direction. My
> advanced troops are now across the Vaal and the main body will be
> on the North side to-morrow.

After crossing the Vaal on 26 May, Hamilton was switched to west of
the railway to approach the Rand and Johannesburg from that direction,
while the main body continued along the line of the rail track to
approach from the east. Hamilton engaged in what many thought a
needlessly direct frontal attack on 30 May at Doorn Kop, where the
Jameson Raid had been surrounded on 2 January 1896. In it the Gordons
lost 17 killed and 80 wounded in a gallant assault, while the City Imperial
Volunteers, using less conventional tactics, suffered few casualties, the
total for the brigade being 28 killed and 134 wounded. On that day
Roberts entered Johannesburg, from which the Boers were withdrawing.
He was met by the town commander, Commandant Krause, who
undertook to ensure that no damage was done to the gold mines,
provided that he was given twenty-four hours in which to effect the
withdrawal of Boer troops from the city. Roberts, anxious both to secure
the mines and to avoid needless casualties, and believing that the war
was virtually at an end, agreed, while the Boers got away all the gold and

which De Wet was the foremost champion. On 30 May Kruger, with his principal ministers, was smuggled out of Pretoria to Machadodorp, 150 miles down the railway towards Portuguese East Africa. On 1 June a council of war was held in Pretoria, from which Smuts and Botha telegraphed to Kruger a recommendation to surrender, while Kruger telegraphed to Steyn, the line to Lindley being still open, to seek his opinion. Steyn's reply was robust. He more or less accused the Transvaal of having forced the Free State into war and then proposed to abandon it. He argued that it was not the capitals that mattered, but the wide, sparsely populated countryside, which provided the possibility of a successful defence of the *Volk* by an aggressive campaign against Roberts's vulnerable communications with Cape Colony and Natal. His argument won over a second council of war next day, and Krause's tactics at Johannesburg were repeated at Pretoria, the Boers being allowed to take away their forces and anything else they wished, before Roberts entered in triumph at 2 p.m. on 5 June, having sent in an advance party of Guardsmen from Pole-Carew's division with their agreement. Before that Winston Churchill had made his way to the camp where he had himself been a prisoner and let the inmates out.

Roberts had been hoodwinked. Before entering Pretoria, he had received a visit from Botha's secretary proposing peace talks, and for the next five days, while basking in the glory of what he thought was a victory that eclipsed those of Kabul and Kandahar, he waited in vain for negotiations of surrender; but there was no sign of them, only disturbing news of attacks on his vulnerable lines of communication. The day before his triumphal entry, Christiaan De Wet, having received an encouraging message of support from Botha, ambushed a convoy taking supplies to Colvile's Highland Brigade at Heilbron, capturing 56 wagons and taking 160 prisoners. Two days later, he attacked at three points on the railway near Roodewaal where it crossed the Rhenoster River halfway between Johannesburg and Bloemfontein, killing 38 soldiers, wounding 104 and taking 486 prisoner, mostly of the 4th Derbyshires, an inexperienced Militia battalion, and seizing or destroying large quantities of ammunition and other supplies. Already, on the day that Johannesburg was occupied, his brother Piet had captured near Lindley almost the whole of the 13th Battalion of the Imperial Yeomanry, one squadron of which was raised from the hunting fraternity of Ireland, including Lords Longford, Leitrim, Ennismore and Donoughmore and the future Lord

Craigavon, with 525 others; 80 men were killed or wounded. Captain the Hon. Douglas Loch of the Grenadier Guards was signal officer at the headquarters of Methuen's 1st Division, and in a letter to his parents of 30 May he told them of Methuen's attempt to go to the battalion's rescue:

> After closing my letter to you last night a telegram came from Lord Roberts to say that we were to march at once to the relief of Gen Colville [*sic*] at Heilbron. Everything had to be altered, wagons unloaded and reloaded so as to be ready for a forced march – We got off at 7 a.m. and marched to Klipfontein arrived about 10.30 am – The wagons got all in by 2 pm – About 1.30 we received news that Colville had fought his way into Heilbron & that he did not want reinforcements. I was rather disappointed as I was looking forward to Lord Methuen relieving the Highland Bde – At 3.30 pm we received orders from Lord Roberts to march at once to the relief of Col Spragge at Lindley – The G.O.C.* determined to move forward at once with three regiments of Yeomanry 45 Battery and two pompoms carrying five days rations and three days forage & supplies in mule wagons – We started half an hour after receiving the order – Gen Douglas with 9th Bde ordered to march straight from Kroonstad to Lindley. We marched till 7 pm when as the guide seemed to have lost his way we halted in the veld till daylight.

31st May
Left our veld camp at daylight and marched till 9 a.m. – baggage got a bit delayed by a badish drift so we had to halt till 11 a.m. when we marched till 2 pm and then from 3 pm to 6 pm when we arrived at a place called Doornkloof – Our scouts came in contact with the enemy but nothing serious except one man was captured – Doornkloof is an abominable place in case of attack as there are high hills all round.

1st June 1900.
Marched at daylight – two bad spruits to cross Doorn Spruit & Elands spruit. By dint of howls and cusses we managed to get across with the wagons fairly fast – We arrived at Paarle Plats 7 miles from Lindley at 9 a.m. we halted an hour for food & to feed and water

---

* General Officer Commanding, i.e. Methuen.

horses. By the way I forgot to say that at 9 a.m. yesterday we met two Yeomen who belonged to Col Spragges Irish Yeomanry who had escaped out of Lindley and were coming to Kroonstad to get help. They brought a message from Spragge to say that he could hold out till Saturday – That he had no bread stuffs but plenty of meat. We were jubilant as we would be with him we hoped on Friday morning – Corpl Hankey the man who escaped walked thirty three miles Wednesday night. After this cheering news we were horrified to hear from a farmer that Spragge had surrendered yesterday at about 2 pm and that the Boers had been largely reinforced – We pushed on at 10 a.m. and came in touch with enemy almost at once. They seemed to be occupying a strong position to our front and right flanks. The G.O.C. heard that they had been largely reinforced – He ordered Chesham to make a turning movement to the left round their right the guns to follow only a very small containing force on our front & right flank. I went with the left. The first Kopje we found held was one about three miles from our starting point. The battery and Pompoms opened fire & the enemy retired at once and enabled the left regiment to occupy it without firing a shot. Meanwhile our left centre Battalion 10th galoped up to a hill without having any scouts out in front so naturally they got a warm reception when they got to the top – but they luckily got off with one man wounded and a few horses hit – We continued to push round the left trying to get to the Boer convoy and our men who were prisoners – But owing to the Battery by some mistake receiving orders from the C.R.A.* contrary to orders given by Ld Methuen there was some delay in getting them on which made some difference – We began to get frightfully scattered we only had about a thousand mounted men at the time we started and at 2 pm they were scattered over about seven miles of country. The Boers began firing heavily at our right rear and got a small force in through ours – I can't describe where our forces got to – I know I was in a desperate funk as we were scattered everywhere but luckily the Boers were in greater funk and went – We managed to collect and get back to Lindley our losses were about 27 killed and wounded – Ld Methuen made a big bid to save Spragge and risked practically the whole of his mounted force and a battery but without success. The town of Lindley is full of our own sick many of Spragge's

* Commander Royal Artillery.

men – Among others Ld Longford who was shot through the neck, it was a close shave but he is practically right now, walking & riding about looking quite fit.

2nd June.
We are living in a house belonging to a Mr Oates a storekeeper – It is one of the best houses I have seen up country at all – We are to stay here I hope for a short time to get things together – General Douglas arrived early this morning with the 9th Brigade and ox wagons – They have done a good march 44 miles in 52 hours – a good march nobody can say we have not done our best to help poor Spragge.

By 10 June Roberts realized that hopes of a Boer surrender were vain and ordered Hamilton and French to advance along the railway line towards Delagoa Bay. They were checked by Botha twelve miles east of Pretoria at Diamond Hill, losing 180 men as Botha's commando slipped away. Raymond Marker described the action of the 1st Coldstream Guards there on 12 June in his diary:

We paraded under hasty orders at 6.30 a.m. and marched East to the position occupied by Genl. Ian Hamilton's Division the previous day, in the following order, 1st Coldstream as advanced guard, 2nd Battn. Coldstream, 3rd. Bn. Grenadiers, the Scots Guards remaining as rear-guard and as escort for the naval and siege guns, while one Battery of Field Artillery accompanied us.

On reaching the above mentioned position we were halted and given orders to march almost due North, i.e. to change direction nearly to the left, and to occupy a long scarped ridge which ran to the South West from the main heights of Donkerhoek. On reaching this ridge we were met by an A.D.C. from Lieut-Genl. Ian Hamilton (Capt. J. E. Balfour, late 11th Hussars) who told us that this ridge was already held by a Battalion from Genl. Bruce Hamilton's Brigade, and that we were to push farther round to the East, up a long valley, at the head of which we should receive fresh instructions from Genl. Ian Hamilton.

He then went off in search of our Brigadier from whom we subsequently received orders to report ourselves to Genl. Bruce Hamilton, and to take orders direct from him, as we should be detached from the Brigade temporarily, under him.

For the last hour heavy gun and rifle fire had been going on in front, and on reaching the head of the valley we found the Derbyshire Regt. halted under cover. We were told to remain in rear of them and follow the advance. On arriving at the crest above this village we found ourselves on the edge of a long basin of grass land about a mile across and terminated to the North by the steep line of echeloned Kopjes, or rather spurs, which form the Donkerhoek heights, and the southernmost portion of which forms Diamond Hill.

Soon after we arrived we saw the leading men of the C.I.V.* advance and occupy the nearer crest of Diamond Hill, and immediately afterwards the Sussex Regiment on their left gained the same position. A very hot fire was immediately opened by both Mauser and Pom-Pom, the latter [sic] on our right, the latter [sic] from left and centre (the Pom-Pom was apparently moved shortly after this as it only fired a few times and did not open fire again). We received orders to advance, following the Derbyshire Regt. The latter moved straight across the open valley, in support of, and rather to the right of the C.I.V., while we followed them but rather to the left. Here we first came under both shell and rifle fire from the far side of the crest, from in front and from our distant left. When we reached the foot of Diamond Hill we were ordered to lie down, and the Derbyshire Regt. moved away to the right, under cover of the high rocks which formed the crest. Here we remained for some twenty minutes, and then advanced to the crest with firing line and supporting Companies – Nos. 5,6,7,8, while Nos. 2,3,4, remained extended at the foot of the hill. Here we came under a very hot gun and rifle fire which enfiladed us from the far right of the Boer position, and also direct fire from their centre.

Luckily it appeared to be mostly unaimed and over elevated, as most of it went into the valley behind us, and the shells did not burst above ground, while the rocks on the crest gave good, but not always sufficient cover for we had several men hit here.

About 4 p.m. we were ordered to move further along to the right and this we did under cover of the crest, and I was then sent by the C.O. to Genl. Bruce Hamilton, who was with Lieut-Gen Ian Hamilton, for orders. He directed a well extended firing line to be advanced

* The City Imperial Volunteers, a regiment of infantry raised for the campaign by the City of London in January 1900.

to try and enfilade the Boer right if we could do it without risk of too heavy losses, and No. 6 sent a half Company to do this, which I accompanied. It came under a very hot fire from its left and front while advancing but not sufficient to stop it until it had advanced about 150 yards from the crest, when fire was suddenly opened on us from some detached Kopjes on our right which had hitherto not unmasked. As this would have become a directly enfilading fire as we advanced further we were forced to lie down under such cover as a few detached boulders and rocks afforded, and the C.O. sent me to report this to Genl. Hamilton. Shortly afterwards the remainder of No. 6. went up into the firing line, as where they were they were under an almost equally hot fire without the power of replying, and about this time the second Battalion came into action on the left and fired volleys at the Boer right. This and the R.F.A. Battery which came into action about the same time, having got under good cover at only 1200 yards range, much relieved us, as the galling fire from the Boer right at once slackened and finally almost ceased. About now Capt. Longueville (No 6) received a message from the Derbyshires that the Boers apparently contemplated a counter attack, in consequence of which report the C.O. sent No. 7 & 8 into the firing line, and in these positions the Battalion remained until dark, under constant fire. As the sun set the Boers opened a tremendous fusillade from all along their line but it was almost harmless. The Battalion actually fired very little as from their great extension, to which our small loss was chiefly due, volleys were impossible and as usual the Boers seldom or never revealed their position sufficiently to offer a target for individual fire. At dusk we were told to entrench on the ridge & throw out outposts & a patrol went from No. 6 towards the centre of the Boer position. We were much hampered in this by the light cast on us by all the grass behind us catching fire, but advanced sufficiently close to the Boer sangars to find they were evacuated, & then returned to report and to bivouac under the hill.

Harry Pryce-Jones was also there and wrote an account of the battle to his mother on 19 June:

We went from Koodoonport from where I last wrote I believe on the 11th & marched about 6 miles & halted all day in extended order, waiting for the Boers to be driven our way but no! they did not come. We slept near there & went on next day & attacked a

Kopje called Diamond Hill near Donkerhook, we got there about 1 o'clock & halted on the rear side, our firing line consisted of C.I.V. & Derbyshire & Sussex, the Boers holding a position in a donga about 1000 yards the other side; by Jove! the Bullets were pretty thick & we were lucky to escape as we did with 9 casualties, 1 since died. we went to the top of the Kopje about 15.30 & went on outpost, we found 'Brother Boer' had gone; so we stopped there 2 days, as we were supposed to be supporting Gen Ian Hamilton, then we marched straight back here about 2 miles E of Pretoria.

Roberts was determined to put a stop to attacks on the railway by commandos helped by farms in the neighbourhood. He signalled to Kitchener, who was acting as Director of Operations from a headquarters at Kopjes, on 14 June:

> We must put a stop to these raids on our railway and telegraph lines, and the best way will be to let the inhabitants understand that they cannot be continued with impunity. Methuen's troops are now available and a commencement should be made tomorrow morning by burning De Wet's farm, which is only three or four miles from the Rhenoster Railway Bridge. He like all Free Staters now fighting against us is a rebel and must be treated as such. Let it be known all over the country that in the event of any damage being done to the railway or telegraph the nearest farm will be burnt to the ground. A few examples only will be necessary, and let us begin with De Wet's farm. Tell Methuen he must arrange for the Heilbron telegraph line to Kroonstad being kept open as well as the one by the railway.

This marked the beginning of the policy of farm burning, the implementation of which raised the practical problem of what to do with the Boer women and children it displaced. The answer was to establish camps for them along the line of the railway, in which the army had to accept responsibility for their maintenance and welfare. It was initially regarded more as a humanitarian than a punitive measure, but, as conditions in these so-called 'concentration camps' deteriorated, they became the source of a scandal, for which Kitchener has generally been blamed. The responsibility for initiating the policy, however, lay clearly with Roberts. From retaliation for attacks on railway and telegraph lines, the policy was soon extended, as a letter from Roberts to the Boer leader Erasmus of 15 August explained, to farms 'used as bases for raids where

Boers in arms seek shelter and obtain food; and whenever our troops are fired upon from buildings, which have the white flag hoisted'. This policy, especially when it was combined with destruction of crops and confiscation of herds, was found distasteful by many soldiers, and Buller refused to implement it in his area, where many of the Boers had been his companions in the Zululand campaign twenty years before. One of those who criticized him for this was Edward Burrows, commanding the Chestnut Troop of the RHA. In a letter to his wife on 18 June from Wakkerstroom, after Buller had entered the Transvaal, he wrote:

> It appears as if this district had really had enough of it – but some things are inexplicable to us of the rank & file – we do not seem to inflict any punishment on the inhabitants of the district & to such an extent spare their feelings that no officer or man is allowed to go into Wakkerstroom and I dont think the Union Jack had been hoisted. The inhabitants of course say they cant control the commando which is somewhere out in the hills & that when we go the commando will return & loot cattle & do damage to them for having surrendered – which I suppose is likely eno' – So one rather wonders why we do not adopt more drastic measures & give them so many days either to bring the commando to its senses & deliver up their arms or take the consequences in the shape of damage to the town & farms & loss of all such stores cattle sheep, forage &c of which we have need & for which we now pay money down – Only a few days ago we found in a farm 1200 sheep the owner was avowedly away fighting against us so we bought the sheep & paid Mrs owner 1200 £ down for them – One does not quite see how this is to stop the kind of guerilla war, which appears now to be going on.

Away to the west Captain M. O'Farrell was with the 5th Victoria Mounted Rifles, raised as the Victoria Battalion of the Australian Mounted Rifles. They were serving in Lord Erroll's brigade in Methuen's force about 120 miles from Mafeking, to which Methuen was returning to refit, when O'Farrell wrote to his brother in Dublin on 31 August:

> I may say his army wanted refitting badly. I never saw such a tattered & torn collection of men. It was strange to see whole squadrons of crack Cavalry regiments marching on foot, the troops carrying their arms & blankets on their backs, & the general want of discipline & order astonished me. The mortality among the horses is appalling,

we landed about 600 men and 800 horses & already have many men marching on foot although we pick up remounts when we can, and commandeer Boer ponies when we get a chance. Both sides here shoot the horses when they can just as eagerly as the men, & the casualties among the former nearly always exceed those among the latter, when mounted troops are engaged.

One of those who did not like the farm-burning policy was Sergeant-Major Cobb of the 7th Dragoon Guards. In a letter to his wife from Heidelberg on 5 December, he wrote:

We are out nearly every day, burning farms, foraging, bringing in suspected farmers & making things generally uncomfortable for brother Boer. I cannot say it is nice work we are on, but of course it has to be done. I don't mind so much when there are no children, but when we have to clear out a farm where there are a whole tribe of children, it comes a bit hard to say the least of it, we had a very hard case yesterday. We went to a farm about 15 miles from here, got sniped at severely wounding two of our men, & found that the owner of the farm who had taken the oath of neutrality, had actually been feeding about 20 of the enemy for the last 3 or 4 days, of course we took him prisoner, & brought him in, the old rascal, but it was a job getting him away, his wife, children & grand-children, about 30 in all, hung around him, tried to get him away from the escort, crying or rather I should say yelling, at the top of their voices, it was pitiful to see their grief, when they really understood the old man had to go, we cleared out the farm of all stock, about 350 head of cattle, 1,500 sheep, & no end of poultry. The cattle & sheep are all sent to the A.S. Corps, but we keep the poultry, the consequence is, that the troops are on, or have been on turkey, chicken, ducks, geese &c. I'm dining late tonight & turkey is the 'piece-de-resistance'. Holding Xmas a bit early isn't it?

Priority was now given to catching De Wet and eliminating the threat to the lines of communication from the remaining Free State forces. Roberts's favourite general, Ian Hamilton, having broken his collar bone in a fall at Diamond Hill, Hunter was ordered to drive them back up against the mountains on the northern border of Basutoland, where the Brandwater River rose. He was given the equivalent of three divisions, Lieutenant-General Sir Leslie Rundle's 8th, of two brigades (16th and

17th), Brigadier-General E. Y. Brabant's Colonial Division of Mounted
Infantry, raised in Cape Colony, and four other infantry brigades
(Highland, 12th, 20th and 21st), with Broadwood's 2nd Cavalry and
Ridley's Mounted Infantry brigades. Unfortunately, while he was waiting
at Bethlehem for his transport to catch up, De Wet and Steyn, with some
2,600 men, slipped through the net back to Lindley, pursued in vain by
Broadwood and Ridley. Hunter pressed on, closing the net by 29 July,
when General Prinsloo surrendered with 4,314 men. A soldier in the
Middlesex Regiment, whose Christian name was Percy, was involved in
these operations and wrote about them to his girlfriend, Florence Keats,
from Bethlehem on 20 July:

> Probably you will have received my second letter by this & know
> where we are, since then we have seen a lot of fighting in fact 6 weeks
> of it & I think have done our share. We were besieged in Lindley for
> 5 weeks & the Boers where [sic] sniping & shelling us every day & on
> Tuesday the 26th they nearly got into the town. We where [sic]
> having our dinner when the order came to saddle up & reinforce the
> Yorkshire Light Infantry who where [sic] stationed on a Kopje
> commanding the town & where [sic] hard pressed, we got there in
> 15 minutes & I am glad to say drove the Boers off fighting till dusk,
> & I am proud to say it was the 57th* that saved the situation, the
> Yorkshires being on the point of surrender after losing ½ of their
> men killed & wounded, including 2 officers. Whilst at Lindley we
> also did a record march to Kroonstad & back through the Boer lines
> a distance of 100 miles in 3 days with a day's rest. The most [? worst]
> thing to happen of interest was on Sunday 1st of July when we
> escorted General Paget out to meet General Clements' column &
> where [sic] ambushed on the way, fighting from 9 AM to 2 PM &
> losing 4 killed and 6 wounded, it was a very hot time for a Sunday
> morning till the Artillery came up & drove them off. The next day
> Monday we joined hands with General Clements & then began a
> weeks hard fighting when we drove them back to Bethlehem & took
> that town the Boers retreating to the hills. The fighting commenced
> every day at dawn & we generally drove them out & occupied &
> bivouaced on their positions at dusk. There was one day especially
> I shall always remember: Wednesday July 4th the Boers nearly

---

* The Middlesex Regiment.

succeeded in capturing the 38th Battery of Artillery, and Guns came
into action & had 3 hrs hard artillery fire with 3 Boer guns but could
not silence them, the fire then slackened down & some men where
[sic] seen coming up towards the Guns dressed in Khaki & where [sic]
taken for our own men & allowed to get within 100 yds of the Guns
when all of a sudden they opened fire on our men at the Battery &
also commenced shelling us again, at this time one company where
[sic] in a dip behind the Guns grazing our horses, when the bullets
commenced to fly & we saw our men retreating, but our Captain
gave the order to advance & the 57th again succeeded in driving
enemy off & practically saving the Guns, but not before they had
killed & wounded all officers & exterminated a section but 1 man of
the artillery, the Battery losing ½ its numbers on this day, after this
it rained for 2 hrs coming down anyhow & wetting us through to the
skin & this is no job when you havent got a change of clothing,
however a general advance was made & we charged a big Kopje &
put the Boers in full retreat & I think we had our revenge for they
buried 78 Boers the next day, there was not a man amongst us that
did not think his time had come when we went into that fire so ably
led by our Captain & not again flinching from doing duty. We have
also burned a number of farmhouses & got plenty of loot especially
in the eating line, turkeys, geese, chickens, sucking pigs etc so we
have a change of diet now again. We had quite a dinner the other
night which included roasted Goose, boiled fowl, stewed peaches &
mealie porridge cooking it over a camp fire & getting it all ready
ourselves. We have also commandeered a harmonium & have some
very nice camp fire concerts the talent being quite up to date. It is
very cold at night time the water in our bottles turning to ice during
the night in fact the difference in temperature is 70 degrees during
day & night. We have lost a lot of our men through sickness &
wounded nearly ½ the company. I have had some very narrow
escapes & have come to the conclusion I was not born to be shot.

When General Prinsloo surrendered, General Olivier escaped with
1,500 men and it was probably he who was the cause of relieving the
boredom which was being felt by Lieutenant C. S. Awdry of the Wiltshire
Company of the 1st Battalion of the Imperial Yeomanry. His company's
task was providing security to garrisons, and convoys of supplies to
them, in the heart of De Wet's country. On 29 August he wrote to his

father from Thabanchu, saying, 'We are really in a pretty ticklish place', and that they had 'a jumpy week'. 1,600 Boers had got away south from Lindley; various outlying parties had been withdrawn to garrisons and on the previous day their 2nd Company had been attacked between Bethlehem and Harrismith and lost 80 men killed and wounded. He added a postscript on the 30th:

> We are absolutely isolated now and, as you probably know, are not strong. We have had an awful night every body on the jump. I was turned out 3 times in the night. The alarms in the night were never due to approaching Boers, but to a desire to give fresh orders, generally contradictory. We are all very angry, but it can't be helped. One time we were told to go up & dig trenches on the mountain, but we could only find one spade and pick, so that was altered.

His boredom was soon to be broken and the trenches to come in useful, as he recorded in his next letter on 9 September:

> You will have heard long ago about things which have happened, still you may like to hear more. I last wrote on Thursday week. Well that night a long patrol came in having been fired on near Mequattinje's Nek, at least 25 miles away. Nothing much happened on the Friday, but we sat in damp trenches from 4.30 to 6.15. On Saturday morning early we moved up into our entrenched mountain. That afternoon a patrol was fired at about 5 miles away & one horse wounded at about 5 o'clock. That showed the Boers were pretty near, & about 7.0 on Sunday they turned up. I saw 9 men about a mile away. They wore military greatcoats, two of them khaki, & had slouch hats turned up on the left with a dark feather, & with a broad white band. They might have been some Colonial corps for all we could tell, for they had rifles carried in buckets [leather sockets] just as we do; they were suspicious, however, for their blankets were of many bright colours, orange being common. Soon after about 80 unmistakeable Boers, in long trowsers, showed on a large kopje near by. I did not note when fire opened, but a shell about 30 yds from me was the first thing, & then 2 more made me scuttle to the trenches under a sharp rifle fire. I got into a trench which was not a good one & was rather enfiladed by riflemen about 800 yds away. During a lull I moved into another place behind some rocks newly built up into a rough wall. That also was a decidedly inferior place, as it let bullets thro'; shone very white, was rather low,

and had a large white rock behind it. The Boers also shelled the white rock from about 2000 yds diagonally & we thought we were done for; however beyond dust & small bits of stone nothing hit us. about 3.0 one of my men was hit by a glancing splinter of bullet off a rock in the thigh. It seemed very painful but it was not bad & we had him moved after dark & he is doing well. All our casualties, only 5, occurred on this day. Our Serg't major had his lower jaw carried away badly by a shell; this was the only severe casualty. The firing on this & every evening stopped at about 6.15. As soon as it was dark & safe we sent for food, water & more amn & started building up our wall stronger. Others in trenches dug nearly all night so as to make them safe from shell fire. Next day firing began about 6.0 & went on till about 6.0: the rifle fire against [us] was much more accurate than on Sunday, we could hardly show our heads over the wall, & the wall & white stone were absolutely covered with marks of the bullets. During the day our wall & rock were deliberately aimed at by a gun firing English 15 pounder & shrapnel shells at about 2000 yds, 4 were fired & all fell within 20 yds of us, but did not hurt us. I forgot to say that the 1st trench I was in the first day was wiped out by a shell from behind & the men had to clear out & shelter among the rocks. On Monday night some Worcesters under an officer named Moss came down & we helped them dig a new trench near ours. He & I went into [it] next day but it did not prove a success & we all had to lie flat in the trench all day to escape the bullets, which came thro' indeed I found two between my head & the wall of the trench. Moss moved up to the old wall trench during a lull, but I stayed there & we only were able to fire about 4 shots each. It was a blessing however that there was no more shelling that day. Next day we had no more fighting & only saw Boers about 5 miles away. We saw some mounted men about 9 a.m. who turned out to be Imp Yeo. We soon lighted fires & had some food & then we started digging again. We also heard our guns & pompoms going. On Thursday we packed up & left Ladybrand.

Lieutenant R. S. Waters of the Manchesters, commissioned from their Volunteers, was serving with the 5th Corps of Mounted Infantry in Ridley's force near Winburg. His diary for 24 August reads:

Pouring morning. Rain stopped & gale got up. Mounted troops moved out about 9.30 leaving the wagons behind & the 2 maxims under me. Was told there was no chance of attack. Thought it safer to prepare. Picqueted farm on L. & low ridge on right of road, moved up a wagon with oatsacks in it. Placed maxims to sweep the road. Searched farm for amm'n picquet having reported occupants attitude as curious. Found some. Put Petrus Leroux under arrest. Obstinate. Had to march him away to bivouac between file of bayonets. Wife howled. Felt brute.

2 p.m. saw few horsemen come over skyline like the dickens. Orderly galloped up with message from Halliwell to say they had been cut off & severely handled & were retiring with the Boers in pursuit & were falling back on my position. Warned the picquets & got up extra ammunition, built oatsack breastwork on road. Gave Collins i/c maxims directions & waited.

In ¼ hour main body came along & spread themselves over the farm, road & the low ridge on R. Heavy firing commenced immediately. Ridley sent me up to hold the ridge to R of road with all my men who were of necessity somewhat scattered. Ridge key of position. Warren one of my men killed stone dead 5 minutes after start. Boers soon all round our positions – rifle fire only. Nasty cross-fire sometimes from 3 directions. Fire ceased sundown. spent night building sangars. Ridley decided not to retreat as we knew Boers were between us and Winburg, Carried Warren down to farm. got water & biscuits. Both maxims put at salient angles of farm. kraal in gun pits. Froze hard at night, no sleep for me, afraid of night attack – men slept fixed bayonets & they snored despite no blankets.

Sunrise rifle fire commenced again & about 6.30 3 or 4 guns opened with common shell & time shrapnel – also a martini maxim from the Boers. Had the devil of a time all the morning. only dared to put head over sangar to fire. maxim the worst. got followed by the thing twice in moving along ridge. Ran. Boer guns constantly moved their position. got several killed & wounded in my ridge. Shell fire devilish at times.

Fire slackened about 3, Boers finding we weren't going to chuck it. Increased & waned intermittently till sundown then ceased totally. Ambulance in farm Winburg. Brought news Roberts had moved Bruce Hamilton's brigade down from Kroonstadt & he might be expected to relieve us tomorrow. Boers sent in a summons to surrender stating they wd: bombard all night with 6 guns if we didn't. Ridley declined. expected attack all night. got a good swig of rum from the wagons for the men & self.

Firing commenced at dawn, rifle only. Observed Boers massing in force betwen us & Winburg with intention of making us think help was cut off. Sent in second white flag asking us to surrender. Ridley said no more emphatically & advised them to go instead. about 10 the Boers melted away, we assisting their departure to the best of our power. Saw Bruce H's advd. guard of mtd. Infy. come rushing over the ridge. Cheered loudly like they do in books.

Prinsloo had asked for an undertaking that the burghers would be allowed to go quietly home and that their private property, including their wagons, would not be confiscated. The former was refused, but the latter agreed. Roberts had given Buller a directive on this subject in 3 June. It read:

My terms with the Transvaal Government are unconditional surrender. With regard to troops, those who deliver up their arms and riding animals are allowed to go to their homes on signing pledge that they will not fight again during the present war. The exceptions to this rule are those who have commanded portions of the Republican forces or who have taken an active part in the policy which brought about the war, or who have been guilty of or been parties in wanton destruction of property, or guilty of acts contrary to the usages of civilized warfare. Principal officers should remain with you on parole until you receive instructions regarding their disposal.

This directive was elaborated at the end of September, when a large number of Boers who had crossed into Portuguese East Africa surrendered. The following order was issued from Army Headquarters on the 28th of that month:

1. General Officers Commanding have been empowered to promise that burghers who surrender voluntarily will not be sent out of South Africa, provided they have been guilty of no acts, other than fighting against us, which should debar them from this privilege. This concession does not apply to those who have taken a prominent military or Political part in the war, nor to foreigners. In the event of a military or political leader enquiring as to terms of surrender, the question is to be referred to Army Head Quarters.
2. All stock, supplies, &c., of those on Commando or of those who have broken their oath are to be taken and no receipt given.

3. In cases where some members of a family, who all live on one farm, have broken their oath and gone on Commando, those remaining are to be warned that, unless the former surrender within a reasonable period, all stock, supplies, &c., will be taken and no receipt given.

4. In cases of sniping, leaders of bands are to be informed that unless it ceases their (the leaders) houses will be burned. A few days should be allowed for this to become known, notices being sent to the resorts of the leaders and to their wives. In the event of its being necessary to burn the farms, further notice should be issued stating why this has been done and giving a list of other houses that will next be burned.

5. All stock, supplies, &c., of snipers are to be taken and no receipt given.

6. Protection is to be given to all inhabitants who have kept the oath of neutrality, remaining quietly at home and taking no further part in the war. Any stock or supplies taken from them are to be paid for or receipts in full given for them.

7. Wives and families of men who are prisoners of war are to be protected, and receipts in full given for anything taken. When a man surrenders, a protection pass is to be given to his wife.

8. Widows of men killed in the war and all lone women are to receive protection passes and to be paid or given receipts for anything taken.

9. Burghers are to be informed that as soon as their leaders submit and when every cannon has been surrendered, peace will be declared and all prisoners of war will then be sent back to their homes. Exceptions only will be made in the cases of Members of the late Governments of the South African Republic and Orange Free State who are responsible for the war and its present disastrous prolongation, and of those who have proved guilty of breaking their oath contrary to the customs of war.

This order did not apply to citizens of Cape Colony or Natal, who were classified as 'rebels' against the Crown and treated accordingly. It was supplemented by a signal of 23 September, stating:

All officers conducting operations against the enemy are reminded that Burghers taken in arms ... will be treated without exception as Prisoners of War and will be deported to St Helena or Ceylon.

Burghers who give themselves up voluntarily will not be deported out of South Africa but will be sent down to Cape Colony or Natal without delay.

*

De Wet now made off to the north-west across the Vaal to join De la Rey, 200 miles away in the Mageliesberg mountains between Johannesburg and Mafeking, in which, on 11 July, De la Rey had surprised and surrounded C Squadron of the Royal Scots Greys, who were holding the pass of Zilikat's Nek. After an action lasting twelve hours, in which the Greys lost 3 killed and 17 wounded, Major Scobell and his 69 men, their ammunition exhausted, surrendered. Kitchener had been charged with coordinating a number of columns intended to intercept De Wet after he had crossed the Vaal on 6 August. Methuen nearly succeeded in doing so, but allowed De Wet to escape, although he had to abandon his guns and all his prisoners. Douglas Loch wrote a description of the action to his parents:

> *12th August.*
> Ld Kitchener was ordered by Ld M last night [he must have meant Lord Methuen was ordered by Lord Kitchener] to march to Rietvlie keeping on de Wet's right. Tilney was sent yesterday morning to explain to Ld K what Ld Methuen proposed & what he wished. We marched at 3 a.m. The enemy were supposed to have laagered at Cyferbuit so we kept away along the Ventersdorp road so as to keep on his left – Benson went and reconnoitred Cyferbuit but duly found a small laager, the remainder having just trekked northwards – We went in pursuit in a Northerly direction after having made our midday halt at Witpootze – We sighted a Boer convoy about 4 miles away trekking in a N.W. direction at 1 p.m. Ld Methuen is hard to find at most times but he was worse than ever today – and when found was in his most eratic [*sic*] excitable mood. He gave and changed orders one after the other – He would not believe the convoy seen was De Wet but at last consented to sending 5th Rgt IY & some colonials to head them – One good thing he did do and that was to absolutely ignore a small commando on our right who were trying to draw us off the convoy – When he gave permission for the Yeomanry and Benson to go on he fell into a sort of 'Don't care' sort of state and kept the guns dawdling back and at last ordered them to

outspan and water, by this time the Yeomanry had got five miles ahead and were held in check by the Boers with rifle fire and gun fire – Hearing the big guns Ld Methuen galloped on himself and then sent back for the guns but much valuable time was lost ... I went back to hurry up guns and then went to Benson and we got guns up. This flanked Boers positions in bush. Boers retired, we pushed on a lucky shot from 70th Battery burst between two centre horses of boer gun as they were bringing up the limber to take away the gun killing all six horses and wounding a seventh – The Boers deserted the gun and were given a happy time as they went away from rifle fire – In the mean time Ld M for some reason had stopped the pursuit but then awoke to the fact that the convoy was really near us, so ordered a hard pursuit – Everybody pushed forward giving the Boers fits – We pursued till dark and even pushed on during dark halting at 8 pm – The country was lit up by burning wagons and exploding ammunition to say nothing of the blazing veld – We had to camp without water – Our wagons arrived at between 11 & 12 – It was an awful day we were all dog tired – 3 a.m. till 8 pm covering 32 miles by the road to say nothing of the extra distances we had to go round and the fighting. Our halting place was Doornplaats – The cavalry at the end of the day were about 10 miles to the right rear. Why they did not push on faster none of us could make out. There we were with Yeomanry and Colonials running circles round the cavalry division – The result of the day being we captured 16 wagons, five being full of forage, 4 others which I believe contained the same, four containing ammunition which were set on fire by the boers, three containing I don't know what, also set on fire, one fifteen pounder gun which the Boers had taken from General Gatacre at Stormberg – about a dozen prisoners and we recaptured over sixty of our own men who had been taken at different times by the Boers –

13th August.
marched at 3 a.m. We did not get much sleep as our wagons did not reach us till nearly midnight – We got some food at 12.30 a.m.. We marched for about 6 miles when the crowing of a cock showed a farm which meant water – We halted just long enough to get water and then pushed on – We had an hours halt at Liliefontein and then pushed on to Rietfontein a 22 mile march – De Wet was on a few miles ahead – Now we really did think we had him tight – It stood

to reason that his animals must be nearly done as he had trekked a tremendous pace – We were driving him up against the natural barrier of the Magaliesberg. We had left a battalion of our own to hold Olifants Nek but this was withdrawn with Baden Powell but Tilney who returned this afternoon from Ld Kitchener brought us the joyful news that Ian Hamilton who was at Hilspoort had been ordered to block the passes over the Magalies Berg – now the only loop hole De Wet has is either to the West to Elands River which he is not likely to try as he would have to pass within a very few miles of us – To the North where he would have to cross very difficult country with bad roads or through Magatos pass which Ian Hamilton may not have had time to occupy – The Cavalry Division are about six miles in rear of us – Why they are there is more than we can tell when they ought to be more to the East – Smith-Dorrien is behind them and Hart behind again – These co-operating columns seem, instead of making a great effort to get up to De Wet, to be content to follow us – Ld Methuen has decided to make another forced flank march to head De Wet from the West, North and Magatos pass – Leaving the Cavalry Division to block the East – If De Wet beats back he will be met by the infantry.

14th August.

Marched at 1 a.m. no lights allowed – we marched first west and then turned N.W. At Waterval we caught some Boers who were just off to the laager having had a night at Home – When we got to near Kortfontein we heard from a Boer woman the exact position of the Boer Laager and we saw some of their scouts – Ld Methuen decided to halt till daylight as the country looked very bad and mountainous – At 4.45 a.m. Ld M sent me with a message back to Gen Broadwood who had arrived at Rietfontein just before we left last night – I was to tell him Ld Methuen's position, De Wet's position and to tell him to block the Eastern road if we headed De Wet that way.

Ian Hamilton, although ordered to block Olifant's Nek, was delayed by having tried to intercept De Wet earlier as he crossed the Rand, with the result that he missed him at both places, De Wet escaping from Methuen and making off to join De la Rey.

While these operations were going on, Captain Jourdain's Connaught Rangers were converted into mounted infantry and stationed at Aliwal

North, where the railway from East London to Bloemfontein crossed the Orange River. His diary for 14 July reports their activities:

Off went H. Company this morning as advance guard, at 7.30 am, followed by E and F. companies (unmounted) with the convoy and baggage. I waited with C. Company behind, as I had to do rearguard.

It was not until 9.30 am that I left our camp of last night, as the waggons, which came up from the drift stretched out a good way. When on[c]e I got under weigh, the pace was very good, and some eight miles were covered with hardly a stop. After passing Charlie's Hope, a small collection of unmarked houses, we came out on to open country. About a quarter of an hour later, I was informed by a galloper from the front that the advance guard had been sniped from some kopjes in front. This was about 11.5 am. Soon after Capt. B.* came back and took my company off to the left front (South) towards some kopjes. We had a stiff gallop up to the front, and then I learned that F. E. and part of H. Companies had gone off to the right front (West) and were engaging a large number of Boers, who were then retiring westwards. Soon also I came upon some men of H. Company who were then halted some 2000 yards from a large hill, on which were some 20 Boers retiring to the West. Sergeant Gilroy was brought back here shot through the heel. He had been held up by some 20 Boers at about 50 yards, but on riding away had his horse shot, and a bullet through the heel. The other man escaped, and came in safely. When I advanced the Boers began immediately to snipe us, and after a while we halted, and dismounted. I was here sent for by Major Moore, and I rode off alone to the right flank, some 2 miles away, but on hearing my company was needed on the right flank (11.45 am), I rode back and told Capt. B. who brought up my company, and also C. Company. After about half an hour's ride I reached the scene of action on the right, this was at 12.35 and was immediately sent by Major M. to take a kopje on the left front. I had only 2 subalterns, and 26 men, and after about a quarter of a mile ride, dismounted, put the horses with eight men in charge in a small donga, entrusted 11 men to Hutchinson my senior subaltern, and took 7 myself on the left. We were to be supported by C. Company. I was given to understand that there were no Boers on

---

* Possibly Captain J. F. Byrne.

this hill, and that only a few wounded were on the summit. I went off at once, and after telling Hutchinson to advance on my right, in echelon, I made for the hill. After about a mile walk, I got within 800 yards of this hill, when suddenly over 30 Boers came round the right of the hill at a gallop, and jumped into a donga. At the same time some numbers of Boers were seen on the summit. I immediately opened fire, but got so hot a return that, after minutes of this unequal combat, I retired about 1000 yards. Here I came upon a barbed wire fence, which caused us much unpleasantness, as the fire was simply galling. At the same time (2.45 pm) I heard the other half of my company hotly engaged on my right. At this time I was lying near some stone pillars to the barbed wire fencing, which only attracted the enemies [sic] fire, so I retired a few yards back. Here we had absolutely no cover, but here we lay trying a shot whenever the Boers appeared. This they did in a most dashing manner, riding out fearlessly, and opening fire without a moment's delay. This state of things continued till 4.30 pm, when I was ordered to retire on the maxim gun by Major M. I fell back some hundreds of yards (4.30 pm) and fell in line with A. Company under Capt. D.* who manned a stone sangar near the gate. Here also we had a hot time, but the chief part of the battle was with E. Company on the right, who were behaving splendidly, delivering a good fire in return, but were hardly pressed. F. Company (4.40 pm) were ordered to retire from the donga in which they were as the Boers were working round the right, and riding fearlessly and firing splendidly. However all along the line the continual rattle of musketry was maintained splendidly. It was a hard battle, but the Boers had a splendid position, overlooking ours, and we had to lie in the open, and return their fire. Here I learnt that my sub. Lieut Hutchinson had been wounded in the thigh and arm, and had been taken out of action. C. Company now (4.50 pm) retired on the camp, about 2 miles in rear taking the led horses. We continued fighting especially to cover the retirement of F. Company, who retired in clusters, and were consequently treated to a galling fire from the Boer left and centre. Heavy fire also went on, on the right, until nightfall. Then we lay quiet awaiting orders. The last shots were fired at 5.35 pm, the Boers actually delivering some volleys before they ceased firing. I collected all my men, and at 6.30 pm got

* Possibly Captain H. R. G. Deacon.

the order to retire on camp, which I reached about 7 pm. After a while I got my company in order as many of my men got to camp before me with [illegible] and pitched my horse lines. I lay down to sleep after a dinner, which after my long fast I had no appetite for. I could not get a wink of sleep all night, as cattle, oxen and horses refused me that consolation. Our ambulance was captured by the Boers, who ordered the man in charge to collect our dead and wounded, and also theirs, and to go into Aliwal Noek.

Attention was now switched to an attempt to deal with Botha in the north-east. Buller, having been released from the 'strictly defensive' imposed by Roberts, and having rejected the latter's proposal that after having already lost Hunter's 10th Division to Roberts's force he should send another west across the Drakensberg Mountains via Harrismith, advanced north up the railway from Ladysmith. Between 10 and 15 May he neatly outmanoeuvred the Boers defending the Biggarsberg Mountains near Dundee, and went on to do the same to Botha's brother Christian a month later at Laing's Nek, where the railway tunnel had been blown up. Corporal Charles Stride of the Volunteer Company of the Dorsets took part in the attack on Alleman's Nek on 11 June and described it in a letter to his parents next day:

No doubt you felt anxious when you saw that the Dorsets were engaged, but am thankful to be alive to relieve your anxiety up to present. We were at Zandspruit yesterday with orders to assault this place 6 miles distant, we were in arms at 7 a.m. & started soon after it was grand sight, the 2nd Brigade on our left, Naval guns, Artillery, Cavalry, Colonials, Machine guns, sample of everything in fact extending miles. We halted for some time for the guns to clear the ground or find the position of the enemy & then started to take up another position in rear of Artillery, while there we were quietly grubbing & all of a sudden a shell came over us then another killing one of our stretcher bearers warned us to take shelter, we silenced there [*sic*] big guns, then advanced across about 1½ miles of open plain, studded with ant hills offering shelter, when we couldn't find anything else, the Dublin Fusiliers were on our right & the Middlesex on the left & the 2nd Brigade on the left when our scouts got within 1000 yards range the Boers opened Rifle fire then commenced a more deafening roar shells whistling & bursting, Pom poms, Maxims & rifles it was a row. when our Company which was on the right of the Regiment got within range of rifles then became our turn firing then double fire again & so on, when within 500 yards I expected to be hit every moment a bullet pitched a yard in front of me sending the dust up almost blinding me, another I could feel the whistle not an inch from my ear, fellers were falling down now & then but not so many just there. At last we reached a Conical hill (passing a Farm flying a white flag) we stormed the top & had a rest from doubling, my word everybody done up, & the kit did seem heavy or rather it was heavy & it included a bundle of sticks that I got so as to make the tea, a thing which everyone gets when they get a chance. Well; after a few volleys we descended to take a larger hill opposite, then came the scene of most of our casualties, we were exposed to a cross fire & bullets did fall thick, one chap (Sorrell) was killed just in front of me, when I got in the shelter of the hill I looked round it was a scene, more than half the Regiment had yet to come & as they were coming across see the fall wounded & killed one of our Company (Williams) was shot clean thro' the calf of the leg & the other (Barrett) in the thigh. Then came fix Bayonets & up the hill as well as we could for it was very rocky, but when we got to the top the Boers were in full retreat in all directions, but some of our fellows managed to empty a few saddles & take some prisoners & things were getting quiet & enough for one day, getting dusk 5.30 p.m. when we had Roll Call that seemed to have a sadness with it, when the questions are asked if anybody knows anything of so & so. after the Roll Call our Com'y for outposts & dead tired, I could hardly move & too cold to sleep long, but am at present enjoying the sun & a short rest to make up for it. At present moment the burial of our killed is in progress & round the otherside of the hill, asked permission to go but refused, expecting to move at short notice. Took 3 snap shots whilst under fire, which I will value more than any, so hope they will be a success. The Farm what I mentioned with the white flag contained 17 sniping at us, when found they begged for mercy (orders to shift)

(Charlestown 13th June 1900) well I was saying about the prisoners one of them was killed by a Hussar in his wrath & everybody felt as if they would like to kill the lot.

After the railway tunnel at Laing's Nek had been repaired, Buller resumed his advance with Lyttelton's 4th Division, and the two armies met on 4 July, Roberts and Buller meeting each other for the first time in their lives on 7 July in Pretoria, which was now linked by rail with Durban, so that Roberts was no longer dependent on the single rail link with Cape Colony.

Edward Burrows was involved in clearing the line for Buller's journey. In a letter to his wife of 8 July from Vlakfontein, he wrote:

On the Tuesday night 3rd inst we got orders to move on to this place about 12 miles further north west so as to join hands with some of Gen'l Hart's B'de who are at Heidelberg about another 20 miles further on. We marched out of Greylingstadt on Wednesday 4th but left a batt'n and a half & about 100 of our b'de there. So we are not now a very large force. We found Boers as I had expected on the line & to the N. W. of us & they had a good deal damaged the line but they were not in much force and didnt seem in a mood for much of a fight, so as we thought our more important job to join Hart we let them alone & came on here across a fine open plain. Thorneycroft & I who were riding together at the front of the advance both expected trouble as the road from Greylingstadt passes under a high hill on each side of it & affords great opportunities for an enterprising enemy. However Dundonald was clear our first job was to join Hart & on we all went, holding the hills until the rear of our column passed through. Next day it was decided to send back a small force of 100 men to a place on the rail way between Standerton & Greylingstadt & off they went a larger force going across the open plain with them to see them safely into Greylingstadt & then return here. When they turned round to return the Boers came down on them & they sent in to this camp for help so out we turned in a great hurry 300 of T.M.I. & 2 guns of mine & we galloped right out into the plain but the Boers seeing us gave up & there was hardly a skirmish. Weber was in command of the 2 guns & I merely rode out to look on as I usually do when only a section goes – The evening showed no guns & it seemed only a poor sort of opposition. Next day Friday Buller was to come thro' from Standerton & go up to Pretoria & see Roberts, as an escort had to take him, it was decided to escort a convoy thro' as well. I was delighted as I hoped for our tents by the convoy and we sent Eden & his section to do the job. All seemed quiet up till lunch. Buller came in all right & went on. I rode up to the hill near our camp & had a good look out but nothing

seemed going on so we came back to lunch. Then we heard firing &
a good deal of it – so went out again & found no chance of 2 other
guns being wanted & walked up hill again to look down and found
the Boers had opened with 2 or 3 guns & a pompom & were trying
to stop the convoy which was slowly wending its way across the open
plain – They seemed to confine themselves to shell fire and it was
soon evident they couldnt stop the convoy – 2 Howitzers of ours had
been sent out to shell them & some of our infantry were down in the
plain too. There were also 2 guns of a Fd Battery with the convoy &
by the time we were there looking on there was not much excitement.
The Boers were shelling the Howitzers who were in the calmest &
most dignified manner slowly walking along apparently utterly con-
temptuous of the shells which burst around them. However they
eventually got one into them & then I got Clery who was looking on
to order them to trot out of the fire & cantered down & sent them
in, thinking this the only job of any interest that had been taking
place. When I came back I found Eden had borne the brunt of the
fight & done very well. He had been the other side of the open plain
& had seen & silenced a gun which the Boers brought up – Then he
was ordered out into the plain to protect the retirement of the M.I.,
who were holding the hills. Directly he came out they, the Boers,
began firing at him – so he galloped – they couldnt hit him moving
and he came into action in the defile & I expect we shall send a
convoy that way to-morrow, so I shall post this & chance its going &
when we get regular communication again will write another line.

Rawlinson described the meeting between Roberts and Buller in his
diary for 7 July:

Buller arrived this morning with Stopford and Sackville-West. They
were shelled by the enemy whilst passing between Greylinstadt and
Heidelberg but got through all right. . . . . Buller we can get nothing
out of – It has not transpired what was the subject of vital importance
which he wished to consult the Chief about. He says he cannot
weaken his L of C, though he talks of sending someone to Bethune.
I trust he will.

Some of Buller's troops were beginning to find life guarding the railway
line from Natal boring. One was Private Harry Walker of the 2nd West
Yorkshires. He wrote to a friend on 24 July from Standerton:

I thank you for the box of cigarettes which I have received this morning from you. we are at a place called Standerton we have just been here a month today we have had no fighting here but I suppose we will have a smash up here one of these days – there are some Boers knocking about here, duty is very heavy here for us, digging every day, making trenches all round camp and where we do outpost, we have made a new railway bridge over the river as the Boers blew the stone bridge up, we are out on outpost 5 nights out of 6 and then we go on picquet and the 7th night we get into camp, but we have to sleep in our boots all the time so our feet does not get much rest and as for a bed we have not seen one since we left England what was last October 20th my bones is proper sore with the laying on the ground & shall not care [illegible] soon it is all over I wish they would stand and fight and then we would soon have it over but they wont we have to race them all over the country and we have had some very big hills to climb, there was a rumer that we were going to be on our way to England this month but it has fell through, so God now when they are going to let us come but I am taking things very easy myself so long as I keep good health. I believe you had a very fine doing at the relief of Ladysmith and Mafeking & I suppose they will be a little to do when all the reservists arrive in Leeds so I think I have told you all there is nothing particular to tell you this time so I will finish and I will try and have an hour's sleep as I am for outpost at 4.30 and there is not much sleep out there so I must conclude hoping to see you soon.

Another rather bored man in the same area at that time was Major Edward de Salis of the 1st Royal Dublin Fusiliers. In a letter to a lady-friend he wrote:

I see by the local paper that two more Boer women have been caught sneaking out of Standerton with mauser rifles up their clothes! Great indignation is felt out here over the tremendous leniency showed to the Boers especially to the women, who are a very dangerous crowd, as they act as spies & hood-wink our people all round. Did I tell you how a patrol of the S.A.L.H. went to search a Boer house and found two women about 22 & 23 in bed, but the S.A.L.H, weren't going to be bluffed by that, & searched the room *under* the bed they found 4 men & in it with the girls 4 rifles bandoliers & 3 or 400 rounds of ammunition!! If I had my way I wouldn't allow any Boer woman staying in a captured town or Farm to wear a skirt longer than 6 inches below the knee, & then they couldn't hid[e] rifles, as it is all the regulations out here are far harder for Loyal Englishmen than for the Boers. some of the women want flogging & a greater half transporting. They are fearful creatures, more ghouls than women. I'd far sooner fall into the hands of 20 men than two women!..... Riccard with 'G' Coy have gone to Volksrust to relieve a Volunteer Coy of the Liverpools who have gone home. I hear he is living at the station Refreshment Room. Mrs Mills* is to live at the Newcastle Convent. Report says the Authorities have kept her down the line all this time & want an excuse to keep her down altogether, they were annoyed at her living in Camp at Colenso, but really no one can say she was the slightest nuisance there. There is great indignation all over the place over the 'Military women' who hang round their husbands like this, Newcastle is full of them, so is Volksrust, & they become perfect plagues when their husbands are wounded. One reg't that came out, brought all their Regimental Ladies, the majority of them did stay in Maritzburg and contented themselves with worrying the Authorities as to the well being of their hubbies, but several followed up the troops as close as they could, this sort of thing leads to a heap of leave getting & accounts for the number of officers on leave in the down country towns, Mrs Bird† of 'ours' came up to Newcastle. I should say that its bad enough for a married man to know his wife is at home, without the extra worry of knowing she is knocking about this benighted country, its not fair on the man or his regiment either and I think of it that way, don't you dear?

*

In August Buller was given the task of dealing with Botha between Belfast and Machadodorp, where he had assembled 7,000 Boers in a strong position at Bergendal, flanked to the north by rocky boulders and to the south by marsh. Buller's plan was for French to move round the northern flank while Lyttelton attacked the main position, the centre of which was dominated by a kopje, held by the ZARPS, the Johannesburg Police, which was not easily supported from the flanks and was vulner-

---

* Wife of the commanding officer, Lieutenant-Colonel C. A. Mills.
† Wife of the Second-in-Command, Major S. G. Bird.

able to British artillery fire. After a prolonged bombardment on 27 August, Lyttelton attacked the hill with four battalions, all of whom had been at Ladysmith, the 2nd Rifle Brigade, 1st Inniskillings, 1st Devons and 2nd Gordons. At a cost of 15 killed and 100 wounded, they drove the ZARPS from the hill and Botha's whole defence crumbled. Sergeant Harry Hopwood of the 2nd Volunteer Battalion of the Manchester Regiment was involved in the action, which he described in a letter to his parents, written on 31 August:

The next day was Sunday and at 8.45 a.m. we marched out of camp, understanding that we were merely shifting so as to be out of range of the shelling. However it soon transpired to be different and our company was extended after going about two miles and formed a support to the Devons who were ordered to form a firing line. We had nothing to do until about 3 o'clock in the afternoon although stray bullets and shells kept coming from the front all day. All at once however an orderly galloped up and told the Captain that we were to form up on the left of the Devons and thus extend the firing line in that direction. We went off to the left about a mile then fronted and in extended order got the word to advance.

The ground in advance of us was a gentle slope upwards so slight as to be hardly noticeable but still forming a cover until you got on the top or skyline. We went forward about 600 yards and nothing happened till we got on the top and then we were met with a storm of bullets.

Of course we had to lie down at once and there was not much cover to be had. So after a few minutes the colours ordered us to go ahead. So we got up and rushed forward, but there was such a terrible fire that we had to get down again before we had gone many yards.

There were anthills scattered about but none near to me. The bullets fairly streamed past one and I saw an antheap about 50 yards in front of where the other fellows had got down so I resolved to make a rush for that on my own. I got up and ran forward but after about 20 yards I had to get down again. How I escaped being hit I don't know as I got nearly all their fire, being the only one standing up then. I laid or rather flopped down in the open and all round me the bullets raised puffs of dust and whistled overhead.

I got desperate and felt sure I should be hit every second. Then I thought I might as well be hit running as lying down, so determined to have another go for the antheap. I got up, and bending down run with all my might forward, and succeeded in reaching it without being touched, dropping down fairly exhausted and breathless. The bullets simply rained past and for about ten minutes after I got there I durst not raise my head. I felt thankful I can assure you when I got down behind that heap. It was not a big one but just big enough being about fourteen inches high and about twenty in diameter at the base. After ten minutes or so the bullets ceased to come so fast and I ventured to look out at the position, and being in front of the other [sic] I could see it quite clearly. We had thought that the Boers were all on the kopje across the hollow in front of us but from where I was I could see about six sangers right down in the bottom which were full of men who were firing for all they were worth. I soon had to get my head down again as they seemed to spot every movement and concentrated their fire on it. Then a pom pom started firing on us from the left front and sent some shells into us, but these did not touch anybody. Before long Holmes of the 3rd section was hit with a mauser in the armpit and soon after that just as I was firing, I heard Alf. Wood who was next to me on the left give a shout and then he called out to me that he was hit in the arm. I told him to bind it up at once with his field dressing which he did. He was quite cool about it and said that I had better not come across to help him as it would only draw their fire on both of us and there was not cover for two. I was rather afraid he would be hit again as he could not help exposing himself in putting the bandage on. All this time the bullets were still whistling round and every time you fired one shot 15 or 20 fell round about you so you had to look handy and get your head down as quick as possible after each shot. About this time two of the Boers opposite me cooly came out of the sanger and started to walk up towards us so I let drive at them and they disappeared very suddenly. It was now dusk and the sun had set and to our surprise the Boers began to creep up towards us taking cover as they came. However they did not come close enough to be any more dangerous, but I was beginning to wonder how we were going to get out of it as I believe the Devons had at this time retired and we were in a very awkward position indeed.

Anyhow the Captain came along before long under a very heavy fire and gave the word to retire one at a time. So I ran across to Alf. Wood and carried his gun and haversack etc for him and we made off back bending down as low as possible. It was during this retirement that poor Munro got killed being shot through the head just after getting up. I cannot tell you as fully as I should like to all the detail, but we landed out of it all right and found the battalion formed up about a mile back and bivou[a]c[k]ed there for the night, three companies going out as outposts. At 2 a.m. firing started again and bullets were flying over our heads. We had to get up at once and were told to retire down the slope as quietly as possible, but the firing ceasing somewhat we did not do this until five o'clock. Firing was continued but our company was told off as supports or reserve rather. We were under fire however all day again and had to dig little mounds as cover. Stirling of the 4th section was shot through the arm in the course of the morning but this was the only casualty that occurred. At about 6 p.m. we were preparing to go on outpost when General Buller came along and said that the Boers were retiring and it would not be necessary to go on picquet so we got off that. We had to march about 6 miles after that to the brigade. Next morning we moved off at 7 a.m. for Machadodorp, but on arriving here at Dalmanutha our regiment halted and is [illegible] yet having been left behind as railway guard so that I suppose we are on lines of communication again.

I am not sorry as we shall get a bit of rest and my heel has been bad with a burst blister which was getting very painful on the march so that it comes in very opportunely for me. We hear that the division went on to Machadodorp and captured two 'Long Toms' and a pom pom there but don't know if it is true or not.

I am of opinion the war will not last so long now, and the Captain said he thought we should be home before Christmas.

Captain Eustace Maxwell, brother of Laurence, the Bengal Lancer, was with the 1st Devons and also wrote home on 31 August:

Sunday [26 August] was a lovely morning and the absence of snipers and the silence of guns made it seem very Sabbathy. We marched out along, or rather below the crest of our ridge, with flankers along the top, and all was quiet for some time, till a maxim began thudding on our right rear, we being leading regiment, and rifles began to go off.* However we continued on our way for some [time], till at last we were faced to our right flank; and advanced to the ridge crest where we suddenly came under a very hot fire; so we lay down. The firing came from a parallel ridge some 1200 yards away, where the enemy were behind a long row of sangars, evidently having the range to our ridge, as their fire was very accurate and prevented our making any proper return, our line being without cover of any kind. My company, on the extreme left of the regiment, was thrown a little forward to try and bring a crossfire on these sangars, and we advanced with much haste to the very sky line, so that if lying down we could not be seen, but if kneeling were exposed; it was impossible to get any fire of consequence on the sangars, as directly a man raised his head there was a small volley at it from the Boers, which constrained him to lie down rather hastily. Meantime Long Tom opened from about 5 miles in front but he took some time to find the range, also a pom pom suddenly made itself objectionable on the left, but was silenced by a field gun before he had done any harm, for which we were very thankful; then Long Tom by a complete fluke burst a shrapnel right over the company, but too high up, and only one man was hit and he but slightly. Our 5-inch guns got to work on him soon after that, and pitched shell after shell on the very spot from which he was firing, and silenced him for the time. The firing on the right was pretty heavy, the maxims being very busy, but I fear it was rather fruitless, as the enemy's sangars were too good; however it was impossible to judge as when one got up to look, several small puffs of smoke from the other side warned one to sit down quickly, being followed by bullets which whistled very unpleasantly close. At length the Manchesters were brought up on our left, but went too far, and had to retire under a tremendous fire from more sangars on their left front, of which the Devons got most of the 'overs and unders' in the way of a cross fire. I sat tight behind the very biggest blade of grass I could find. At last the howitzers tried to get on to the sangars in front of us from a long way on our right, but they did no good, pitching shell after shell exactly halfway between us and the Boers; I suppose they would [sic] not see their target, and were acting on directions, for as a rule they are very accurate. However the

---

* The battle was spread over two days, the 26th and 27th; the 27th is known as the Battle of Bergendal.

smoke of their lyddite enabled us to fire rather more, so they did some good. Then old Long Tom opened as gaily as ever on our big guns, who had a sort of duel with him till dark; our guns again seemed to throw all their shells exactly where Lengthy Thomas was firing from, but I suppose they did not, as the old boy did not seem to mind a bit. As the short twilight came on, the firing became tremendous; there was a perfect chorus; big guns, howitzers, maxims, pompoms, and rifles. Suddenly, as if someone had smacked the heads of two little quarrelling boys, all was silent, and the day was over. The regiment had 35 casualties including 8 killed – Four men of one company were missing; an ambulance went out next morning to look for them, and was fired on, a Eurasian apothecary being mortally wounded, and compelled to retire without effecting the object. Also some of the Boers were using explosive bullets all the day. Are they not a splendid enemy?

We were very lucky to be in the firing line, as I think most of the casualties were amongst the companies in support, much of what was intended for us going over our heads into them. Still, I confess I was glad when the night came, as it was not much fun being potted at without being able to make any return to speak of.

That night we remained where we were on piquet, digging trenches under cover of the darkness; in the middle of the night The Manchester picquets suddenly opened a tremendous fire, but there was no return, so I expect their men had the jumps, and were firing at nothing, a not unusual occurrence.

I do not quite know what was the object of the day's fighting, or whether we gained anything by it; any way we did not lose anything, and I comforted myself through the rather cold watches of the night by the reflection that I had at last being [sic] under a proper fire.

Lieutenant E. Longueville of the Coldstream Guards was now ADC to Major-General Inigo Jones, commanding the Guards Brigade in Pole-Carew's 11th Division. His diary records their experience in the battle on Buller's left:

Aug. 26th.
We marched at 7 am to the monument. There was a certain amount of confusion, as first of all they decided that we should only make a reconnaissance, and then it was changed and we were to go right on. We had a long wait behind the monument while the cavalry came

over from the right flank, when they did come they worked all round the hills on the left, and it was very pretty to watch as we had a good view of a big boer laager and as soon as they discovered that the cavalry were coming they quickly packed up and went off under cover of a rearguard. We amused ourselves while waiting by shooting off the 4.7[in] gun at a few boers who were hanging about in our immediate front – it pleased us and didn't hurt them! We then had luncheon during which spent ricochets kept dropping around with awful buzzings and whistlings. Just as we finished the order came to advance. The Scots Guards led, Henry's M.I. being in front. We occupied a long ridge extending east from the monument. A lot of unaimed bullets were dropping all along the slope behind our position and the 2nd Coldstream who were lying down in support had 5 men hit by them. I was kept pretty busy running about. In the middle of the afternoon I had the pleasure of seeing our precious mess cart come blundering up and get bogged just where these unaimed bullets were thickest, however they only had one mule shot, in the mouth. As soon as it got dark I was sent for the transport and we camped.

Aug. 27th.

We were shelled by a long tom while having breakfast. The shells came unpleasantly close to our camp so after breakfast we moved further back. They continued to shell us most of the day; but we had no casualties except an oxen which was hit in the leg, and Hooper's (doctor) pony which was killed. These were shrapnel and burst well though rather too high. One of the fuses picked up was set to burst at 40 seconds, so they must have been firing at 11000 yards or thereabouts. Late in the afternoon I saw a boer waggon trekking across our front about 3000 yds away. I galloped down to the artillery camp; but although they hooked in a section at once, and we raced back we were too late as they were out of sight.

Aug. 28th.

We marched early, and camped at Elandsfontein. We had a long halt in the middle of the day, and I believe a battle was expected, however nothing came of it. There was some difficulty about our camp, and a little unpleasantness between staffs. The 1st Coldstream had to go back some way to guard the baggage. In the evening the cavalry occupied the hills where the boers had been, and found a letter stuck on a rock – 'Dear Mr Kahki [*sic*], we are not feeling very well today; but trust we shall meet you some other time. Yours ever—'.

Aug. 29th.

A very foggy morning and we had a long wait behind the cavalry. When we at last got to the top of the hill, the mist lifted a little, and we found a lovely view of a wild mountainous country with a fearfully steep descent before us. We got down all right and then had to go up another long hill. I was then sent back to the rear to tell the Grenadiers to go back up the first hill (some two miles) to guard the baggage, they were naturally not very pleased! When we got down on to the plain I went over to a farm on the right and found a garden full of lovely violets. While I was picking a bunch I heard guns, and riding back to the column, I saw the naval 12 prs shelling a boer pom-pom, which had suddenly appeared on the right of the Lydenburg road, away on our left. This was a smart piece of work by the boers, they brought this gun up unobserved, shelled the column, and got away without damage. We camped at Helvetia Farm, Buller's force also camping there. In the evening the General walked round the water supply and we saw a misterious [*sic*] figure squatting on a kopje just above the brook, on going to investigate, we found that it was Mac Hay digging for bulbs.

Aug. 30th.

Marched to Waterfall Onder. There were several burning farms in view dotted about the country. In the morning a rumour went round that if we got to Waterfall in time we should catch Kruger. When we had marched some distance we began to go down hill, and suddenly found ourselves at the edge of a deep valley, with the village of Waterfall at the bottom. On the other side of the valley there were several snipers hidden in the big rocks on the face of the hill who shot at anyone who went into the village, and although we shelled them and fired long range volleys at them, they did not leave till after dark, and some cavalry who had got into the village had to lie low all day, in spite of our having a division and the rest of the cavalry on the hills behind them.

Lord Dundonald's mounted brigade was involved in the pursuit, as Major Birdwood records in his diary:

28 August.

Force marched for Dalmanutha. we were to have done left flank & ½ front but at last moment got orders to do the front and push on through Dolmanutha along Machadorp road, S.A.L.H. in front: about 4 miles beyond Dalmanutha we found the Boers holding ridges over the road, with High velocity guns and Pompom in action. We brought up 'A' troop & blazed at them while we tried to work round their flanks, when they fell back & this soon happened at next ridge & we got on hill overlooking Machadodorp, the Boers abandoning one of their ammunition waggons: they then got their guns in position on ridge beyond towing & shelled us as we went down to it: I galloped up to try & get Strathcona's behind a kopje they got in front of, but as I got there a shell burst just in front of me a piece going through my horses neck & cutting his jugulla [*sic*] vein & another piece into his chest & out behind his rt. shoulder & into my right leg just below & inside of knee. I got on to Orderley's [*sic*] horse & tried to go on, but felt sick & faint so had to get off and lie down. Knox – Dr R H A & MO of MI [Mounted Infantry] came up, cut my breeches open & dressed wound from wh. blood & fluid were coming. Rogers SALH – MO. then came & had me carried to their ambulance & later to Mach: got cup tea Italian ambulance & then went on across spruit to 3rd Mtd Bde F.H. [Field Hospital] where Branigan dressed me.

Further to the north Walter Kitchener's 7th Brigade had been operating near Lydenburg. His ADC, Captain A. W. Speyer of the West Yorkshires, wrote an account of the brigade's operations, in which he described the events of 16 August:

At dawn on the 16th one of our native scouts reported that he had seen the Boers trekking, and almost simultaneously a signal message from Lt. Col. Aylmer was received, saying that his outposts could see a column of dust travelling in a South-Westerly direction. Thereupon the 19th Hussars received orders to get in touch with the enemy, whilst our force at once left Commissie Drift for Uyskraal on the Elands River to act as support to the cavalry.

We arrived there after four hour's [*sic*] march and halted for a short space to water and feed the horses and mules. Then we continued our march, following in the wake of the Hussars who had taken a path running parallel to the river and upstream. We had hardly proceeded three miles, when an orderly on a much-spent horse, galloped up with a message from Col. Aylmer to the effect that the Boers were attacking him in great force and asking for immediate assistance. The General at once gave the order to push on as quickly as possible, and every horse was put to its best pace. Five miles of ground were covered at full gallop, several more messengers being encountered en route urging us to bring reinforcements with all speed.

The noise of the firing, which had been faintly heard for some time, now gradually sounded closer and closer, and suddenly we came upon the scene of action. The General and Staff were with the leading troop of the 19th Hussars and we distinctly saw some of the enemy gathered round the 19th Hussar transport, which they had captured. On our approach these Boers retired and joined the rest of their men who had surrounded the 19th in the dense bush and were shooting at them at close range. The leading squadron of the 19th now dismounted, and leaving their horses to be led on, the men advanced on foot in extended order through the bush, the troops behind following in a similar formation in support. At the same time a squadron was sent to the right to outflank the enemy, and a maxim having been brought up in the centre, a heavy fire was opened on the enemy. At first the Boers replied vigorously but perceiving the troops advancing in a long line, which extended well beyond their left flank, they soon saw that the game was up and bolted, the two field guns arriving just in time to give them a few parting shots. . . . The Boers retired about 3 miles S.W. to the strong Kopje position of Vrieskraal, which commanded the road running parallel with the Elands River. It was now fast getting dark, so our force withdrew some four miles, and bivouacked at Slagboom. Our casualties were 2 men killed and 6 wounded (four of whom died), and 4 officers and 25 men of the 19th taken prisoner. All of them were released that evening after they had been stripped, receiving the Boers' dirty rags in exchange for their uniforms. The officers stated that they were well treated, and that Commandant Muller had forbidden his burghers to take their clothes. The practice of taking our men's boots, putties [*sic*], breeches and tunics had become the rule now whenever any of our troops were unfortunate enough to fall into the enemy's hands.

Kruger escaped over the border into Portuguese East Africa, as did 1,500 Boers and 500 foreign volunteers, abandoning their artillery and setting fire to 1,500 railway wagons. Roberts was particularly concerned that they should not destroy the railway bridge at Koomati Poort on the frontier, and the Portuguese authorities were cooperative in seeing that this did not happen, as they were generally. Kruger and the foreigners, including MacBride's Irish, set sail for Europe, Oom Paul in a Dutch navy cruiser. Most of the Boers returned home after taking an oath of allegiance, the Transvaal having been declared a British colony on 28 October, by which time Buller had sailed for England, where he resumed his command at Aldershot until sacked a year later after a row with Roberts, who had returned in January 1901 to succeed Wolseley as Commander-in-Chief. He had originally planned to hand over to Kitchener in October and then leave after a visit to his son's grave at Chievely, but his departure was delayed by the illness of Queen Victoria's grandson, Prince Christian Victor, son of her daughter Helena, wife of Prince Christian of Schleswig-Holstein, and of Robert's daughter Aileen, both of enteric. When the Prince died on 28 October there was a further delay, as Roberts thought that he might have to bring the Prince's body back in SS *Canada* with him; but the Queen ruled that he should be buried in Pretoria, as he had himself expressed the wish that, if he died in South Africa, he should be buried alongside his comrades in the ILH. Rawlinson, who was due to return with Roberts, was very frustrated at this delay. In his diary for 27 October, he wrote:

> I had arranged everything for the Chief to start after Church tomorrow but the serious condition of Christian Victor coupled with the fact that Aileen also has a temp're of 102 today induced him to wire to Lansdowne that he was obliged to postpone his departure 'sine die' – This is to my mind very unfortunate, it is almost a calamity but it may have one good effect, it may make him embark at Durban instead of coming all the way back to Elandsfontein by rail – Ward this morning was authorized to warn the Canada that it might be wanted to come to Durban which is a good indication. This evening we have better reports of the Prince and we hope he may pull through but the next 24 hours will be the critical time for him – There is a consultation of doctors tomorrow. The Chief made a great mistake in not sticking to his original plan and starting before Sir A. Milner came up – He would have done better to leave as he meant to about the 12th and have seen Sir A. in Capetown. Now it is

impossible to say when he may get away and if Aileen gets typhoid we shall be another 6 weeks in the country.

Neither of Rawlinson's hopes were fulfilled. Roberts did not finally leave South Africa until 10 December, after a great send off from Cape Town. By that time he was beginning to have doubts as to whether the war was over, as he had believed it to be six months earlier. It was not: it had been transformed into an entirely different type of contest, and Kitchener was left to get on with the dirty work, as indeed it proved to be.

Back in July, on the 4th, Roberts had written a confidential letter to Milner, in which he made some recommendations about his successor. He wrote:

> With regard to the officer best fitted to command in South Africa when I leave, I would name Kitchener, but I am aware that he looks to India for a career, and I am under the impression that he will be given a high appointment in that country when the war is over.
>
> Failing Kitchener, I would recommend Ian Hamilton or Neville Lyttleton. The former I consider one of the most promising officers in our Army, but he has no fancy to remain in South Africa, and I am strongly in favour of his going home, where he would be available for any future war in which we might be engaged.
>
> Neville Lyttleton I do not know so well, nor has he had the same opportunities as Hamilton for showing what he is fit for during the present war, but men who have served with him in Natal speak in his favour. He is sensible, discreet, and above all he is a gentleman. Would you approve of him as your first Commander?
>
> For head of the Military Police and of any local troops that may be raised, Baden Powell is far and away the best man I know. He possesses in quite an unusual degree the qualities you specify, viz; 'energy, organization, knowledge of the country, and a power of getting on with its people'.
>
> As a member of the Government you would find Baden Powell most useful. I understand that he is prepared to remain in South Africa for a time, and, if I have your permission, I will sound him as to his willingness to accept such an appointment as we are both thinking of him.

Baden-Powell was subsequently employed to raise and command the South African Constabulary, a force of 10,000 armed men, recruited in Britain and the Colonies, as well as in South Africa itself, designed to take over guard and general security tasks from the army.

7

DIRTY WORK

November 1900 to May 1902

By the time Roberts handed over command to Kitchener at the end of November 1900, a basic disagreement had arisen between Milner and the latter over strategy. Kitchener's plan was to concentrate on military action to eliminate the commandos, so that the war could be brought to an end as quickly as possible, both to save money, for which the Tory government, re-elected in October 1900, was pressing, and so that he himself could achieve his ambition to be appointed Commander-in-Chief in India. He still had hopes of this, although the outlook was obviously uncertain. In a letter to Roberts on 4 December, he wrote: 'I am afraid my chance of India is small but am sure you will do the best you can for me when you get home. I cannot be sufficiently grateful for all you have done.'

Two months later those hopes appeared to have been dashed, and, when Roberts offered the prospect of a home command when the war was over, he turned that down, replying: 'As the Indian command is obviously impossible some more civil work would be more what I should look forward to.'

Kitchener's strategy was to be implemented by the use of military columns, 1,000–2,000 strong, centrally directed by himself and supported by an increasingly widespread application of farm destruction. Milner, on the other hand, thought that priority should be given to establishing a sound administration, including security for the inhabitants, where it mattered most, and to working gradually outwards from there, so that eventually the commandos, if they had not by then been eliminated, would find themselves in remote and infertile areas of little importance. High priority should be given to implementation of this policy in the Rand, so that gold mining and other industry could flourish as the prime resource of his future Federation, and that a white population would be encouraged to come to the country and outnumber the Afrikaners.

Kitchener had no wish to see industrial revival of the Rand absorb precious rail capacity, which was barely sufficient to meet his needs both for movement of troops and for their supply. He shared the attitude of many of his officers in a distaste for the nouveau-riche Uitlanders and a feeling of affinity with the Boers, whom they tended to think of as another species of country gentlemen like themselves. He prevailed, although he did not succeed in persuading the British Government to provide the additional troops he thought would be needed to implement his strategy and achieve rapid results. Many of the reserve and volunteer forces that had been raised in Britain, such as the Imperial Yeomanry and the City Imperial Volunteers, had completed the period for which they had been called up or volunteered, and there was little patriotic appeal in this phase of the war. Kitchener would have liked Indian or Egyptian Army soldiers, but the political objections to that were too great. Such reinforcements as he did receive tended to be merely replacements for those departing. In the new year the government agreed to provide 30,000 reinforcements, many of whom were to come from Australia and New Zealand, the first 10,000 to arrive by March. Baden-Powell's South African Constabulary would relieve the army of some of its guarding commitments. Nevertheless Kitchener had some 200,000 men, including 140,000 regulars, with which to chase 20,000 Boers; but, when all the line of communication and logistic commitments had been met, he could only make about 22,000 available for the columns, and only 13,000 of them were in combat units. He had many frustrating exchanges of correspondence and signals on this matter with the new Secretary of State for War, St John Brodrick, Lord Lansdowne having been transferred to the Foreign Office.

Roberts, as Commander-in-Chief, had to pass on to Kitchener some of the less realistic views of the Cabinet. In a letter of 29 June 1901, he wrote:

> They are influenced by a feeling that the nation will resent the present heavy expenditure when it is brought home to them in the shape of fresh taxation, and when they realize that the Boers fighting against us do not now number more than 16,000 or 17,000.

The idea of the Cabinet is, now that you have so completely

devastated the country, that during September a beginning should be made to reduce our troops very considerably, and confine ourselves to holding the several lines of railway and the principal towns – and in addition to organize a sufficient number of small but efficient movable columns under carefully selected officers, and in positions from which they would be able to act against any body the enemy might bring together.

The first thing that seems to me essential is to clear the Boers out of Cape Colony, and this I hope French will succeed in doing. Their presence in the Colony must cause considerable unrest, give them hope of being able to raise the people against us, put heart into the waverers, and discourage those who may be loyally disposed. Besides, I imagine that the Boers can get food fairly easily, and possibly ammunition in the Colony. Anyhow, no reduction of our force would seem possible until the whole of the country south of the Orange River is in our hands, and I am sure you will agree with me that all our efforts should now be directed towards that end.

You can of course judge best on the spot what troops can be spared for this purpose but, as after the end of August, the Government will insist on our practically vacating all the district not immediately on the line of rail, it seems to me that perhaps Rundle's and Elliott's columns might be moved South of the Orange River. Harrismith must be held but between that place and Kroonstad we can have no troops, nor between Harrismith and Standerton to the North and Ladybrand to the South.

The South African Constabulary, which you mention in your letter of 31st May as gradually getting into order, will, I hope, be able to pacify the country between Jacobsdaal & Ladybrand. South of that line we shall not be able to hold much at first perhaps, but we must have strong posts all along the Orange River to prevent another invasion of Cape Colony. That I look upon as the most important part of the programme.

In a letter a week later, he wrote:

They [the Cabinet] are getting alarmed at our spending a million and a quarter a week, and at the possible outcry when the British public realize that we require between two and three hundred thousand men to cope with the eighteen or twenty thousand men now left in the field against us without giving thought to the enormous area over which this comparatively small body are scattered. . . . . The idea of Corps d'elite is Chamberlain's. I told him you might not find it possible to carry it out but I was sure you would do your best. You have not mentioned Plumer recently but if he is still in good form he would probably make such a corps a success.

By that time Kitchener's numbers had been reduced to 189,000 and he was being pressed to reduce them further to 140,000, which he maintained he could not afford to do until the situation in Cape Colony had been cleared up.

On the other side of the hill an important council of war was held at the end of October 1900 at Cypherfontein, a farm in the Zwartruggen Hills, seventy-five miles west of Pretoria, at which Botha, Steyn, De la Rey and Smuts were present. De Wet was also invited, but did not manage to get there before they dispersed when information that a British column was approaching reached them. There had been considerable discussion of the pros and cons of pursuing De Wet's and De la Rey's strategy of commando raids, which had resulted in farm burning. Although the latter imposed suffering on women and children, it committed burghers who were victims of it to continued commando service, and revulsion to it encouraged others to join; but there were doubts about the period for which the strategy could be maintained. Eventually it would make life intolerable both for the families and for the commandos themselves, and could lead to them becoming too weak to protect themselves against the native 'Kaffirs'. One solution, especially favoured by Smuts, was to extend commando operations into Cape Colony and Natal. The British would surely not burn farms within their own colonies, and there were plenty of sympathetic and well-supplied Boer farms there which would provide shelter and supply. It could also bring about a political crisis in Cape Colony, where the Afrikaners provided the majority of the white population and held power in the legislative assembly. Botha, who had initially been sceptical, was won over. Their hurried departure appears to have prevented consideration of another suggestion by Smuts, an attack on the gold mines.

From this council of war Steyn joined De Wet near Bothaville on the Valsch River, where both of them narrowly escaped capture on 6 November. It was a case of repetition of Sannah's Post, but in reverse. They knew that Major-General Charles Knox's column was nearby, but

33. Armoured train.

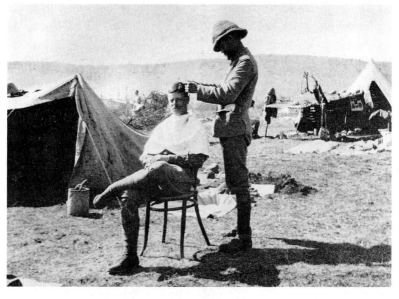

34. Captain Tracy, 1st Coldstream Guards,
having his hair cut by Private Harker near Diamond Hill.

35. 'A welcome drink'.

36. Bringing in Boer families.

37. Building a blockhouse.

38. East Yorkshires signalling from New Zealand Hill to Rensburg, 14 January 1902.

39. New South Wales Lancers bringing Boer prisoners into Pretoria.

40. Rimington's Tigers.

41. Natal Garrison Artillery at Modder River Bridge, 6 February 1900.

42. Bheesties (water-carriers) for South Africa, kit inspection.

43. Native runners.

44. Basuto scouts.

45. Sergeant-Major ?Harris (?10th Hussars) and Dutch guide.

46. Christmas presents, Modder River, 1899.

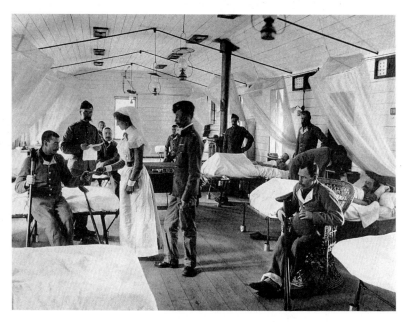

47. Presentation of Queen's chocolate, Wynberg hospital.

believed it to be seven miles away on the other side of the river, and few precautions were taken while the commando slept. However, Knox's vanguard from the 5th and 8th Mounted Infantry, commanded by Lieutenant-Colonel P. W. J. Le Gallais, surprised them soon after dawn. De Wet, Steyn and most of the 800-strong commando managed to get away, protected by a rearguard of about 150 men, who, unable to find their horses, were defending De Wet's guns. A fierce fight at close range ensued between this rearguard in one farm and Le Gallais's men in another. The latter's staff officer, Major William Hickie, contacted Knox by helio to ask for help. When he returned, he found both commanding officers, Le Gallais of the 5th and Wally Ross of the 8th, and several other officers, badly wounded, and so assumed command himself. It was another two hours – not until eight o'clock – before Knox arrived with reinforcements. Hickie and Major Lean of the 5th then ordered their men to fix bayonets and charge across the forty yards that separated the two positions, whereupon the Boers put up the white flag. The action had lasted for about four hours, the British casualties being 13 killed and 33 wounded, Le Gallais among the former: 25 Boers were killed and 100 surrendered, many of them wounded. Knox prevented Hickie from ordering that two of them should be shot when he discovered explosive bullets in their pockets. De Wet's six guns were taken, two of them captured British ones, one ironically at Sannah's Post. Knox made only a half-hearted attempt to pursue De Wet, who crossed the railway and made his way towards Ladybrand on the Basutoland border east of Bloemfontein. South of there, on 23 November, he attacked the isolated garrison of Dewetsdorp, where 480 men, most from the 2nd Gloucesters and 1st Highland Light Infantry, surrendered after resisting for forty-eight hours.

In operations not far from there Corporal Jack Morgan of the 34th (Middlesex) Company of the Imperial Yeomanry was wounded on 19 November. A friend, Basil Napier (probably a sergeant: he was later commissioned) described the action in a letter to Morgan's mother on that day:

> By the time you get this you will have heard of Jack's wound by cablegram. Dear old boy, he has had a very close shave & throughout today & always he behaved with the utmost pluck and calmness. He wont be able to write just yet so I will tell you just how it happened.

You know we have been fighting for the last 3 weeks ever since we
left Harrismith for Vrede & Standerton. We have been with Gen.
Boyes taking a convoy to Vrede. The poor old 34th have up to now
lost 20 killed & wounded besides many more down with enteric etc.
Today No 2. sect. under Mr Grey, 15. N.C.O & I were left advance
guard leaving the infantry & guns about a mile in rear. Capt Brune
& No. 1 sect were on the right of the road & us. About 10.45 (we
had been marching since 4.45) Brune sent word by Jack who with
me formed a connecting file between 2 men on the road & us, that
the enemy held the low line of hills ahead by report & that we were
to keep on advancing. At about 800 yds from the ridge our scouts
saw Boers on the skyline. There was only one thing to do so we
galloped ahead to a low rise, dismounted & 8 of us went up. I & my
officer being in front got there first & saw nothing, Jack was not then
with us. I built up a little heap of stones & then walked a few yds
back to see if all the others were up. Without any warning the hidden
Boers as near as I could judge some 30 or 40 opened a heavy fire.
We all flopped down just where we were & those of us on the crest
opened fire. I was on the extreme right furthest out too far behind
the shanty for shelter & Mr Grey just behind. Before we had been
there 2 minutes Grey called out 'Napier I'm hit!' 'Where Sir?' 'In the
arm.' I looked round & saw him lying on his face & the bullets
kicking dust spots all round us. I yelled out to keep on firing as it
was our only chance. I knew it was no good attempting to move
Grey as it was certain death so we all lay on our faces & stuck it out.
Directly afterwards up came Jack Heaven knows how or why except
that he knew his pals were in a hole. Cpl. Morgan was always cool &
quiet under fire, no gush or chatter, every one knew that & were glad
he came. Things went on like this for perhaps another 5 minutes.
Suddenly Jack called out from somewhere to my left rear 'Basil I'm
hit' I forget what I answered. Someone called 'In the face & shoulder'.
I dont *think* I ever felt so angry & vicious before for I knew we could
do nothing so I started (foolishly) cursing the Boers as only a soldier
on service can. Their fire at last began to slacken & Grey & I
alternately begged & cursed the men to let 'em have the— – — –
swine. Well; I looked round & saw Jack half crawling, half rolling
down to the horses who were also getting a share. The Boers were
chucking it! & yet there was noone helping us. Jack d— someone on
the way down who tried to help him & said 'D— it keep under

cover, I'm all right' good old Jack. Squash who was with 4 led horses as soon as he saw Jack well down the hill jumped on his pony & went for the ambulance.

They were still firing on us so we made it hotter & hotter, soon they ceased & I went down & found they had tied up Jack, face & right shoulder. I was frightened that they were coming round on our left flank & got him round on the right & made him comfortable & went off to get some water.

Thursday Nov. 22.

Jack is going on splendidly. I have seen him & fed him on porridge & rice every night. 2 days ago they put him under chloroform & found the bullet had gone through his right cheek just missing the eye & from there into his shoulder where it missed all bones & went through a small artery & cartilege & out again. The Doc. told me his arm would be stiff for a few months *but nothing more.* He is very fit, talks eats & drinks champagne. Of course travelling in the waggon gave him jifs! but thank Heaven that ends tomorrow when he will be in a comfortable hospital. I am wiring to [illegible] for him tomorrow. Poor old 34th 1 killed & 5 wdnd this trip, less than ½ our original no. left.

[Morgan was invalided home on 30 November]

De Wet continued southward, intending to enter Cape Colony; but Kitchener had reinforced the more obvious crossings of the Orange River and heavy rains swelling both it and the Caledon ruled out crossing elsewhere. De Wet returned to Dewetsdorp by 12 December. Two days later, now with 4,000 men, he moved north again, Knox pursuing him, hoping to catch him as he had erected a blocking line from Bloemfontein to Ladybrand; but De Wet managed to force his way through, after which his men split up into smaller commandos to the north-east of the Orange Free State. His activities had provided a diversion, under cover of which Hertzog, with nearly 1,200 men, and Kritzinger with 700 slipped into Cape Colony, the former moving west, raiding rail and other communications, and the latter south towards Port Elizabeth, pursued by the 17th Lancers, now commanded by Douglas Haig.

While Knox had been chasing after De Wet, Major-General R. A. P. Clements was on the trail of Smuts and De la Rey in the Mageliesberg, in cooperation with Broadwood, based at Rustenburg. On 2 December

Smuts discovered that a convoy of supplies was on its way to the latter, and on the following day he and De la Rey attacked it, inflicting 64 casualties and capturing 54 men and 118 wagons. Taking 15 wagons filled with the supplies they coveted most, they burnt the rest and released the prisoners. A week later they returned to the attack after they had discovered Clements encamped with 1,200 men in the gorge of Nooitgedacht. Making a careful reconnaissance and joining hands with General Christiaan Beyers, with another 1,500 men, they surrounded Clements on the night of 12/13th December, prepared to attack at dawn. A premature attack on the 300 men of the Northumberland Fusiliers, who were picketing the heights, gave the alarm. Beyers then launched his attack, and Captain Yatman of the Fusiliers, greatly outnumbered, was forced to surrender by 7 a.m. Clements was now swift to act. Early morning mist and then the loss of the heights prevented him from signalling by helio to Broadwood for help. By energetic action he succeeded in concentrating part of his force with all his guns, including a 4.7in which was just rolled down the hillside, onto the key position called Yeomanry Hill, which he successfully defended against an attack by Smuts. Inexplicably this was not followed up by a concerted attack by the three Boer commandos, partly, it would seem, because Beyers's men were too busy looting the British camp, which Clements had left as he moved to the hill. At 4 p.m. that afternoon Clements withdrew unhindered, and, with 1,000 men, made his way towards Pretoria, having lost 74 men killed, 186 wounded, of whom 14 later died, and 368 captured or missing.

Kitchener was angry at this setback, and was at first inclined to support a demand from Roberts that Clements should be sacked; but, after seeing Clements, he relented and eventually took Clements on to his staff. He was severely critical of Broadwood for not moving his 2nd Cavalry Brigade to help Clements and wrote to Roberts on 21 December:

> I think I shall have to send Broadwood home and put Knox 18th Hussars in his place. Broadwood has never been the same since Sannah's Post and French thinks he ought to go. Poor fellow he is a splendid soldier and I fear it will hurt him very much.

It was intended that Broadwood should leave, with two other brigade commanders, Major-Generals Douglas and Talbot Coke, a week later;

but Kitchener relented and Broadwood remained in command of his brigade for the rest of the war.

Dr S. V. Robinson, a civil surgeon serving with the army, was in the first action and wrote an account in a letter to a friend in England from Rustenburg on 29 December:

> I hope my 'guv' forwarded my last letter to you telling you all about my little escapade on Dec. 3 when the convoy was lost. I had so little time to write so I thought that would be the best to do. Well! the empty convoy returned on Dec. 6th & is now within a day's march of here on its return journey so at last we shall get some news & our Xmas letters. We have practically been in a state of seige [*sic*] for the past 3 weeks. The enemy as no doubt you have seen from the papers have been in force all around us. We could see the shells bursting on the Magaliesberg when Clements was attacked. All his men that were taken prisoner came in here too. Over 300 of the 'Fighting Fifth'* – I am afraid they hardly can claim that title after this war as this is the second time that they have come to grief. We have been very busy & have over 200 patients in at the present time. At last we have taken over the Church & it will hold over 50 beds which are on this convoy. I have most of the wounded that I brought in from Buffelspoort & they are all doing fairly well. Only 4 of them will stay here – the remainder will go down by next convoy – Evans goes with it – my next one won't be before the end of the next month. I am quite ready for another one although I never want to have such a fire poured all round me again. It was very hot – & I did feel it when the poor little mare dropped. I do miss her! Haven't tried to replace her yet.
>
> I have taken some photos of the guns that did so well & also of the camp kettle that was hanging under a gun limber there are 22 separate bullet holes thro' it (that is 44). There were 15 in one gun wheel alone. Pretty hot fire. Eh! I believe the papers said that only 6 out of 150 wagons were saved – they imply that the whole convoy was not lost but it was moving in two sections. The whole of first part was lost except those 6 wagons. The mails were saved at much personal risk by the Postal men. I lost everything except what I stood up in & my camera – found a shirt & 3 or 4 pairs of socks here. My suit isn't fit to be seen – tunic dirty & torn & breeches in rags. You know we don't wear our best on the 'trek'.

* The Royal Northumberland Fusiliers.

I also lost most of my trophies. I expect to have a nice lot of photos – am sending the films home to be developed. Broadwood has left this district & gone to Krugersdorp thank goodness – his men are done up & we usually get 50 a week from him. Clements is to operate between here & Commando Nek & look after our convoys. We shall probably stay here – Well, for ever! as things are going on. There have been quite 8,000 Boers round about here lately & some of them are not more than 20 miles away now – de la Rey! There are a few snipers outside our pickets & it isn't safe to go very far. As you may guess we had a very quiet Xmas on ¾ rations. We had managed to keep one bottle of whiskey though, to drink her majesty's health & that of 'absent friends'. Had a couple of Chickens & a blancmange – Had a concert in the Church (unconsecrated). I sang 3 songs & got encored twice.

Kitchener ordered French into the area to clear up the Mageliesberg. Beyers moved off to the north, while De la Rey dispersed his commando and Smuts organized a new one to operate near Johannesburg.

Hertzog's and Kritzinger's irruption into Cape Colony inevitably caused considerable alarm, which provoked the declaration of martial law, except in the native areas and the ports. Milner had always been sensitive to the threat of an Afrikaner uprising in the colony. There had been a short-lived one at Prieska on the Orange River in a remote area of the north-west in March 1900, accompanied by a raid by 1,000 burghers from the Free State under General Steenkamp, but it had soon petered out. Milner welcomed the new opportunity to mobilize 'loyalists' in the colony, even though it might be limited to guarding railways and other vulnerable points. But Hertzog, who had got as far west as Lambert's Bay, 100 miles north of Cape Town, and Kritzinger found that although they were given supplies and shelter they could not raise recruits for their commandos in the colony nor provoke a general uprising, and they began to retrace their steps to the Orange River.

Major O'Farrell was appointed staff officer to the Commandant of the District round Prieska later in the year and described it in a letter to his sister in September 1901:

We have to look after a piece of country 250 x 100 miles in extent, larger than Ireland is it not? German territory & Bechuana Land are on the North, & Naqualand on the West. The country is of course very thinly peopled being cut up with large grazing farms, where the people raise horses cattle sheep & ostriches. They are almost all Dutch & disloyal, a great many of them are in the field in open rebellion, & I fear most of them who [are] still on their farms are sympathisers. There is of course a large black population & a number of half breeds (half Dutch half Zulu) they are called 'Bastards' the term carrying no idea of reproach or insult. These Bastards are largely used as scouts & for defensive purposes, & are organised under European officers & armed & mounted by Gover'mt, it is 'war to the knife' between them & the Boers who seldom give them quarter. The Kaffirs are born orators & actors & it is most amusing to see a group of men & women talking, the conversation is accompanied by the most energetic & generally graceful gestures. I was watching the examination of one of our black scouts a few days ago (he was one of three who went out & was ambushed by the Boers, who captured the other two & shot them, & this man lay hid among some rocks & heard all that went on) I did not understand a word he said but could follow his story quite easily from his acting. He used to crouch down & look round as if in a great fright with his eyes nearly starting out of his head, then imitate men beating others, then spring up to his full height & pretend to run, & so on all the time talking as fast as he could. The Boers searched for him, sometimes coming within a few yards, & when they could not find him drove the others away a short distance & shot them, he acted the whole affair in the most dramatic manner. Acting a telegraph operator is not altogether a pleasant billet just now particularly in some of the lonely villages, the wires are constantly being cut & men have to go out on horseback & repair them. Two girls in charge of offices in this district behaved very well lately. One is a Miss Devenish at a place called 'Omdraai Vlai' about 40 miles from here on the De Aar road. The Boers suddenly put in an appearance, & while they were actually in the house & her father delayed them, she ticked off the news that they were there. The next moment they had smashed the instrument to pieces. Another girl at Van Wyk's blei also got off a message before a party of the enemy could stop her, & they threatened to thrash her with a Sjambock I believe. The work here is very interesting and you would enjoy it I think as you have had a legal training, Clarke & I are the head of the law department as the district is under Martial Law, but we have of course the various Police Magistrates to act under us & assist the Military Courts. Nine tenths of the population are graded as First or Second class Rebels, & are under surveillance & even now & then we have to try, & sometimes execute rebels taken in arms. We have also to see to the provisioning of the district as the country has been pretty well cleared of all food supplies, & at present have a convoy of 140 waggons stuck up on the bank of a flooded river 80 miles away while we are very short of food.

De Wet had not given up hope of joining the other commandos in Cape Colony. On 27 January 1901 he set off south again from Senekal, 100 miles north-east of Bloemfontein, with 2,000 men, eluding Knox's and Bruce Hamilton's columns sent by Kitchener to intercept him, and crossed the Orange River on 10 February, 800 of his Free State burghers refusing to go further. Moving west, he was helped by bad weather, which hindered pursuit by Plumer, who, with 1,070 mounted troops, mostly Australian, had been sent south to catch him, Kitchener himself following to coordinate the fifteen columns, totalling 15,000 men, which he had brought to the area. De Wet was forced to abandon his wagons and by 19 February had given up hope of operating successfully in Cape Colony. He doubled back eastward, trying in vain to find a crossing over the flooded Orange River, until, having joined up with Hertzog on 27 February, they both crossed at Botha's Drift in an area lightly guarded by Byng. By 2 March he was back at Senekal, having covered 800 miles in forty-three days, rivalling the Scarlet Pimpernel in his elusiveness. On his visit to these operations, Kitchener's train narrowly missed being attacked itself.

Major Birdwood, having recovered from his wound, had been posted to his staff in October 1900, when the 3rd Mounted Brigade was broken up and Lord Dundonald went home. Birdwood's job as DAAG was to look after the affairs of the mounted troops, but he seems to have been particularly close to Kitchener, with whom he went riding almost every day. He records in his diary:

16 February.
Set off with Lord K. by train, pilot engine in front & armoured train in rear. Left Pretoria at 6 a.m. reached De Aar 7 a.m. next day. Set off back at 7.20 on 17 February, stopping at Naauwport to confer with General Inigo Jones, Commanding Guards Brigade. Arrived Bloemfontein 7 p.m., met Tucker. Travelled all night & reached

Vereeniging at 5.30 a.m. (18 February). Hear Boers had just crossed line between there and Meyerton – just after leaving Klip River we saw about 250 Boers galloping from E to W & presently we heard an engine being blown up. We backed into Klip River Station & our escort of 60 men of Hampshires went on to scene of train, when Boers cleared: they had a pom pom in action, which nearly hit our engine, & presently armoured train came from Elandsfontein, but Boers had blown up engine, derailed about 4 trucks & burnt 1 of meat. They carried off a lot of clothing: engine driver badly scalded & 1 man of our escort killed: we changed to armoured train in which we went to Naval [?] Spruit & then in trucks to Elandsfontein, where we got special to Pretoria, arriving about 3 p.m.

Another railway incident occurred at about the same time, but on the line to Natal. It was described by Captain Samuel Rowlandson of the 4th Durham Light Infantry in a letter written from Vlakfontein to his brother Oswyne:

22 Feb.
On Wednesday morning the mail train steamed in here about eleven o'clock. There were a good many people in it including two women, a girl and a small boy. The train started off for Heidelburg. It went merrily past Snickerbosch Spruit (where Cook's brother is) and when it nearly got to Kraal – Bang! – one of three trucks was blown up by dynamite and at the same time a volley of bullets was poured into the train.

Fortunately there were about 30 men with rifles in the train and they all scrambled and took cover and a battle began.

The armoured train with its pom-pom went out from here and protected the mail train's left flank the big fat gun on Edenkop poured shells into the Boers, a pompom went out from Snickerbosch and shelled them too, and a fifteen pounder blazed away at them from Kraal. So you can imagine there was a good noise going on. The Boers got within 150 yards of the train but were beaten off, they crept up in the grass & were I hear most difficult to see.

The battle lasted 4 hours or more & then under a heavy fire the armoured train was coupled onto the wrecked mail and brought in here at least most of it, the remaining part on the other side of the break was taken by an engine & construction truck into Heidelburg.

So the Boers were really beaten. The mine which they had laid on the line must have been done very well. It was fired by means of an electric current as the armoured train brought in two or three hundred yards of isolated [sic] copper wire which got entangled on the cowcatcher.

It was dark when the armoured train came back here dragging the mail train with its broken windows and six wounded men two so badly wounded that one of them is certain to die and the other very likely will die.

We had to rummage out blankets & rations for them and as there were 6 or 7 officers on the train they came & dined with us. It was an awful scramble and most uncomfortable.

This morning I was out at four o'clock along the line and came in about six. One of the native scouts had been shot this morning so there are still Boers about. I suppose they will end in getting a train.

Your present of a packet of ripping chocolate arrived safely actually on my birthday, so I nibbled a bit of it in honour of the occasion very many thanks. The pompom of the armoured train on Wed fired about 500 rounds.

On the western side of the Transvaal, Methuen was actively engaged. Lieutenant R. S. Britten of the 37th (Buckinghamshire) Company of the Imperial Yeomanry wrote to his father from Klerksdorp on 21 February:

As expected we arrived here Tuesday morning. Before we left Wol-meranstant we had very exciting times. All our outposts were attacked at one time about 11 A.M. but before 2 A.M. we drove them all off with the exception of one where there were about 300 Boers & a gun at far end of a very long & steep kopje – We managed to get a Squadron & a Pompom up in support or they would have been surrounded – No one had any idea that the Commandos had guns, but it appears that several Commandos had got together & intended to hammer us before we got to Klerksdorp – the four Commandants were L[? J]olly du Beer – De Villiers Smith & Douthwaite – We moved out of Wolmeranstant by a different road to that they expected as we had received information from our prisoners that they intended to have Methuen's convoy & that the four Commandos were to attack simultaneously & at different points but a few volleys from us soon brought out the white flags – the capture consists of 5,000 head of cattle – 15,000 sheep – 64 waggons – 10 Cape carts 20,000 rounds small rounds ammunition – 1 ton pompom – do – 64

live Boers with arms & sundry horses etc – We camped on the spot
& our Convoy joined us that night – We had left now only two days
provisions on Convoy & we still had to get this lot safely through to
Hartbeestfontein before we could get to Klerksdorp – You can
imagine what a lot of keeping to-gether [*sic*] all these sheep etc on
the Veldt would take – we captured a lot of blacks & they drove this
lot between the mule & ox transport – Barnums Show was nothing
to it[.] We started next morning with 500 mounted fighting men &
400 Infantry – The 3rd Yeomanry were in advance & then we came.
After we had gone about 4 miles, they opened fire on our scouts, the
whole concern was drawn up under a hill & infantry put to guard it
– We had no sooner done this than the Dutch opened fire in our
rear, this apparently was a blind to take our attention from the front,
anyhow it was damned unpleasant.

The Boer position was extraordinary; there was a gradual slope to
them from our side & the mountains went down straight on their
side so they had perfect cover.

Immediately firing started the General ordered our Regiment to
hold the Kaffir Kraals on the road between the hills & if possible to
hold a kopje on the left & the 5th Yeomanry were sent with Pompom
on the right – As luck would have it I was leading troop of 37th,
which always marches first then 38th 39th 40th. I was sent with my
troop (which now consists of a Sergeant, Corporal & 12 men) down
to hold one of the Kraals. When I got within 300 yards, I was fired
on from three sides so you can guess bullets came thickish, by a
marvellous prick of luck we got behind a Kraal & only got 2 horses
shot & of course we were galloping quite 40 miles an hour – (I
should like you to ask Gilbert's brother what he thought of that
gallop)[.] We got inside these huts & made holes all round & soon
let them have it, all the time bullets were flying over us, & when we
came out we saw 100.s had gone into the wall – The Regiment turned
left handed & held Kopje on left. The guns were playing on the Boer
positions for 8 hours & still the shooting was just as heavy from their
rifles – At this point Methuen ordered the 10th to advance on the
left & rush positions which we did & cleared the brutes out, the
Infantry were in support on the left, the devils knocked 35 of us over
18 in our regiment & 17 in the North Lancs – Of course we have
seen nothing to touch this before & the General says he has heard
nothing like the fire since Modder. The Fifth did much the same on

the right but they had better cover & positions not so strong against them. Eustace Fiennes led the Oxfords in gallant form & they got within 10 yards of Boer position with fixed bayonets – The General couldnt say too much for Xth, when it was over. I hear he has mentioned the Regiment which is a great thing, being the first *Regiment* mentioned. Lord Kitchener will be sick when he hears of our casualties but no good can be done here without a few. We accounted for & buried 42 Boers on that trek & know of 70 wounded.

*

During this period Kitchener's attention had also been focused in another direction, the eastern Transvaal, where on 29 December the garrison of Helvetia on the Delegoa Bay railway had been attacked and overwhelmed by Commandant Ben Viljoen's Johannesburg Commando, 235 men surrendering. Kitchener was furious when he got the news, and wrote to Roberts on 4 January 1900:

> A most outstanding blow came on us last Sunday when we heard that Ben Viljoen's men had surprised and rushed Helvetia at 2.30 a.m. on Saturday and captured the 4.7[in] gun without a shot being fired. The sentries must all have been fast asleep and as there have been many cases lately of men sleeping on their posts I have issued a warning that I will confirm death sentences in such cases.

Three officers were court-martialled as a result and one of them was found guilty and dismissed the service.

On 7 January Ben Viljoen and Botha attacked Belfast, but were driven off by Smith-Dorrien's men, who suffered 140 casualties in the action. These attacks provoked Kitchener to organize a major operation at the end of January, directed by French, to eliminate Botha's commandos from the whole area south of the Delagoa Bay railway and north of that leading to Natal, giving him 8,500 mounted men, 6,000 foot soldiers and 63 guns, with 6,000 more men to supply them, divided into seven columns. While five of them drove from west to east, two (including Smith-Dorrien's) would move south from the Belfast area to cut Botha's escape routes. However, Botha broke through the net with 2,000 men in thick fog near Ermelo on 6 February, dispersing Smith-Dorrien's column as he did so, and made off to the north. The drive went on until it petered out in foul April weather in the Drakensberg Mountains on the

Transvaal's border with Swaziland and Natal, the bag amounting to 272,752 animals, 2,281 wagons and carts, 11 guns and only 1,350 Boers, the majority of whom had surrendered voluntarily.

One of the columns was commanded by Brigadier-General Alderson of the Mounted Infantry and included the 14th Mounted Infantry, with which Lieutenant Waters was now serving. The men came from the West and East Yorkshire, the Middlesex, Lincolnshire, Gloucestershire, Essex and Manchester Regiments and the Royal Fusiliers, the officers from those regiments and also from Australia, Canada and the Indian Army. With the 13th Mounted Infantry they formed the 5th Corps of Mounted Infantry under Colonel Jenner of the Rifle Brigade, totalling 800 men. With two field artillery batteries, the 4th King's Own Yorkshire Light Infantry and 200 men of the Canadian Scouts, they formed Alderson Column, one of six working eastwards from Pretoria towards the Portuguese frontier and Swaziland at the end of January 1901, one of which was commanded by the future Field Marshal Allenby. Waters's diary takes up the tale from the start of their operations on the 26th:

> Came in touch with Boers 3 days out about 1000 strong, I should say. They would not fight tho' it looked like it. They couldn't give a battle without being flanked on the R. or L. by the other columns. Alderson didn't press them very hard as he had orders to hold them. Only shelled them with R.H.A. Moved on due East clearing all families & stock & burning all farms. Finally reached Mooifontein (pretty spring) 7 miles from Ermelo. Stopped 3 days. Sent in sick including King & Whylock to Standerton, also our own & Smith Dorrien's wounded from fight at Bothwell when L. Botha made night attack on him & got through outposts into camp. Smith Dorrien had 20 killed & 50 wounded but beat off attack. Sent families into Standerton. Went into Ermelo & country round for grain & mealies & anything worth taking, Got lots of mealies. Forgot to say I took on job of Quartermaster & Transport Officer just before this vice Gretton doing adjt. as well. Got 2/- a day extra pay.
>
> Lots of peaches about in farm orchards. Rather coarse as a rule.
>
> Moved on slowly to Amsterdam a hamlet, then to Derbe on the Swaziland Border. Had bad time with the waggons the mules dying R & L. Bad drifts etc. Stopped Derbe 10 days. Rained all and every day bar one. Everything swamped. Got toothache; had tooth out in tent by Ingall, Pulled it straight.

Cleared & swept country all round of everything. Found lot of gin we doled out to the men in a store. Couldn't get convoys to us owing to rain, so very short of food. Got plenty of sheep & mealies however. Left Derbe & moved on through town of Piet Retief over Assegai River to Marienthal. The distance of the 1st march was 12 miles & it took 48 hours to do. Worst 48 hours I have ever spent. Exclusive of Assegai River we had six drifts about. Crossed Assegai River by the a.m. drift 4 feet deep, stony & current flowing about 4 miles an hour. Sides very steep. About 4 p.m. it came on to rain in the S. African fashion & the country was a bog [took] us ½ hour and the thunder & lightning were appalling. Didn't have my coat in my saddle that day of course.

The country from Assegai River up to Marienthal that slopes up with some very steep ascents 20 degrees or more at times & you go up through a wide cleft in the hills. When darkness fell this cleft was a jumble of groaning oxen, braying mules, yelling natives & cursing officers & to add to the joy of it the Boers were about. They hit 4 K.O.Y.L.I. in the afternoon. At midnight I gave it up till day light as all my wagons were up to their axles in bog. Slept for two hours in the mud, two inches deep – a cleaner spot comparatively. Woke at about 3 & stumbled on Wardrop in the dark. I got into a cape cart with him & with some of the gin from Derbe we got to sleep. It tasted like paraffin but I swigged it down neat, I was so cold. Slept till daylight, worked all the day on a mealie cob and a tin of pea soup I found & by evening just got the last wagon into Marienthal. I ate a supper that night & slept.

By this time Kitchener had contacted Botha through his wife, who, with Kruger's, had stayed in Pretoria, to suggest a meeting. Earlier attempts to initiate peace talks had failed, including one in January through General Marthinus Pretorius, son of Andries Pretorius, founder of the Republic. It had elicited the bleak response from Botha and the acting President, Schalk Burger, that they 'would not discuss any question of peace: they were fighting for their independence and would do so to the bitter end'. Kitchener's message was that he would discuss anything other than the annexation of the two republics, which was not negotiable. Botha agreed to meet him at Middleburg on 28 February. Kitchener had already suggested to London the points that he thought Botha would raise and the line which he proposed to take. They were, first, the legal position of the natives: he recommended adoption of the native laws of the Orange Free State, which he described as 'very good', being slightly more liberal than those of the Transvaal. Secondly, he wished to compensate the Boers for war damage, remarking that the Rand should easily be able to pay for it. Thirdly, he wished to reassure them that their destiny would not pass into the hands of 'the capitalists', particularly not the Jewish gold magnates; and finally and most controversially, that an amnesty for the Boers who had fought against the British should include the Afrikaners from Cape Colony and Natal who had done so, referred to as 'colonial rebels'.

Milner was not in favour of a meeting with Botha at all, and was firmly opposed to the last proposal. Kitchener argued that at least a distinction should be made between those 'rebels' who had joined the commandos while Boer forces had been occupying parts of Natal and Cape Colony in the early phase of the war and those who joined them from other parts or later on, when the Boer forces had been driven north. Milner was not sympathetic. He and Kitchener met at Bloemfontein before the latter sent his telegram to London. Under the threat from Kitchener that his soldiers could not be relied on to continue to fight with enthusiasm if the war went on indefinitely, Milner reluctantly agreed to Kitchener's line, except for the amnesty for 'rebels'. In that he was supported by Chamberlain in London, who also disagreed with Kitchener's proposal to apply the native laws of the Free State. He accepted a formula that initially the states would be governed as colonies, but that they would be granted self-government in respect of internal affairs 'as soon as circumstances permit', and that both the English and Dutch languages would be used in schools and courts. Chamberlain's objection to the native laws proposed was that it would deny them the rights enjoyed by natives in Cape Colony and Natal.

In its place, the words used in the proposal put to Botha were:

> As regards the extension of the franchise to Kaffirs in the Transvaal and Orange River Colony, it is not the intention of His Majesty's Government to give such a franchise before a representative government is granted to those colonies, and if then given it will be so limited as to secure the just predominance of the white races, but the legal position of Kaffirs will be similar to that which they hold in the Cape Colony.

These revised terms were put to Botha on 7 March, who then left to consult his colleagues. On 16 March he rejected them, principally because of the absence of an amnesty for the 'rebels'. Kitchener blamed Milner for the failure and threw himself urgently into the prosecution of the war, which he was longing to bring to an end.

By this time he was in trouble with London over another issue, which has blackened his reputation to the present day, leading even to accusations that he pursued a deliberate policy of genocide. There is no doubt that he shared the view of many of his subordinates that female influence was a potent factor in steeling the determination of the Boers not to abandon the struggle; but it was bureaucratic complacency and inefficiency, not deliberate policy, which led to the 'scandal' of the camps. The intensification of action by Kitchener's columns, with the erection of a network of wire fences joining block-houses to restrict Boer freedom of movement, had swollen the population of the camps for Boer families, now called 'concentration camps', the term used for similar camps which the Spanish had established in their campaign against Cuban guerrillas. Conditions in them had been bad from the start. By the time of the Middleburg Conference they had become much worse. A South African Women and Children Distress Fund had been set up in Britain to alleviate their plight, and its representative, Emily Hobhouse, a forty-nine-year-old spinster from Cornwall who had influential relatives, came out in February, and, with Milner's encouragement, toured the camps. She was horrified by the conditions and alarmed at the high death rate. Travelling back to England in May in the same ship as Milner, who was on his way on leave, she saw both Brodrick and the Liberal leader, Henry Campbell-Bannerman. The latter was not prepared to make a major political issue of it, as he was trying desperately to hold together his party, split between pro- and anti-war factions. But no such hesitancy applied to David Lloyd George, who was supported by other radical MPs. The Government, while bombarding Kitchener with questions about the camps, to which they received consistently complacent replies, sent out an entirely female commission headed by Mrs Millicent Fawcett, a feminist Liberal Unionist, one of its members being the wife of one of Kitchener's brigade commanders, Major-General Sir William Knox (colloquially known as 'Nasty' Knox to distinguish him from Major-General Charles 'Nice' Knox).

Kitchener had already had to face criticism about the extent of farm-burning and had written to Roberts on 8 February:

> The reports on farms being asked for by parliament go home this
> mail – totals Transvaal 256 and Free State 353 – this includes every
> hovel or building of any kind, mills etc and does not really mean a
> genuine farm in many cases, at the same time there may be some
> unrecorded – I think if 50 were added for this it would be a liberal
> estimate.

When he heard about the proposal to send out the commission, he wrote on 19 July:

> It is only the families of surrendered burghers that we have to keep
> in camps by agreement. I see a number of ladies are coming out, I
> hope it will calm the agitators in England. I doubt there being much
> for them to do here as the camps are very well looked after. Kendal
> Franks was quite astonished at the excellence of some camps he saw,
> he only wanted the sick forced to go to the camp hospital they now
> refuse to do.

In another letter, he wrote: 'All the agitation about the refugee camps seems to me to come from subsidies in Holland.'

Between August and December the commission visited thirty-three camps, presenting their report at the end of the year. They were stringent in their criticism and made a number of practical recommendations. The result was to transfer responsibility for their 154,000 inmates from Kitchener to Milner, although the army remained the only organization capable of providing for their maintenance. Another result was to bring about an end to farm-burning and the removal of families. Ironically this worked in Kitchener's favour. The commandos found themselves having to provide for them in the areas which were not closely controlled by the British, restricting their freedom of movement and imposing a burden of responsibility which they found irksome.

That the policy of farm-burning was in full force in 1901 is shown by a letter, dated 30 March, to his mother and sister from Second Lieutenant Thomas Preston of the East Lancashire Regiment, based at Vet River in the Orange Free State:

> I have not got your mail of last week yet so we are now 2 mails overdue
> as I believe the boat which was carrying them broke down near

Ascension Island, but I expect they will arrive soon. I will give you my diary for this week. We have had three small engagements & ought to have had a fourth but it was badly arranged & did not come off.

Sunday March 24th
The Boers are reported to be at a farm about 1½ miles from camp with 2 waggons as the gun & mounted infantry go out to try & capture the waggons, but when we get to the farm the waggons are gone but some Boers are near another burnt farm about four miles from camp so the gun shells them out of it & we drive in about 50 horses, about five or six miles further on in the distance we could see 400 more Boers which De Wet left here last time he came up as they were all knocked up & unable to go further. I & some other fellows get a few shots at some of the Boers across the river but at a very long range. On the way to camp we met a party of Bethune's column coming towards Vet River bringing 17,000 head of cattle with them collected in the neighbouring districts the whole of the column is about 2000 strong but the part that came to the Vet River was only 110 Mounted Infantry, I think if the Boers had known it they would have attacked it to recapture some of the cattle, but having all the cattle with them made it look much stronger they had about 4000 oxen & 100 horses, but the sheep had to be left about 2 miles from camp as between them & camp was a stream which the sheep could not cross owing to heavy rain, but the other cattle were got across all right, just before the column reached camp it began to pour with very heavy thunder rain far harder than it ever rains in England & all the men of the column were of course drenched to the skin without any chance of any shelter of any kind as there is not a spare tent in camp & those we have are worn out & full of holes & as it was evening then there was no chance of getting dry that night or of lighting a fire as everything was wet, I don't think I have seen every one in a worse condition than they before this war, as they had been treking all day & had not had any food since the previous night 24 hours before, & that night they had not even any blankets with them to put round them so had to lay down where & as they were in about four inches of water their officers tried to get them under the shelter of water tank where the engines get water but most of them would not stir as they were already soaked & could get no worse, of course they got food & rum here. One of their officers fell down a hole,

between the rails where the engines put out their ashes, in the dark & was carried to hospital, The sheep had to be left where they were as the stream got still more flooded & ten men were left to guard them. Next morning *Monday 25th* the 10 men guarding the sheep 2 miles away were attacked by the Boers & about 6000 sheep were captured by them so we went out with our M.I. to help the men of the column to recapture them & drive off the Boers, the Captain in charge sent about 50 men to cross the stream & reinforce the ten men on the other side while we & the rest went up this bank, the stream was then in full flood & two men got drowned while crossing, one of their officers named Fern who was crossing with them jumped in with all his clothes on & just missed catching hold of him as he was sinking for the last time & then dived for him & almost got drowned himself as some one else had to go in & get him out, their horses swam out on the other side the other man's leg got caught in the stirrup & he was held under & both washed down with the current, we then went on after the Boers & the party on the opposite side of the stream found them in some Kraal & drove them out of three lots of Kraals after some rather hard fighting one man being wounded & three horses shot & one man missing, the missing man being last seen in a patch of mealies in which were four Boers as well, having lost his horse, I think four other men were missing, when the man was first missing they were fighting at 100 yds range, Fern who jumped into the river went on fighting all day with nothing on but a Mackintosh as all his clothes & boots were of course wet, & then had his horse hit as he made rather a target riding in front in his black Macintosh, We then went on to Easthaven's woman whom I told you about last week & brought her in. She was very angry at first as the Boers were not there to protect her this time & said she would get her husband & sons on commando again & is now in Bloemfontein jail. In the evening the doctor went out in a Cape Cart to bring the wounded man in, he was hit in the foot, the bullet first going through the but [sic] of the rifle.

*

Kitchener's strategy of great sweeps, combined with his blockhouse-and-fence network, was beginning to pay dividends.

Rawlinson, after a spell back in England, returned to South Africa to assume the same post on Kitchener's staff that he had held in Roberts's time. On 31 March 1901, to his great pleasure, Kitchener gave him command of a column, previously commanded by Lieutenant-Colonel Shekelton, consisting of 800 men and 6 guns, which brought him promotion to local Colonel. He was under the command of Major-General J. M. Babington in the south-west of the Transvaal. His diary for 14 April describes the action at Brackspruit:

Our plan was to march to Kaffirs Kraal 135 by night swing round to the S.W. by Paadeplaats 189 and then come home by Geduld and Buisfont'n. We started at 1 A.M. – As I was to lead I was in my place at the hour named but Babington's troops were 40 minutes late so we were somewhat delayed – we marched up the Kaarl spruit crossing to the N. bank at Reitfontein and halting every hour for 5 or 10 minutes – It just began to dawn as we passed Syfer Kraal 42 – Babington told me to push on and take Kaffirs Kraal if I could – This I did and surprised and captured a boer outpost of six men there asleep in the farm – I saw there was no one on the hill to the S.W. of the farm so, as it was obvious that this was the Key of the position I sent Cookson off with the 6 Corps to sieze [sic] it ordering Gosset with the 8th Corps to support his right rear. Cookson got the hill without firing a shot by 7 A.M. and pushed on over the top – I therefore left Gosset to follow on and myself went after Cookson – As I got to the top of the hill I met an orderly who said there was a boer laager just over the hill and that the guns were wanted at the front so I pushed them on as fast as possible – At that moment I heard heavy rifle and pompom fire on my right which meant that Gosset was engaged – an orderly also came from him to say that as he could see 10 wagons trecking away before him he was turning off to his left to capture them – I had sent Montgomery to him to tell him to draw to his left towards Cookson but he had left me before I heard of the 10 wagons – I then galloped on after Cookson hearing the guns in action. On arriving at the scene of action I found that Kitchener's and Roberts Horse had galloped into the boer laager and captured a 12 pounder gun and a pompom whilst the 2 M.I. had gone off across the plain chasing the flying dutchman. The troops were rather scattered but the enemy were in full retreat – Shortly afterwards the general turned up and ordered me to get my force together saying I was too much extended and that when we had assembled he would turn round and march via Geduld to Buisfont'n.

I therefore sent off three messengers to Gosset to call him up to me
– this was about 9 A.M. – However the general had told him to
remain where he was with the result that he Gosset did not rejoin
me till 12.30 – It was then getting late – Meanwhile whilst we had
been sitting still in our extended position Grey having come up
between Gosset and myself some 200 boers who had heard the firing
and come up from the direction of Geduld crept up to within some
500 yards of the guns – I had sent a party of Kitcheners horse to hold
the Southern edge of the hill and feeling anxious that they should be
in the right place I rode off myself to see where they were – A few
heads were visible above the grass which I took to be K's horse and I
rode up to them thinking they had gone exactly where I wanted them
– What was my surprise on coming within 20 yards of them to find
that they were boers – Two men jumped up from the grass with their
rifles at the present shouting hands up – I at once turned and bolted
though I think they were as surprised to see me as I was them – They
fired, and hit my horse which was the one that had been captured
from the boers 3 weeks before – He rolled over leaving me sprawling
on the ground – My boer friends came on me with leveled rifles and
being unarmed I was forced to surrender – They were fairly civil but
demanded my watch and haversack which I had reluctantly to hand
over to them but the watch was only a 25 bobber so I did not mind
– They then asked me for money so I gave them 5/- – All this I did
very slowly for I knew my men were all round them and that there
would shortly be a row and sure enough just as one of them had got
my horse (wounded) bang went one of the 12 pounders and away
went Mr Dutchman as hard as he could go. It was rather a narrow
squeak and I should not have minded if they had not bagged my
horse with my zeis [*sic*] glasses makintosh [*sic*] and telescope on it –
If they had only killed the horse they would have been bound to
leave the saddle but he was only wounded I fear – for he trotted off
lame – having walked back to where the guns were I was congratu-
lated on my escape &c – there was no sign of Gosset till 12 Noon
when he appeared coming along the valley round under Grey's
people -- by 1 P.M. he was formed up between Grey and myself and
at 1.30 we started off for home – I had to do rearguard which with
2500 sheep and 500 cattle to bring in was not a cheerful task especially
as the boers sniped us most of the way back to camp till 8 P.M. dead
tired.

It was a successful day. The boers were completely surprised but there were a good many more of them than we had been led to expect – I must have seen 1000 altogether during the day for at one time they were all round on three sides of us – I do not think Babington handled us very well – He would I think have done better to go out West into the open country beyond Brack [illegible] and hunt them a bit more – We might easily have done this but it is easy to be wise after the event – He made no use of Grey whom he kept sitting on the hill in the centre all day without hardly firing a shot – B. seems slow in action and in making up his mind – He is rather wanting in dash and I should say his nerve was not very good – On the whole I was not impressed with him as a leader and do not think he would be a good man in a tight place. It was a hard day and I was very tired after it but it was a great experience.

His diary a month later illustrates further what these sweeps entailed:

May 12th Sunday Geysdorp
Up to 5 P.M. this evening we have done 132 miles in 112 hours – Not bad marching on the whole and with a loss of only 52 horses out of a total of 1900 – Our bag has been 8 Prisoners, 5 Rifles, 20 Wagons, 210 horses 6 mules 750 cattle 18000 sheep which is not as much in prisoners as I could have wished – Today we marched in here 21 miles and were lucky enough to find a good pan of water which will be useful to us in the future. I shall go in to the railway tomorrow and get supplies – This evening I sent off wires to Kitchener & others reporting what we had done – Mules and horses though tired are well and with a couple of days rest will be ready to start again – Strong wind blowing all day but not too cold tonight – country round here very flat and open with patches of bush here and there – Passed several tracks of Boers all going South – They have evidently broken up in small parties and will collect in the Wohner-ranstraat [Wolmeranstant?] district.

That the removal of Boer families to camps was still continuing is shown by the entry in his diary for 8 July:

I did not march till 10 A.M. this morning in order to give them a chance to get the cattle we captured yesterday divided into teams and put into yoke – The transport have received 200 really excellent trek oxen which has quite put my transport on its legs again – I sent out

Logan with his company to clear some farms before we started and he got sniped on his way back – Then I marched with the horse commando as far as the drift over the Marico which we reached at about Noon – I had heard Williams in action nearly all the morning – Dissultory [*sic*] Rifle fire and an occasional gun – After crossing the drift I moved south to Driefontein 90 which turned out to be a very rich farm – This I cleared of all food supplies and the men had a good go at the chickens pigs and oranges – One lady whom I found there was very recalcitrant and refused to come along – She lay in her bed saying she was sick until the doctor went to her and reported her in 'robust health' and in bed with all her clothes on – I ordered her to be taken bodily bedding and all and placed in the ambulance which was done – We then marched on about a mile crossing two small drifts when the flankers and advance guard were suddenly opened on by 10 or 20 boers away on the left front – I at once moved the guns up on top of the shoulder on our right and a few rounds soon silenced the snipers; but they hit one of the scouts through the thigh and wounded two horses – Tomkins company, who were doing left flank guard to the convoy were also fired on and had three horses wounded and Denne hit through his field glasses.

The unnamed sergeant of the Royal Dragoons had been taking part in sweeps in the south-east of the Transvaal. He describes one in March:

On the 15th the convoy being ready, we inspanned & trekked, the Royal Dragoons being the advance guard, & my troop, the advanced scouts. Spread well out with ears and eyes well on the alert, we moved forward several miles; all was calm and peaceful. Halting presently by a clear, crystal stream, the Squadron leader, who was with the advanced troop, said 'You had better fill your water bottles here', and had hardly finished speaking, when the flip flop of the Mauser was heard & bullets came singing around our ears. 'Dismount' was the order, & away went the horses, one man to four, to a donga, where they were out of sight. We ran forward dropping down behind ant hills, small rocks or anything that afforded cover & there wasn't much: whiz,whiz,whiz, came the bullets striking the ground with a flop & throwing up little spurts of dust, or with a crack & a shrill scream from a ricochet off a rock. My party of twelve men were lying widely scattered & we soon located the enemy on a ridge 1,300 yards distant, & returned the fire. After a few minutes up came our Maxim & commenced grinding out bullets at the rate of 400 a minute. Then our 'Cow' gun came into action on a hill in rear, the shells humming and shrieking over our heads, & bursting along the ridge, which, if nothing more serious, had the effect of disturbing the Dutchmen's aim. After half a dozen shells, the Boers ceased fire & we galloped up the ridge just in time to give them a parting shot. On the other side of this ridge was a farm, & we returned to our bivouac with a couple of fat geese on each saddle. Up to this the weather had been fine, but on the 16th the clouds were low on the berg, & it commenced raining.

We went out early in the morning but could not see 50 yards except at short intervals when the clouds lifted. We returned at midday, the Convoy remaining stationary; a regular beast of a day; cold, wet and miserable. Next morning we were up at half past three. It was still raining & thick, but we moved off at 4.30 am my troop being escort to the naval gun. The weather cleared a bit at midday, & our advanced scouts were fired on from the Elandsberg, a big mountain range we had to cross. One gun came into action, also the other guns, but we ourselves had nothing to do except watch the shells bursting on the mountain. As the convoy had outspanned near where the guns had been in action, we had not far to go. The clouds settled down & it rained steadily all night. The following morning was again wet and thick, & we started out at 4 am & forded the Pivaan [?] river, a deep, swift stream with a lovely waterfall, & rode up the mountain. After reconnoitring & seeing no trace of the enemy, we returned to the convoy which did not move.

On the 19th the convoy got across the river & on to the berg. In some cases three spans (forty eight) of oxen had to be used to pull the wagons across, the rain having made the road almost impassable. These roads are mere tracks of course they are not metalled. My troop was on the left flank of the berg, about 4 miles out, we became fog bound for two hours. We had to halt & put sentries, on front, flanks, rear.

Next day the 20th the convoy managed to get down about a mile. We were out all day & once more got wet to the skin. Fifteen Boers surrendered; they all had long waterproofs & some waterproof overalls reaching well up the thighs. Our cloaks were absolutely useless to keep one dry becoming soaked after a few hours rain – a long waterproof would certainly be a more useful article in this

Country except for the cold weather when of course we swear by the Cloak.

It continued to rain all night & the following day. The troops were in a deplorable condition, wet through to their skins. No shelter, no place to sleep, except in mud, & nothing to cover them except a soaked cloak, & an equally wet blanket. By the 22nd the wagons were hopelessly stuck, some only up to their axles, others deeper. The troops were put on half rations; but in spite of their being cold, wet & hungry, they never lost their spirits & sat round in the mud & rain, singing songs, & laughing & chatting as if they were on a picnic. On the 23rd we saw the sun & a bit of blue sky for the first time for seven days. We managed to get a dozen wagons through the Chakas Spruit on the Pongola River near Luneburg. We had to sling the boxes & sacks across by a wire cable. General Dartwell's Column was on the other side & with General French's force had been living for a week on mutton & green mealies & water. I have nothing further to add at present except that it's still raining.

Another sergeant, involved in operations in the Orange Free State at this time, was P. C. Jonas of the 43rd Company of the Imperial Yeomanry. He was later to earn the Distinguished Conduct Medal and be commissioned. In his diary he wrote:

On the 20th [May 1901] we had our first taste of fighting we, the Hants & another Squadron were on the right flank & had got some way ahead & to the right of the main body. the advance scouts came in touch with the enemy & we were sent on to locate their positions & draw the fire we went over several ridges & at last after galloping down a slope & up another short slope we dismounted at a farm & crept up a gentle slope in front & were very soon under fire we were in well extended order & we lay down taking what cover we could find which was not much & opened fire we could see nothing to fire at & were told to fire at 1500 yds at the line of the ridge in front we had a very warm time of it for about ¼ of an hour & we found out afterwards that we had been within 50 yds of some of their advanced posts & even then we had not the least idea where they were, their fire got a bit too hot & as we could not advance & our guns were a long way back we were ordered to retire, we were under a very heavy rifle fire all this time & while we got our horses & then after leaving the farm we had about 2 miles of open country to cross before we

got to cover as soon as we got out of rifle fire they opened on us
with guns & pompoms: they gave it us pretty hot we went across the
open like blazes with the pom poms bursting just behind us all the
way, they had got our range to a nicety but they did not allow for
the pace that Yeomen could travel when they liked I think our friend
'Tin-belly' & our worthy Sgt Major were running a neck to neck race
for first place 'Tin-belly' went like fun all arms & legs & although
their weights were rather against him he came in a very good first.
a pom pom is an excellent weapon when you are using it but it is a
horrid thing when the other chap has got it. I really dont think it has
ever done much harm on either side out here but the moral effect is
great: [Further thoughts about the pom-pom]

Well we got behind the ridge . . & waited there while they dropped
a few shells which all went over us. Our colonel was very anxious to
get onto the rise in front. I dont know what for but they would not
let us, we galloped out once & got about 400 yds but as they dropped
a few shells & pompoms at us & we knew they had the range we got
back, our gun arrived about 3 hours after this & got into action
somewhere on the rising ground above the place where we afterwards
camped. We had done what we were supposed to do that is drawn
the enemy's fire & located his guns, & then had the pleasure of seeing
our shells bursting round their positions, as we went back to camp
in the evening they dropped a few shells just over us. I must say from
the experience I have had I dislike rifle fire much more than I do
shell fire.

The Yeomanry and Mounted Infantry played a major part in the
maintenance of security throughout the whole area. Trooper William
Grant served with the Ayrshire & Lanarkshire Company of the 6th
Battalion of the Imperial Yeomanry, cooperating with the 7th Mounted
Infantry Regiment, formed from the Manchester Regiment. They were
based at Bethlehem in the north-east of the Orange Free State. His diary
for 16 April 1901 records:

This morning our company with part of the 7th M.I. were to form
a patrol to take some Dutch families from their farms where they
were suspected of feeding the Boers and also giving them clothing.
We had safely taken 3 families from as many farms but on
approaching the 4th which was situated about 3 miles distant from
the last we had left, the M.I's who were the advance screen fell into

an ambush and before they could extricate themselves had lost 2 killed and 1 wounded, besides 7 horses which bolted. This threw the column into confusion and we had all to retire on the gun which accompanied us. The Boers emboldened by their success followed up and at one point were within a half mile of our position and if they could have managed to reach a little hill, which they attempted to do, they could have driven us off. Suddenly 50 or so of them broke cover and galloped for the aforesaid hill; our section of 35 men (being No 1 section) received orders to mount and also make a rush for the same hill. Their 50 men was backed up by a lively rifle fire while our 12 pounder supported us. In less time than it takes to tell we had reached the ridge and the Boers seeing the game was up, attempted to take a ridge to the left but here they were met with a heavy fire from some M.I's who had taken shelter here after they had been ambushed. On our reaching the top of the hill we opened fire but did not do much damage as the Boers were fleeing back to their main body which held a strong position behind the farmhouse, on a hill, with plenty of cover in the way of shrub and large boulders. This was where the work came to be done, as our forces had nearly a mile of open ground to cover before they reached the farm and to add to the difficulties the ground in front of the farmhouse was all cut up by dongas which during the rainy season carried the water off the hill. Our M.I's to the number of 150 working up on the right of our position took fine cover and made it hot for the Boers in the farm and kralls [sic]. On seeing the forward movement of the M.I's, Capt Boswell our sectional leader ordered us to gallop to the left front and take cover in an orchard there. Hastily mounting and forming up we, extending as we galloped, got within 500 yards of the farm when a terrific fire was directed against us from the kopje and kralls which seemed to be full of Boers. The bullets were spluttering all around us, whizzing past and over us, and it does not say much for the Boer markmanship when they only managed to give one of our men a bit of lead in the thigh. My old Bombi (a name I had given my nag) was going along in fine style not galloping but bounding, when suddenly one of our men who was about 15 yards ahead gave a call and instantly reigning [sic] up his horse turned, the rest of us coming behind, being warned, drew up as quickly as we could and not a minute too soon for old Bombi was just on the edge of a very deep donga

Boers rode up to the Yeomanry's farm – they fired & killed one Boer – then no end of Boers appeared & opened fire on this farm – one of the I.Y. officers' horses bolted so he sent over to us to help him out as the Boers were getting round behind him – so we made for a Kraal close to them & opened fire whilst they sneaked out of the farm & retired – they went back to a kraal about 1 mile off whilst 8 M.I., myself & the Intelligence officer kept up the fire. then we retired to the kraal – the Boers came to the kraal we left & were only about 500 yds behind us – then bullets were whistling all over – I noticed one of the M.I. turn absolutely green with fright – when we got to the next kraal the Yeomanry retired again to a farm whilst we kept the Boers off – then we cleared – they got as far as the kraal, but not any further as we were in range of the big gun – All we lost was one horse, the one that bolted, one we had to leave on the veldt as it was done up & could hardly stand up & one horse shot through the near hind leg – We got back here at 1 o'clock just in time for lunch – I dont think claret & soda water ever tasted so excellent – the Yeomanry were not a great success – in fact when we were covering their retreat they wanted to leave us & go straight on for Eden's Kop; – but one of our subalterns, who came out with us, ordered them to wait.

*

The success of Kitchener's strategy forced the commando leaders to contemplate afresh moving into the colonies, Smuts to Cape Colony and Botha to Natal. A council of war was held at Standerton in the eastern Transvaal in June in reaction to a message from Kruger, after the Middleburg Conference, urging a steadfast war effort. Smuts's plan was to slip into the east of Cape Colony and join hands with Kritzinger, who was just managing to survive in that area. They would then move west, where they would be joined by De la Rey, and all together would provoke an Afrikaner uprising. Botha would create a diversion by crossing the Drakensberg and invading Natal.

A few weeks after this, Steyn had a narrow escape when his laager at Reitz was surrounded by Broadwood's cavalry. Twenty-nine members of his government and all its papers were captured, Steyn himself getting away in his shirt-sleeves. Soon after that, Rawlinson paid a visit to Pretoria and was told by Kitchener what had been going on, as he records in his diary for 22 July:

I have had a most interesting day, and do not return to Klerksdorp till tomorrow. I find the actual situation far more satisfactory than I had guessed or even hoped that it could be. K. has been very kind and communicative in telling me all that he has been doing and shewing me all the telegrams that have passed between himself Roberts Brodrick & Chamberlain – the correspondence that has been captured with the Free State officials at Reitz, between Botha and Steyn coupled with the telegrams that have been sent by Botha to Kruger and the latters reply shew that the leaders regard their position as hopeless. Botha like the gentleman that he is would surrender like a shot but Steyn when he wrote on the 14 July was strongly against it. Kruger in his answer to Botha said there was no hope of European intervention though he did not advocate an immediate surrender – He laid great stress on the fact that Botha should not take any definite action without the approval of Steyn – They all seem to harp on the 'National' feeling and the preservation of a sentiment of Africander-dom [*sic*] but Botha admits they cannot go on much longer for want of ammunition and war material – Steyn however is the man that has and is standing out against surrender but as this was prior to his narrow escape of capture he is perhaps less inclined to maintain his obstructive attitude now. K. saw the members of the O.F.S. gov't that were captured at Reitz and impressed upon them that unless they soon brought the war to a close we should commence deporting the families never to return. We are also putting this about the burgher camps which will I am certain have a good effect. We might hear any day that the thing was over though it might also go on for months.

One of those who had been chasing Kritzinger in Cape Colony was Sergeant-Major Cobb. In a letter to his wife of 25 February he had written:

We have been literally all over the place between Prince Albert Rds & Mount Stewart, on the South, & as far North as De Aar, chasing a commando under a 'slim' Dutchman named Kritzinger, we have only been in touch with him on about 3 occasions, each time we gave him a severe doing, but he is not down here for fighting purposes, he's simply trying to make the Cape Dutch rise, but I rather fancy, he has been greatly disappointed in his mission, we don't believe he has had more than 70 recruits the whole time he has been going about, but all the same, he has led us a nice dance after him, he either slips round or over the hills, or double back, of course he has the advantage of having no transport, he simply lives on the country, so where we have to keep to the roads more or less, country no matter how bad, is of no concern to him or his, we have driven him North, so in all probability he will fall in with some of our other Columns, let's hope so. We have just heard the glorious news, that French is after Botha, & giving him more than he wants.

After his visit to Pretoria, Rawlinson's column was operating in the eastern Orange Free State, where he found himself on the trail of Smuts, although he did not at first realize it. His diary for 25 August records:

We started this morning [from Sterkfontein] under the firm convic- tion that there were no boers about – and certainly up till 2 P.M. there was not a vestage of a dutchman. But just as we were ascending a ridge of Kopjies on the other side of which I expected to see camp laid out, we heard an explosion – Then another and then a third – It was evident therefore that it was not Fair blowing up ploughs so I at once galloped to the top of the Kopjes and saw that Gosset with the elswick* was shelling some 100 boers who were just disappearing round the shoulder of the Kopjies to our right – The line of hills I knew from the map ran about 5 miles north of where I was to Holfontein and as I did not think the burghers had seen us I descended the hill by the way I had come up and galloped like fury to cut them off – I sent Brooke with 2 Coys 2 M.I. on ahead whilst I followed with the guns as fast as we could go – When Brooke reached Holfontein he found the whole of the burghers in the plain below him about 500 yards off so I set to and galloped them across the open. He captured 18 prisoners 20 rifles and 30 horses of Smutts [*sic*] commando of transvaalers – If I had known at the time that it was Smutts I would have pushed on again for his horses were very beat and I was sorry now I did not however I am sending Gosset with a pompom and Kitcheners horse and rations to the 29 to pursue and keep touch of Smutts – He may catch him up tomorrow and if

---

* The 'Elswick' was one of six 12-pounder guns originally intended for the Japanese navy, which were bought by Lady Meux from Armstrong Whitworth's Elswick works at Newcastle-on-Tyne in 1900 and used by the 1st Northumberland Volunteer Artillery, many of whom were employed at Elswick. One of them is in the Museum's collection (NAM. 1991–11–42).

so he will probably bag some more of his men. Anyway he will be
able to let us know at Reddensburg on the 29th in what direction he
has gone – We have been lucky today so I hope our luck has turned
and that in future we may get at them better – I march into
Edensburg with the 2 M.I. and the baggage tomorrow.

His diary for 7 September, written at Gelukfontein, records his
frustration at failing to catch Smuts:

We have had a long and tiring day also a fight. I sent Gosset off with
the 8 M.I. at 4.30 A.M. towards the Elandsberg to get between the
enemy and that range whilst I took the 2 M.I. the 37 Batty elswick &
a pompom at 5 A.M. to Hebron a high spur running North from the
Koesberg. By 8 A.M. I was on the Hebron hill and had got Crum
with Gosset who was about Homesdale – He reported about 20 Boers
away on his right so I sent him after them and followed with the 2
M.I. as fast as I could. When Gosset reach[ed] a point somewhere
near the 'H' of Harvey in Harveys Hoek he believed that he could
see 300 boers so I galloped on and arrived just in time to see them
disappear between a high ridge of Kopjies which runs from Wear
Kop up to the Elandsberg – The position looked a very strong one
and I think perhaps I was wrong in having a go at them but it was
so long since we had had a fight that I could not resist the temptation
– I sent Gosset & 2 Coys down to get hold of a ridge of Kopjies in
the low ground beyond a deep spruit that ran right across our front
– The enemy's left rested on the Elandsberg which was impregnable.
He got the low ridge but when he topped it and tried to push on to
the next ridge he came under a very hot fire – I shelled the boers for
about an hour and sent Gosset down another company to turn their
right with but he was not able to do it Harwick not going far enough
round – So I had eventually to go down there with the 2 M.I. and
the guns. The moment I did this the boers cleared at once and Gosset
occupied their position – Our casualties were one man killed and
two wounded and we know we hit at least two boers – It took some
time getting the troops assembled and it was 5 p.m. before we started
back for camp. The road was a very bad one – Just as it got dark we
had a horrible gorge to go up and it was necessary to wait a long
time at the top for the tail to close up. Eventually we moved on again
but had to put two R.A. horses in the ambulance to help the mules
along – Then it was very difficult to find Camp amongst the Kopjies

– The night was dark – no moon and there were Veldt fires all over
the place so that it was just 11 P.M. before we got in – They had not
taken the trouble to keep fires lighted or send up a rocket Balloon
thinking we should remain out the night – It was a long, tiring, and
not very satisfactory day. I have halted today to rest both men and
horses.

Smuts, with 250 men and 500 horses, had crossed the Orange River on
3 September by a drift near the Basutoland border, which was not guarded
as it led into a native reserve, where he found the inhabitants hostile.
Driving them off, Smuts moved south-west in terrible weather to the
Stormberg Mountains, from which he was fortunate to escape. One of the
original purposes of the operation, to join hands with Kritzinger, was no
longer valid, as the latter had been driven out of the colony several weeks
earlier, although a number of small bands, totalling some 750 Boers, were
still at large. One of them, 130 men commanded by the 'rebel' Commandant Lotter, was tracked down by the enterprising Colonel Scobell's
column near Petersberg on 5 September and attacked by a squadron of
the 9th Lancers as they were startled out of their sleep. 13 Boers were
killed, 46 wounded and 61 taken prisoner; 8 of them, including Lotter
himself, were later executed, the fate for rebel leaders decreed by Kitchener
in a proclamation on 8 August. Smuts's men and horses had been reduced
to a miserable state when, on 17 September, in the Elands River gorge,
they came upon the 200 men of C Squadron of the 17th Lancers,
commanded by Captain V. S. Sandeman. In the mist the patrols of the
latter mistook the Boers for irregulars of another column, Colonel
Gorringe's, as many of the Boers were wearing captured British clothing
and carrying British Lee-Metford rifles, ammunition for their Mausers by
then being hard to come by. Smuts decided to attack, and a fierce battle
at close quarters resulted, in which the Lancers lost 29 killed, including 4
officers, and 49 wounded, while Smuts lost only 1 and 6. The latter's
greatest gain was the supplies of food, fodder, clothing and ammunition
for their British rifles. He burnt what the Boers could not carry as they
rode away out of the mountains, while Haig hurried to the rescue, finding
Captain Lord Vivian, whose sister he was later to marry, among the
wounded. With his three columns, totalling 2,000 men, Haig hounded
Smuts as the latter, after a number of narrow escapes, made his way to the
Western Cape, waiting there in vain for De la Rey to join him.

Meanwhile Botha had embarked on his invasion of Natal. By that time he had reached the area of Utrecht on 14 September. His horses were exhausted and the rains had flooded the Buffalo River, which he planned to cross. As soon as Kitchener's intelligence told him that Botha had moved towards Natal, he sent Lieutenant-Colonel Hubert Gough's 24th Mounted Infantry by rail from Kroonstad to Dundee, from where they marched to De Jeger's Drift on the Buffalo River, where local intelligence reported that Botha, with 700 men, was planning to cross. Having himself crossed it, Gough, on 17 September, saw a party of 200–300 Boers riding north towards Vryheid. Calling for help from Lieutenant-Colonel H. K. Stewart, who had another 450 mounted infantry nearby, he decided to attack, not realizing that Botha's 700-strong main body had seen him and ridden round his flank, entrapping him. He himself was captured with 6 other officers and 235 men, after losing 20 killed and 24 wounded, including 3 officers who died later.

Botha took what he wanted, but let the prisoners go, finding their horses too exhausted to be worth exchanging for his own and Gough's two guns too cumbersome. But he felt too weak to cross the Buffalo and ride towards Ladysmith. Instead he continued southwards as the rain poured down, until, on 26 September, he came up against two British forts, Forts Itala and Prospect, on the border of Zululand. Misled by locals who said they were weakly defended, he attacked and failed to take them, losing 58 men at Itala, which was defended by the Durham Company of Militia Artillery commanded by Lieutenant R. C. M. Johnson, who lost only 9 men. He suffered another rebuff at Prospect, and after this demoralizing defeat set off back to the Transvaal, where Colonel G. E. Benson's column of 1,400 men (about 1,000 of whom were mounted), acting on intelligence provided by the Uitlander Colonel Woolls-Sampson, had been lowering the morale of the burghers in a series of raids by night.

On 30 October Botha caught up with Benson's transport, which had become bogged down and was protected by a rearguard of 280 men and two guns. Benson himself was with them, while his main body was with Woolls-Sampson in a defended camp at Bakenlaagte a mile away. Botha split his force, part attacking the camp while he himself, with 1,300 men, went for the rearguard. Although the main body successfully defended the camp, they were prevented from moving to the help of Benson and his men, who fought gallantly to the last, Benson and 65 others being killed.

This sequence of setbacks affected Kitchener's morale. In a letter to Roberts, Kitchener expressed his dismay that something like this could happen to one of the best of all his column commanders: how could the war be brought to an early end, when most of his commanders were far less able. Birdwood wrote in his diary: 'Lord K. much upset & said he really didn't know what to do, only fearing what might happen next.' Raymond Marker confirmed this in a letter to his sister on 20 September:

> I am afraid I can not as usual say that everything is going very well out here – as the last two days have brought a series of mishaps – nothing serious in any way – though we have lost 4 guns in all – but I am very sorry for Lord K as both occurrences might have been easily avoided with proper precautions, and it is always a blow to have these sort of things happening at this late period of the war – & he probably feels it more after two years continuous strain of this work put here. He is always wonderfully even minded over everything & never 'murmurs' in any way – at the most merely says – I do wish people would use a litle common sense. Of course any success gets the Boers tails up again – but as they invent the most astonishing tales of victory daily, it matters little if for once in a way they have a substratum of truth to build on.

Kitchener's mood was reflected in his letters to Roberts. In almost every one he wrote despairingly about his intense wish to find some way to bring the war to an end: of his annoyance with the authorities in Cape Colony whom he accused of not doing enough to help the war effort, including his disappointment that Baden-Powell's South African Constabulary did not take over static security duties adequately. He constantly stressed his wish to see more drastic measures taken against members of commandos, such as confiscation of their property. He dismissed the suggestion of threatening permanent banishment, as he thought that the Boers would correctly guess that if a Liberal Government came to power they would all be allowed to return. Instead he suggested that the French Government should be approached to allow Boer prisoners of war to be settled in Madagascar, where they could be joined by their families. He complained of a hostile press, notably the *Daily Mail*, and a lack of appreciation by the British public of the importance of the war.

Roberts did his best to encourage him, and Kitchener appreciated this, replying on 17 August:

Many thanks for your kind letter of 20th July. Sometimes one feels rather low and disappointed at the results of so much labour on the part of our men; but I really do not think that we could have done more.

A similar letter of Kitchener's, dated 11 October, must have crossed one from Roberts of the 19th of that month. Kitchener had written:

It is very good of you to say that you wish I could get a rest. I certainly feel sometimes rather done up and there is no doubt the war is a most tiring and trying one – I only fear that there may be something I might have done to hasten the end which I have neglected, and that someone else might do it better – However if I retain your confidence I hope with all my heart to be able to see it through.

Indications of Kitchener's mood seem to have reached Roberts also from other sources, possibly from Rawlinson, who visited Pretoria in September and wrote in his diary for the 18th: 'I find K. rather altered and aged from the long strain. He badly wants a rest but cannot possibly get it I fear.'

On 19 October, Roberts wrote a secret personal letter to Kitchener:

The Government are getting anxious that your health would not be able to stand the strain you are now undergoing, and I have been consulted as to what would have to be done in the event of your requiring a rest.

The responsibility of the last eleven months has, of course, been tremendous, then you were severely tried for some years previously in the Soudan [*sic*] and as Chief of the Staff in South Africa, so that it would not be surprising if you found a change necessary. My hope is that you will be able to hold on and bring the war to a satisfactory conclusion, but we cannot afford to lose your services, and whenever you think you have had enough, don't hesitate to let me know.

I have told Brodrick that I am prepared to return to South Africa to take your place, and though I have no wish to leave England again, I should like you to know that you can depend on my doing anything in my power to help you after all the valuable assistance you afforded me last year.

   P.S. I am sure you will understand that it is only on account of your health that a temporary rest is suggested, no one could have done better, and we all have perfect confidence in you. I only want you to know that I am quite ready to act as C-in-C in South Africa until you return refreshed.

This letter would not have reached Kitchener when he wrote on 1 November:

I see the papers say I am not much good as a strategist. . . . . Can you get anyone to do it better, if so please do not hesitate. A new man at the head might evolve some new ideas for finishing the war. I try my best but I am afraid it is not much. Would a considerable increase to the troops finish it? It would I think hasten the end but not finish it for some time. Since Benson's affair I am inclined to ask for more troops.

By this time Kitchener's policy had gradually been transformed into that which Milner had originally favoured. A colonial administration operated with a fair degree of security within the area bounded by the network, which by May 1902 was to number 8,600 blockhouses, covering 3,700 miles of fence, manned by 50,000 white soldiers and 16,000 armed Africans. By November 1901 the area effectively cleared of commandos had increased to 14,450 square miles in the Transvaal and 17,100 in the Free State. The tally of Boer soldiers captured increased every month, rising to 453 in December. Kitchener was confident as he embarked on his next major sweep in the eastern Transvaal, coordinated by Rawlinson, his columns adopting many of the tricks of the commandos, as Benson had been doing. By the end of December 1901 they had dispersed most of Botha's commandos and turned their attention to the north-east corner of the Orange Free State, where De Wet and Steyn were still at large in the area of Lindley, Bethlehem and Reitz, near which they held a council of war at the end of November. The decision was to attack with 700 men one of the many columns, one of which was commanded by De Wet's brother Piet, who had changed sides, the overall total of which amounted to 20,000 men. The place and time chosen, ironically, was Bethlehem on Christmas Day, where Lieutenant-General Rundle had a weak force engaged in extending the blockhouse network to

Tweefontein, dispersed into four locations several miles apart. The principal force, 400 men of the Imperial Yeomanry with two guns, commanded by Major F. A. Williams of the South Staffordshire Regiment, heedless of the lessons of Majuba and Spion Kop, occupied a kopje called Groenkop. After a careful reconnaissance, De Wet sent his men up the steep, unguarded western face during the night of Christmas Eve. The result was a disaster, the Yeomanry losing 57 killed, including Williams, 88 wounded and 200 taken prisoner. David Maxwell described what happened in a letter to his parents, written on 26 December:

We spent a gloomy Christmas spending the whole of it in picking up & burying a lot of Yeo boys who let De Wet rush their camp at night & collar everything – including gun & pom-pom. We were ordered out at 5 a.m. & got there by 6.50–12 miles – but of course too late, as they took the camp at 2.30 a.m. We got one waggon back & shelled them, but could not follow up as they were in a very strong position & we were too weak. It is a horrid thing to talk of but one can't help dwelling on it a little. The force was about 400 strong – with a gun & pom-pom – covering the building of Blockhouses – Rundle with a smaller force & a larger hill to hold was about 2 miles to their right & a string of Blockhouses away to their Rear. We couldn't believe it was possible to take the hill – which was a natural impregnable fort – Precipice on 3 sides with a flat open plain all round & a muddy boggy river about 400 yds to their front – De Wet was known to be near & Williams who was in Command told Rundle that he hoped he would attack as no one could ever turn him out of such a strong position. The whole of their sentries must have been asleep, as it was a full moon & a clear bright night. The Boers climbed up one of the precipices – formed line about 200 of them & then walked thro' the camp – shooting down every one that got up – most were shot in their tents. 60 were killed, 68 wounded & 15 natives killed. numbers are still missing & some officers are known to have been taken away by De Wet – He got all their transport – mules, horses, arms – ammn (70 boxes S.A.A. 2500 rounds pom pom – 100 shells) 6 days food for 400 men & horses & all their Xmas presents. I am afraid that there is no doubt that they killed numbers of wounded – as many of the dead had bayonet wounds as well as bullets – & the Boer doesn't carry bayonets – also many heads smashed in with buts [sic] of rifles – One of the surviving gunners states that many of them got drunk on the officers whisky & Rum for issue on Xmas day & then rushed about killing the wounded. The Boers only took off about 2 waggon loads of dead & wounded & we picked up 2 dead boers – so I am afraid their casualties were very small. The more one looks at the position the more inconceivable it seems.

We came back about 5 miles – camped here for the night – our waggons getting in about 9 p.m. so we had our Xmas dinner – breakfast & lunch all in one & a rather gloomy one.

Tweefontein was an undoubted setback, which Kitchener felt deeply, but it did not seriously affect Kitchener's plans to continue the pursuit of De Wet and De la Rey. Early in 1902 he organized a major operation, with 9,000 men in four columns, commanded by Rawlinson, Byng, Rimington (now a colonel) and Major-General E. L. Elliott, to sweep the area from Frankfort down to the Basutoland border from east to west in order to drive De Wet up against the blockhouse–fence line of the railway, issuing minutely detailed orders for its conduct; but De Wet slipped through, only 286 Boers being taken. However De Wet and Steyn had a narrow escape later in the month when Kitchener repeated the operation with a total of 30,000 troops, including those manning the blockhouse line. They got away, cutting the wire in the south-west corner of the area, but lost 50 killed and 778 captured. This naturally annoyed Kitchener, but by this time his gloom had been dissipated by the news that he received from Brodrick on 31 January 1902 that he would after all be appointed Commander-in-Chief in India in October. Commenting on this to Roberts, he wrote: 'I think we must have finished here in lots of time for me to be ready to go out by October, but if anything happens to prevent it I should prefer to stick to this until it is finished.'

While these sweeps were in progress, Trooper Charles Barnard of 5 Troop of the South African Constabulary was involved in a clash with Grobler's commando near Cypherfontein. He wrote from there to his mother on 1 February about the action:

You will no doubt have read in the papers of a convoy of two bullock wagons and one mule waggon being captured on the 28th out this part by Grobler's commando: I was there.

The waggons came out from Val escorted by six of 16 Troop and about three of 20 Troop, when they got here seven of us including a sergeant Atkinson (from Gloucester) went on with them and took another six men on from No 4 Troop (under Corpl Sherwood of Australia) and four men from 16 troop who had been captured & stripped the day before rode on the waggons. All went well until we were within a mile of 20 Troop & could see the camp when we heard two shots fired on the left advance. I and two others who were riding beside the waggons started to gallop forward to see what the row was (the skyline was only about 200 yds away) when all at once we saw a party of about sixty riding in a line straight at us over the rise with our advance guard riding like mad towards our left flank one of us dashed back to the waggons to turn them & the other (an Australian) & myself let fly at the beggars off our horses next moment we were treated to a volley from further to the left; it went high: we both fired again then turned & went like '*Lord Flower*' [?] for about 1000 yds back along the road to a few mud kraals where nearly all the rest were or were going to; the shots meanwhile singing round us like an angry nest of bees. We don't mind them when they go 'bings' but they are very unpleasant when they sound '*plop*' that is when they strike the ground just against you. During the first rush Corpl Sherwood got off his horse about 200 yds from the waggons behind an anthill and was surrounded by five boers he shot one & next minute was hit in the top of his skull when we got to the kraals most of us sat on our horses & kept moving about & firing as often as possible afterwards we got down & round the kraals. We drove the beggars off the wagons once but they came back & took them away over the sky line a strong force about 100 of them then stayed behind & formed a rearguard far too strong for us to do any thing against so we started straight across for No 20 after we had made another attempt to follow the beggars & got chased back again to the kraals but on that trip out I brought back the wounded Corpl on my horse; they had taken his rifle & bandoliers from him.

Before we could get to No 20 we could hear a sharp fire start over on our left again so we swing round & dashed up to see what was on & found that it was about 60 SACs from No 4 No 20 & No 16 & 17 come up along the main road & joining together were having a go at the boer rearguard which had been strengthened & they were in the spruit & the boers on a ridge 500 yds away, of course down we went for it into the spruit getting a sharp peppering but no casualties our party coming up & joining the firing line the boers fell back & our boys rushed up the ridge on foot & peppered them as well as they could; they hung on there for about an hour then rode on another mile after them in the dark but they got away with the wagons: the officer in charge reckoned that he could have got back the wagons if there had been another hour of daylight.

The boers suffered heavier than we did for during our little dose I saw three dropped & along the track they went two bullocks & two horses were found dead next day. All the damage we sustained was one man hit & one horse hit in the hock with a splinter. When we got into camp at No 20 at ten o'clock I only had ten rounds of ammunition left!

The boers attacked very prettily & with great spirit but they funked us twenty men in the kraals although there were at least two hundred of them. They had a fine haul one waggon being loaded with Lady B.P's christmas presents of 'plum duff & backy' for Nos 20 16 & 17 troops. A case of whiskey for some officers & a jar of rum for troop issue.

Yesterday ten Australians from a column which is lay [sic] between 4 & 20 today chased two boers & took one then four kept on after the other (a Cape rebel) who suddenly disappeared (down an anthill hole) and while the Australians were looking for them shot them all down & then made off on one of their horses. One was shot dead, one died last night, one went through here today for Standerton having been shot with a soft nosed bullet which passed through the horses head through his hand up his arm out at the elbow & into his chest. One was so close to him when he shot him that the devil hit him across the mouth with the rifle!

While almost all the active operations were north of the Orange River, life was not entirely quiet south of it. Second Lieutenant H. C. Rees was serving with the 3rd East Surreys at Beaufort West in Cape Colony just south of the river. His letter to his mother on 10 February describes recent events:

We've had what the papers call another 'reverse'.... About the 30th of Jan Crabbe started out of here for Fraserburg – 80 miles off. Capper & Lund's columns were North & South of Fraserburg & Major Crofton followed an hour behind Crabbe with the convoy of 77 waggons & 150 men. Crabbe soon got ahead, & was held up by the Boers about 60 miles out. On the 4th Feb Crofton was attacked

by about 80 Boers. He laagered his waggons & sent a message to
Crabbe to say that he was in a bad state. At 12 that night about 500
Boers under Hugo & Millen attacked the convoy & after a very fierce
fight in the pitch dark the Boers under Hugo charged the position &
took it. This was about 4.0 a m. The major was shot dead at 5 yds
just as he got up to surrender. He just said: 'It's all up boys, you've
done very well – stick up your hands' & he fell dead. I think that's
what he said anyway something to that effect. We lost there 4 killed
& 16 wounded. Hugo treated the men very well & sent them to
Beaufort West in waggons. The Boers then burnt the convoy taking
only the waggons. Then Crabbe did a mad thing to try & retrieve
this disaster. He left 200 men to guard his camp & took 200 men &
2 guns to attack the Boers. Of course the Boers smashed them. He
lost 50 killed & wounded another 20 or more taken prisoners. Luckily
Capper's column, who had marched 68 miles in two days, & Lund's
column came to his assistance but every officer either in the fight or
in the other columns said that they were galloping all they were
worth with about 1000 Boers after them. The moral effect is tremendous. For the Boers to be able to say We took a convoy in the teeth
of three columns & routed one column is great. Most of Crabbe's
column is in here now, & the hospital is full of wounded. We buried
poor Major Crofton with full military honours yesterday, there was a
tremendous crowd, everyone appeared. He's a great loss to us, he
was always so keen about sport & so full of fun. He was very good to
me too. I'm very sorry for his wife. I believe he wasn't long married.
Anyway, perhaps its better so, if he'd lived its quite on the cards that
he would have been made the scapegoat, as is the way of the British
army. He must have fought splendidly. Of course he might have got
a lot of praise, but it's very doubtful.

Meanwhile De la Rey was active against Methuen in the north-west
of the Transvaal. At Yzer Spruit near Klerksdorp on 24 February he
attacked a wagon convoy, inflicting heavy casualties, 58 men being killed,
129 wounded and 194 taken prisoner. Only 1 officer and 108 men
escaped. Soon afterwards he clocked up an even greater success. He had
observed Methuen starting off from Vryburg on 2 March with a convoy
of 39 oxen-drawn and 46 mule wagons, escorted by 1,400 men, mostly
irregular cavalry from eight different units, intending, after a five-day
march, to join up with Colonel Grenfell's column of 1,200 mounted

men from Klerksdorp. De la Rey attacked Methuen on 7 March at Tweebosch. The irregulars panicked, while the remainder, from the Northumberland Fusiliers, the Loyal (North Lancashire) Regiment and the Royal Field Artillery, stood firm until 68 had been killed and 121 wounded, including Methuen, some 600 being taken prisoner. Methuen was the first and only British general to fall into Boer hands. De la Rey treated him courteously. Kitchener took it badly. It was rumoured that he wept when he heard the news. Major Birdwood's diary records:

> *March 8th.*
> Heard that Lord Methuen with Paris column had been taken by Delarey [*sic*] near Maribaga. I am so *very* sorry for Methuen. Was to have gone for ride with Lord K. but he had a headache & wouldn't go out.

> *March 9th.*
> Hear Methuen was wounded in thigh & a prisoner with Delarey, all his men released, Was to have ridden with Lord K. but he wouldn't come out again & I only got him to take a short turn in the garden.

> *March 10th.*
> Lord K. a bit better.

> *March 11th.*
> K well again [word indecipherable]!

One of his ADCs, Francis Maxwell, recorded much the same:

> 8 March. K very down & didn't dine with us. 9 March. K v. down still: ate no breakfast, didn't come into lunch or dinner. 10 March. K. on the mend & nearly all right at dinner. 11 March, K quite recovered.

But he had no need to be depressed. Two weeks later he learned that a deputation of Boer leaders wished to come to Pretoria to discuss peace terms. Burger, Botha, Steyn, De Wet and Smuts arrived by train on 11 April, but Kitchener had not invited Milner, who did not join them until, authorized by London to do so, he arrived three days later. In the interval the Boer delegation had proposed 'a perpetual treaty of friendship and peace' preserving the independence of the two states. Kitchener cabled the proposal to Brodrick, who naturally turned it down flat. Milner meanwhile had cabled London, advising that Kitchener should

be firmly tied down to the terms agreed for his guidance at Middleburg.
London agreed, the only concession being on the subject of amnesty.
The answer was given to the delegation on 17 April, when Kitchener
agreed to a temporary armistice while they returned to consult the
burghers. Birdwood attended the talks and recorded in his diary for that
day:

> Meeting at 10 a.m. Have telegram read. Steyn said loss of Indepen-
> dence a great blow to them – immediately adjourned & discussed
> among themselves. Met again at 3 p.m. Milner nearly spoilt whole
> show by getting on the high stool. K said it made his blood run cold
> for fear he should ruin everything: after rest had left K continued
> meeting with Botha, Delarey, De Wet to discuss the means of getting
> at Commanders to give them terms.

Meanwhile another of Kitchener's great sweep operations had been
in progress against De la Rey in the western Transvaal. Four columns,
commanded by Rawlinson, Kekewich, Colonel A. N. Rochfort and
Walter Kitchener, had started parallel sweeps on 26 March, but met with
little success, De la Rey slipping through the net after inflicting 178
casualties on Colonel Cookson's largely Canadian column in Walter
Kitchener's force on 31 March. His brother, who had himself been
present in his armoured train at the start, realized that there was a need
for better coordination between the thirteen columns into which the
four main forces were divided. He therefore gave the task to Ian
Hamilton, who had been his chief of staff since November 1901. The
sweep started again on 10 April, heading south-west between the Great
Hart's River and the Vaal. Beyond Tweebosch, at Rooival, on 10 April,
Kekewich's two columns of almost 3,000 Mounted Infantry, supported
by six guns, came upon a mounted Boer force, some 1,500 strong, under
Generals Potgieter and Kemp. The Boers attacked in a Balaclava-like
charge and, in spite of poor marksmanship and some panic among
Kekewich's men, they suffered heavily, Potgieter and 50 of his men being
killed. Although Rawlinson and Hamilton were riding together and,
about 7 a.m., could hear the firing, Hamilton gave no order to Kekewich
or Rawlinson to pursue the fleeing Boers until 9.30 a.m., nor for Walter
Kitchener, twenty miles away, to join in until two hours later, by which
time all hope of catching them had been lost. Rawlinson's diary does not
give a very clear picture of this action. He wrote:

April 11th Friday Noitgedacht.

We marched from the line of the Brackspruit at 7 A.M. – Before we had gone half-an-hour I heard very heavy firing in the direction of Kekewich's camp – I was riding over Cookson's Battlefield with Johnny Hamilton and when we went to join Briggs we found him galloping off to see what Kekewich was at – on reaching there we found that Keke had been attacked by Potgieter and a large commando of 1500 men – On our arrival the boers fled – I drew Scott over to the right and Dawkins too in case they were required but Keke beat off the attack himself with a loss of 5 killed and 30 wounded – Boers lost at least 30 killed and 60 wounded – We then pushed on South after the Boers as hard as we could, and after a gallop of about 14 miles captured ten guns and a pompom as well as about 30 prisoners – Boers scattered in all directions – Walter Kitchener had been ordered to Vleck Kraal but did not turn up – A good day but hard on horses – Some discussion as to who captured the guns.

Shortly before this action Rawlinson appears to have been upset about some doubts about his future. The entry in his diary for 22 March read:

I have been thinking over what Gwynne told me yesterday and have settled in my mind that whatever happens, I will serve K and Johnny H to the best of my ability throughout the war and that after that I dont care a d--n what happens – I have written this to Johnny – But what most distresses me is that Hammy* for whom I have done so much is as great an enemy as any of the others – I am sorry for this as he will suffer for it for I cannot forgive such underhand work and I shall be just as unmerciful to my friendly enemies as I am to the boers – I respect men of ability who are arbitrary but I cannot take a lenient view of the man who has no ability & is merely a jack in office. I have been busying myself about remounts all day and find I can turn out 1600 men with which I am satisfied.

The failure to catch more of the Boers in this action was no longer relevant. On 19 May De la Rey joined the other members of the Boer

---

* Probably Lieutenant-Colonel H. I. W. Hamilton, Kitchener's Military Secretary, brother of Major-General Bruce Hamilton.

delegation when they returned to Pretoria to resume peace talks, which Milner was doing his best to frustrate. In this he was aided by De Wet, who remained intransigent, while Steyn was ill and unable to attend. The lawyers of the two sides, Smuts and Herzog for the Boers, Milner and Sir Richard Solomon for the British, hammered out a draft agreement, which was accepted by the generals and cabled to London. On the difficult issue of amnesty for the 'rebels', Milner, having agreed it with the Cape government, conceded that their leaders would not be imprisoned, but merely deprived of a vote. The fate of Natal 'rebels' would be decided by the courts. The delicate issue of political rights for natives was glossed over by an amendment to the Middleburg terms which deferred any consideration of giving them a vote 'until after' the new colonies had been granted self-government, which would effectively postpone it for ever, as long as Afrikaners controlled that self-government. Finally the financial subsidy to cover pre-war debts of the two states would be increased from £1m to £3m.

In spite of Milner's protests, the Cabinet agreed the proposed terms, although Chamberlain had jibbed at the change over native rights, and they were formally put to the delegation on 27 May. A representative body of sixty burghers was assembled at Vereeniging at 2 p.m. on Saturday 31 May. They considered a motion proposed by the Transvaal which recommended acceptance of the terms and explained the reasons why: the lack of food for families outside the camps; the conditions within them; the general lack of resources; the growing threat from the natives; Kitchener's proclamation of 7 August 1901, threatening confiscation of the land of burghers in or supporting the commandos; and the hopelessness of any thought of victory. Botha and De la Rey persuaded De Wet to support this, and it was passed by fifty-four votes to six. The Treaty of Vereeniging was signed at Kitchener's headquarters at 11 p.m. that night by Burgher for the Transvaal and De Wet for the Orange Free State before Kitchener and Milner for Britain. The war was over. Kitchener was created a Viscount, promoted to full General, and awarded a grant of £50,000.

On 17 June a dinner was given in his honour by the Johannesburg Town Council, the Chambers of Mines, Commerce and Trade, and the Stock Exchange. The menu displayed a map of Africa, showing a continuous stretch of red southwards from Alexandria through the Sudan to British East Africa, south of which there was an unfortunate gap, before continuing through British Central Africa and British South Africa all the way to the Cape. It listed the courses:

Hors d'Oeuvre
Consommier Printanier Royale
Filet de Sole Frite à la Magado
Pommes Parisiennes
Vol au Vent à l'Ancienne
Filet de Bœuf Piqué à la Barigole
Coq de Bruyère Rôti
Salade Alexandra
Pièce Monté à la Versailles
Charlotte Russe
Gelée Melange Glacé de Nougat en Bombe
Patisserie
Café à la Turque

To wash all this down, the guests were offered Amontillado, Liebfraumilch, Château Lafite 1891, Perrier Jouët 1895, Pommery and Greno (Extra Sec) and liqueurs. One wonders if any of the guests reflected on the contrast with life in Ladysmith, Kimberley or Mafeking under siege.

8

AFTERTHOUGHTS

The Boer War must be considered, as it was by many at the time, to have been an expensive failure. Expensive it certainly was. In financial terms it cost the British Government £210 million. Both the Afrikaner and the native population of the Orange Free State and Transvaal lost heavily in terms of property of all kinds. The compensation paid out after the end of the war covered only a small proportion of the real losses and was, without doubt, unfairly distributed. In terms of lives lost, whether in action or by disease, and physical injury it was also expensive. A total of 448,895 white soldiers served there, of whom 256,340 were regulars or regular reservists, 45,556 Militia, 36,553 Yeomanry and 19,856 Volunteers. 29,395 were recruited from the colonies, over 16,000 from Australia, about 6,400 from New Zealand and some 6,000 from Canada. 52,414 were raised in South Africa itself, mostly Mounted Infantry and Light Horse. In addition 7,273 men from Britain and 1,258 from Canada were recruited into the South African Constabulary. Deaths totalled 20,721, of which 7,582 were killed in action or died of wounds and 13,139 from disease. Total casualties, including wounded, amounted to 52,156: of them, 1,400 were Australians, 507 Canadians, 421 New Zealanders and 8,187 from South Africa itself.

87,365 men are believed to have served in the Boer commandos of the Transvaal and Orange Free State, including 13,300 'rebels' from the colonies of Natal and the Cape and 2,120 foreign volunteers. It is believed that over 7,000 died. To these must be added deaths in the 'concentration camps', estimated at 18–20,000, although some of them would have died naturally during that time. 10,000 armed African natives served as scouts, guides or guards with the British, and 30–40,000 as transport drivers or general labourers. Any of the former who fell into Boer hands were usually shot, as were many who helped the British in other ways. Estimates of African deaths directly attributable to the war vary from 7,000 to 12,000. For all who took part, whether combatants or not, it was undoubtedly expensive.

And what did it achieve? Certainly not Milner and Rhodes's vision of a rich British South Africa within the Empire, dominated by an immigrant white population of Anglo-Saxon origin, as pictorially represented on the menu of Kitchener's farewell dinner. Two factors combined to influence that: first, the immigrants did not come in the numbers needed to dominate the new colonies: secondly, Campbell-Bannerman's Liberal administration, which came to power in Britain in 1906, implemented to the letter the promise in the Treaty of Vereeniging to grant internal self-government to the new colonies. These factors ensured that the Afrikaners would hold political power not only in the Transvaal and Orange Free State, but in the whole of the Union of South Africa, created in 1909, until a combination of pressures forced them to hand it over to the despised 'Kaffirs' nearly a hundred years after the war began. The European population of Anglo-Saxon origin, although strong in Natal, remained throughout either in opposition or as a minor partner. The Africans, until the final reversal of their fortunes, suffered most. Milner's introduction of the stipulation that they should only be enfranchised 'after' internal self-government had been granted not only ensured that they were denied it in the Transvaal and Orange Free State, but that, when the Union left the Commonwealth in 1961, they lost their rights in the Cape Province and Natal. In the balance against the disappointment of Milner's hopes was the fact that a high proportion of the Afrikaner population was content with the prosperity and degree of independence they enjoyed as a Dominion of the British Empire and was prepared to fight on Britain's side in both world wars, although there was a significant minority which opposed that. Milner himself, ironically, was finished off by a tsetse fly on a visit to South Africa in 1924. What the Boer War did certainly achieve was a thorough reorganization of the British army. Its organization, equipment and training had clearly proved inadequate, and some of its generals too old, slow and incompetent. Half a century of only minor wars against unsophisticated and ill-armed opponents had left it unprepared to meet an enemy who, although inferior in numbers (although not initially) and in logistic backing, had superior weapons, was more mobile, was familiar with the terrain, both locally and generally, and led a life which made him tough and skilled in fieldcraft, marksmanship and endurance.

The British generals, promoted by seniority, flavoured by the favouritism of the two rivals at the top, Wolseley and Roberts, were not an impressive lot. Roberts himself did not think much of many of them. In a letter to Lord Lansdowne on 1 March 1900 he wrote of Buller:

> I send you a file of telegrams which passed between Buller and me the last fortnight, from which you will see he is a difficult person to make any arrangements with. He never seems able to make up his mind what is the right thing to do.
>
> I quite see the difficulty I have placed you in by my covering letter to Buller's Spion Kop despatch. But I feel I should have failed in my duty had I allowed it to go on without expressing an opinion. Personally I should be glad to see both Buller and Warren leave the country, but it is not easy to get rid of them, without a storm being raised, which I would rather avoid for the credit of the Army.

In a subsequent letter (on 31 March) he wrote:

> I fully recognize the difficulty which has arisen in connection with the Spion Kop despatch, but if Buller and Warren were ordered home, I do not know how they could be replaced, unless comparatively junior and untried officers were selected, who possibly might not do better than their predecessors.
>
> At present affairs in Natal seem quieting down, and though I shall probably require one or two divisions from Natal to cooperate in the advance on the Transvaal, these would come under my immediate command on entering the Orange Free State.
>
> My advance will probably cause the enemy to withdraw altogether from Natal and consequently neither Buller nor Warren is likely to be involved in difficult operations in the future.

Before that, he had told Lansdowne of his decision not to retain the services of White, either as Governor of the Orange Free State or as a corps commander, and to sack two cavalry brigade commanders, Brabazon and Babington, although he appears to have relented in the case of the latter. He had also passed on an anonymous comment (almost certainly from Ian Hamilton) that 'confidence is much shaken in Buller and all the other Generals [in Natal], except Lyttelton, Hildyard and [Walter] Kitchener'. His views about some of the others were given in the letter in which, before he started his offensive in February, he recommended Kitchener as his successor.* He sacked Gatacre and

* Page 199.

Colvile (after the latter had been promoted to command the 9th Division) before he left. Before and at the time of his arrival in South Africa he wanted to sack Methuen, but neither he nor Kitchener did, which is surprising considering Methuen's consistent lack of success. In fact Kitchener came to respect Methuen, writing to Roberts on 30 August 1901: 'Methuen has been to see me. I never saw him looking better and he has done very well lately.' However, it is astonishing that both he and White eventually became field marshals, Methuen perhaps because he was protected by Wolseley or, as a Guardee, by the Court.

Two generals about whom it is difficult to make a certain judgement are Buller and French. Buller was severely criticized at the time and for long after for his indecision and lack of resolution in not pressing harder to break through to Ladysmith. It is not surprising that Ian Hamilton and Rawlinson were of that school, having been shut up in Ladysmith and being favourites of Roberts, while Buller was Wolseley's man; but, as some of the previous pages show, they were not alone. At Colenso he was surely right not to persevere after the double fiasco of the loss of Long's guns and Hart's deployment into the Loop; but he must never-theless take the blame for an unimaginative and unrealistic plan. His performance in the Rangeworthy Hills–Spion Kop–Twin Peaks–Vaal Krantz battle can only be described as lamentable; but both the plan and execution of the final battle which led to the relief of Ladysmith deserve great credit as pointing the way to a tactical method which was unfortunately seldom repeated in the First World War. Although criti-cized by several of his immediate subordinates and their staffs, he remained to the end popular at lower levels, perhaps because they realized that he would not demand that they 'push on' when the odds were clearly against them. Roberts's relations with him were never happy, culminating in Buller's dismissal from Aldershot Command and the army when Roberts was Commander-in-Chief over a public argument as to whether or not Buller had ordered White to surrender Ladysmith, instigated by Roberts's supporter Leo Amery.

Roberts started off admiring French, but changed his mind after the relief of Kimberley, as has been recorded.* French seems to have had a tactical flair, but to have been unsound in judgement and weak in administration, characteristics which he was to demonstrate later both as

* Page 139.

Chief of the Imperial General Staff and Commander-in-Chief of the British Expeditionary Force in France.

Ian Hamilton is another enigmatic figure. He was clearly highly regarded as a staff officer by, in succession, White, Roberts and Kitchener, but his record as a commander, apart from bravery in action, was less certain. His star, which had consistently risen until then, was to plummet at Gallipoli, where Majors Birdwood and Hunter-Weston were to shine, the former as commander of the ANZAC corps and the latter of the 29th Division.

At lower levels, the opportunity to exercise independent command in every field with mobile columns sifted the wheat from the chaff and brought into prominence commanders who were to dominate the scene in the First World War: Haig, Rawlinson, Allenby, Plumer, Byng, Smith-Dorrien and Gough; but they made their mark in the second part of the Boer War, when mobile operations were the order of the day, and perhaps paid less attention to the lessons of the earlier battles, in which direct attack on entrenched and concealed enemy led to heavy losses.

Kitchener was as critical of his subordinates as Roberts had been and discussed their shortcomings frankly with the latter in his weekly letters. Soon after taking over, he wrote about some unsatisfactory commanding officers. On 14 December 1900 he wrote:

> I hope you will remove Colonel Phillips and some other incompetent COs. I could then use regiments that are comparatively fresh but have now to be kept on garrison duty owing to the impossibility of trusting the COs in the field.

A fortnight later he wrote:

> Phillips of the Norfolks is evidently no use whatever also Curran of the Manchesters and Gosset of the Derbyshire the latter is believed to be slightly mad and has resigned his commission.

Two weeks after that, he wrote:

> Hart has I heard quite surpassed himself.* I think he had better go home as he is really hardly sane.

---

* He had allowed the Boer anthem, the '*Volkslied*', to be played at a function.

A week later, when Brigadier-General J. R. P. Gordon's 3rd Cavalry Brigade had failed to surround Beyers's commando, he was removed from command. At the same time Kitchener expressed dissatisfaction with Lyttelton. He was consistently critical of Babington, but reluctant to get rid of him, and, when he was told by Roberts that Smith-Dorrien was to go to India as Adjutant-General, he wrote:

> [He is] a most excellent man in the field, but on paper or in an office I do not think he is at all in place. He writes very rashly and then regrets it.

He held a low opinion of Baden-Powell. On 5 April 1901, he wrote to Roberts:

> Baden-Powell does not appear to do anything with the S.A.C. men beyond dressing them up. I am trying to get Milner to urge him on to doing something however small. They have now a lot of men and horses but I fear B.P. is more outside show than sterling worth – he is spending a lot of money.

In the same month he wrote that the commanding officer of the 17th Lancers, Lieutenant-Colonel Herbert, must be removed, as a result of which Haig replaced him. In the same letter Kitchener wrote, 'It is very difficult to find good commanders for all the columns', but said that Lieutenant-General Sir Bindon Blood, Major-General E. L. Elliot and Colonel Beatson 'are good'.*

Finally, what of Roberts and Kitchener themselves? Neither can be said to have covered themselves with glory, whatever the applause they received at the time. Apart from the relief of Kimberley, for which the credit must go to French however badly he may have overexerted his horses, neither came well out of the conduct of operations from the time they left Ramdam to their arrival at Bloemfontein, which included Paardeberg; and, after that, there was no serious resistance on the way to Pretoria. Roberts earns credit for firmly sticking to his strategy of giving priority to that drive, if necessary at the expense of Natal, although his attitude to the need to relieve Ladysmith was equivocal. From his communications with Lansdowne, he appears excessively self-satisfied.

---

* All three came from India.

Kitchener is more difficult to assess. His position as virtual deputy to Roberts was ill-defined and not an easy one. His handling of the battle of Paardeberg does him little credit. Unfortunately the archives of the National Army Museum contain no papers either of his, other than correspondence with Roberts after the latter's departure, or of his immediate subordinates, so that one does not get a clear picture of how he handled them and what they thought of him. Crude as his methods in the second half of the war may have appeared, their essential strategy, that of separating the guerrilla forces from the population which supported them, was one which the British army found itself forced to follow in many subsequent cases of colonial insurgency. That he was a man of single-minded determination is not in doubt.

But it was not just personalities, and the selection of them, which needed changing, it was the whole organization of the army from top to bottom, and this was set in hand even before the war had finished. When St John Brodrick succeeded Lansdowne as Secretary of State for War in 1901, he put forward a proposal to reorganize the army in the United Kingdom into six army corps, some of their divisions being a mixture of regular and 'auxiliary' troops. His proposals met with considerable opposition and had not got far when the war came to an end and the Prime Minister, Lord Salisbury, set up two Royal Commissions, one, chaired by Lord Elgin, to report on what had actually happened, and the other, by the Duke of Norfolk, to report on how the 'auxiliary forces', the Yeomanry, Militia and Volunteers, should be organized and maintained 'in a condition of military efficiency and at an adequate strength'. The former reported in July 1903, and, as a result, Lord Esher, who had been a member of the Elgin Commission, agreed to chair a committee to recommend a reorganization of the War Office in the light of the Elgin Commission's recommendation that the post of Commander-in-Chief should be abolished and replaced by an Army Board similar to the Board of Admiralty. Esher worked quickly and recommended an organization in which Directors, with clearly defined responsibilities, should exercise authority delegated by the Army Board through its principal members, of which the chief was to be the Chief of a General Staff created to exercise responsibility in the fields of operations, intelligence and some aspects of organization. Its framework has survived almost to the present, although significantly altered in the 1960s and since by a series of centralizing measures in the joint service Ministry of Defence. Disgusted, Lord Roberts went off to make a nuisance of himself in retirement.

These attempts to reorganize the general structure of both the regular and the 'auxiliary' army did not crystallize until Richard Haldane became Secretary of State for War in Campbell-Bannerman's Liberal administration in 1906. His complete reorganization of both, including the concentration of the Yeomanry, Militia and Volunteers into the Territorial Force, became effective in 1909 and made the army infinitely better prepared for war in 1914 than it would have been if the Boer War had not taken place to shake it out of its complacent nineteenth-century pattern. Unpleasant as the experience of the Boer War had been, and tragic for its casualties, it was undoubtedly a blessing in disguise for the British army.

In the tactical and equipment fields lessons were also learnt, but not to the degree that they should have been. The mobility of the Boers made a great impression. In the earlier stages, it was their ability to shift their forces rapidly from one point to another, while the British could only trudge along on foot, followed by creaking ox-drawn wagons, all in clouds of dust visible from miles away, that made an impression. In the second half of the war, it was the elusiveness of the commandos and their ability to strike out of the blue, and the need for our forces to be equally mobile, that dominated the scene. These impressions tended to obscure the fact that it was the superior firepower of the Boer rifles and artillery, fired from concealed and entrenched positions, which had held up Buller and Methuen and caused Kitchener heavy casualties at Paardeberg. Haig and his fellow column commanders therefore held an exaggerated view of the effectiveness of cavalry in 1914. Although neither the lance nor the sabre proved of much value in South Africa, Haig opposed their abolition and continued to express faith in the charge as the ultimate aim of cavalry training. When, as Director of Military Training in 1907, he supervised the production of *Field Service Regulations*, he did not make it at all clear what the cavalry soldier was meant to do with his carbine, the shortened Lee-Enfield rifle with which he was equipped, and poured scorn on the concept of Mounted Infantry, who dismounted to use them as they had done on so many occasions in South Africa. He can perhaps be forgiven for not foreseeing that it was the combination of obstacles, in the form of wire-protected trenches, and a far more intense use of machine-guns and artillery than had been seen in South Africa, which was to sound cavalry's death knell. The superiority in firepower which the Boers enjoyed, at least in the earlier stages, arose from the Jameson Raid. That alerted the Transvaal and the Orange Free State to the obsolescence of their armament and led to orders from both in 1896, mostly through the German firm Krupp, for more and better artillery and small arms.

As far as artillery was concerned, at the outbreak of the war the Transvaal had the following field artillery: six Creusot 75mm, eight Krupp 75mm, four Vickers Mountain 75mm, four Nordenfeldt 75mm, one Armstrong 12-pounder, and four Krupp 120mm howitzers, as well as some obsolete mountain guns (four Krupp,) six 7-pounders (two captured from Jameson), and three 5-pounders. They also had twenty-two Maxim repeating 1-pounders, universally known as pom-poms. They fired an explosive shell to a range of 3,000 yards, the gunner being protected by a shield. The Boers found them particularly effective against British machine-guns, which, when they were deployed at all, were generally sited in their front lines. As fortress artillery, which they converted to use in the field, they had four Creusot 155mms, known as Long Toms, firing a 94lb shell,* one 150mm mortar, one howitzer firing a 64lb shell and six Hotchkiss 37mm guns. The Orange Free State had fourteen Krupp 75mm guns, five Armstrong 9-pounders, three Armstrong Mountain 3-pounders, one Krupp 37mm and three pom-poms. Neither state was able to increase its arsenal during the war, except by captures from the British.

The British army's standard artillery organization was based on the battery as the unit, batteries of six guns being loosely brought together in brigades. French's cavalry division had one Royal Horse Artillery brigade consisting of two batteries each of six 12-pounders. Infantry divisions had one Royal Field Artillery brigade of three batteries, each of six 15-pounders. In addition Buller had a Corps artillery consisting of one RHA brigade of twelve 12-pounders and two RFA brigades, totalling eighteen 15-pounders and eighteen 5in howitzers. There were also some 5in field guns. The 12-pounder fired shrapnel to a range of 3,800 yards and the 15-pounder shrapnel to 4,100; although both guns were capable of firing high explosive, they were not supplied with it in South Africa.

---

* Although a formidable weapon, its effectiveness was limited by defective fuses, so that many of its shells proved to be 'duds'.

The 5in howitzer fired a 50lb lyddite HE shell to 4,800 yards and the 5in gun a lighter shell to 10,500. In the second stage of the war, the 5in batteries were converted to Mounted Infantry. The army's lack of longer range artillery was partly remedied by the deployment of a Naval Brigade with guns removed from the cruisers *Terrible*, *Powerful*, *Monarch* and *Doris*. They were 4.7in, firing a 45lb shell to 10,000 yards, and 12-pounders with a normal range of 8,000 yards which could be extended by digging in their trails to 12,000. At Kitchener's suggestion, when he joined Roberts, the British army bought a number of pom-poms: by May 1900 Roberts had fourteen and by 1901 there were about fifty deployed, usually one or two to a column. There was also the one battery of the volunteer Natal Field Artillery, equipped with six 7-pounder rifled muzzle-loaders.

Both sides had machine-guns, although neither in such numbers as to be very significant on the battlefield. The Boers appear to have had no more than twelve Maxim .303in and eight .45in, the latter captured from Jameson. They also had one Swiss 7.5mm Maxim. There was no regular scale of deployment in British units, but an indication is given by the fact that at the end of 1900 there were thirty-one machine-guns, almost all Maxim .303s, distributed among thirty-nine columns. Their use was restricted by the ungainly design and weight of the carriage. Some Volunteer units bought their own and used the lighter tripod mounting, which the Boers also used, and some acquired American Colts or Hotchkiss guns.

Both the Transvaal and the Orange Free State had placed large orders for rifles in 1896. The former ordered 50,000 German Mausers through Krupps, but only 37,000 had been delivered when the war started, and they had bought 34,000 Martini-Henry rifles from Westley-Richards. They also had 7,500 Portuguese Guedes 8mm and 2,700 Lee-Metfords, some of which they had captured from Jameson. The Orange Free State ordered 18,000 Mausers, only 8,000 of which had been delivered by 1899. They also had Martini-Henrys and Lee-Metfords, supplied to them by the Transvaal.

The standard British rifle was the Lee-Metford and the Lee-Enfield, the latter gradually replacing the former and some Metfords being fitted with Enfield barrels as they were refurbished, the rifling being better suited to the new cordite ammunition. Colonial units had Martini-Henry rifles and carbines and some had Martini-Metfords or Enfields which fired the .303 round. Mounted units initially had the shorter Lee-Metford carbine, later replaced by the Lee Enfield.

The characteristics of the principal rifles were as follows:

Mauser: calibre 7mm, muzzle velocity 2,719 feet per sec., sighted to 2,200 yards: 5 round magazine: smokeless powder.

Lee-Metford rifle: calibre .303in., muzzle velocity 1,830 fps, sighted to 1,600 yards: 10 round magazine: initially black powder, later cordite.

Lee-Metford carbine: as for rifle except m.v. 1,680 fps, sighted to 1,580 yards: 6 round magazine.

Lee-Enfield: calibre .303in. m.v. 2,060 fps, sighted to 1,600: 10 round magazine: cordite.

Martini-Henry: calibre .450in, breech-loading (i.e., no magazine): m.v. about 1,500 fps, sighted to 1,400 yards.

One of the handicaps under which operational commanders laboured was that of inadequate information, while they suspected that their opponents were well informed about their own movements. This was partly because Boer mobility and the superiority of their rifles, at least in the first half of the war, prevented British mounted troops from carrying out effective reconnaissance, and partly because the Boers were operating in their own country, helped by their compatriots. Nevertheless the British employed 'loyal' whites and natives as scouts, guides and messengers with a fair amount of success. Boer forces were seldom so thick on the ground that they could not penetrate enemy lines. An interesting innovation was the Observation Balloon, operated by the Royal Engineers, forerunner of aircraft.

The telegraph, most lines following the railway, was the principal method of communication for everyone. Once away from that, the only alternative to using messengers on horseback was the heliograph. Much use was made of the latter, and when there was no sun flashing Morse messages by searchlight reflected off clouds took its place, a technique to be used in both World Wars to produce artificial moonlight for night operations. Pigeons were also used, certainly from Ladysmith.

The problems of supplying and moving the army over huge distances, much of them barren country, dominated the war. A huge proportion of the army's effort was devoted to keeping itself supplied with food and forage, ammunition being less of a problem as expenditure was never very large for long. Most of the army's manpower was involved in guarding the railways and the slow convoys of wagons drawn by oxen or mules, winding their way along rough tracks in clouds of dust when dry or struggling up to the axles in mud when wet. In spite of Roberts's criticism of the Army Service Corps, it fully justified its recent formation and it is not surprising that Buller paid it high tribute and became its father figure.

The same cannot be said of the medical service, certainly not in the first half of the war. Treatment and evacuation of casualties was crude and badly organized, as were steps to combat the ever present threat of disease by field hygiene. Dysentery, enteric and typhoid took a heavy toll. The unsatisfactory state of the Army Medical Service had been recognized before the war and the Army Medical Corps had been formed in 1898 in an attempt to improve it, but had not made much impact by the time the war broke out the following year. 850 doctors accompanied the force in 1900, many of them civil surgeons, paid £1 a day. By the end of the campaign, numbers of all ranks in the Corps in South Africa totalled 8,500, providing 21,000 bed spaces.

Finally the men themselves. Reading their letters and diaries, one is impressed by how cheerfully and philosophically, whether they were regulars, regular reservists or volunteers, they accepted their duty and the often harsh conditions in which they fought or just passed their time. If some of their attitudes seem strange today, one must realize that they were the products of their time and its attitudes, although perhaps they were more literate than those who did not keep diaries, or whose letters, if they wrote them, are not in the archives of the National Army Museum. But those letters and diaries are not all that different from what soldiers wrote in the time of Marlborough and Wellington, were to write in the First and Second World Wars, and might write today. The soldier's self-respect, his concern that his comrades should hold him in high regard, his genuine concern for them, and his pride in his own unit shine through. It is that spirit which, whatever the conditions of life and the cruelties of war, makes the life of a soldier on active service rewarding and challenging, as it was for the soldiers who fought, survived or died in that war, which should never have taken place.

Maps

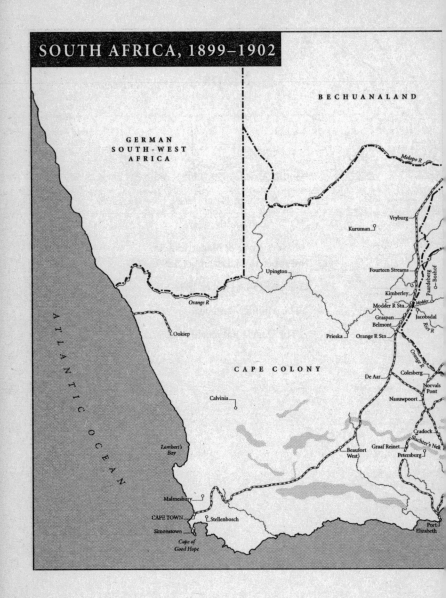

SOUTH AFRICA, 1899–1902

BECHUANALAND

GERMAN
SOUTH-WEST
AFRICA

Molopo R.

Vryburg

Kuruman

Fourteen Streams

Upington

Kimberley

Orange R.

Modder R Stn

Modder

Ookiep

Graspan

Jacobsdal

Belmont

River R.

Prieska

Orange R Stn

Orange R.

CAPE COLONY

De Aar

Colesberg

Norvals
Pont

Calvinia

Naauwpoort

Cradock

Slachter's Nek

*Lambert's
Bay*

Beaufort
West

Graaf Reinet

Petersburg

ATLANTIC OCEAN

Malmesbury

CAPE TOWN

Stellenbosch

Simonstown

*Cape of
Good Hope*

Port
Elizabeth

Paardeberg

o-Boshof

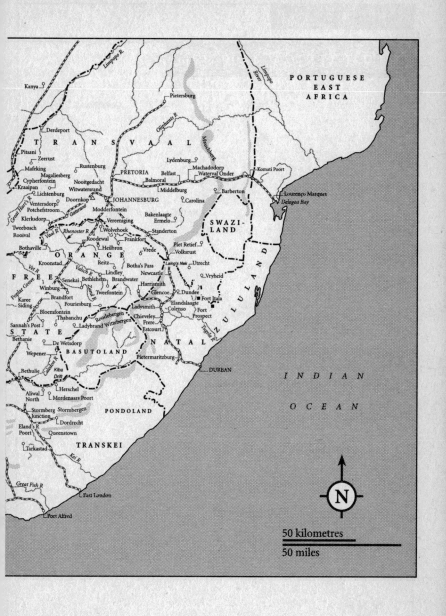

PORTUGUESE EAST AFRICA

Kanya
Pietersburg
Limpopo R.
Limpopo River
Derdeport
TRANSVAAL
Oliphants R
Pitsani
Zeerust
Lydenburg
Machadodorp
Komati Poort
Mafeking
Rustenburg
PRETORIA
Belfast
Waterval Onder
Magaliesberg
Nooitgedacht
Balmoral
Cypherfontein
Witwatersrand
Middelburg
L. Lourenço Marques
Kraaipan
Lichtenburg
JOHANNESBURG
Barberton
Delagoa Bay
Ventersdorp
Doornkop
Carolina
Modderfontein
Potchefstroom
Bakenlaagte
Klerksdorp
Vereeniging
Ermelo
SWAZI-
Tweebosch
Vaal R.
Rhenoster R.
Wolvehoek
Standerton
LAND
Rooival
Roodewal
Frankfort
Bothaville
Heilbron
Vrede
Piet Retief
ORANGE
Kroonstad
Botha's Pass
Laing's Nek
Utrecht
Volksrust
FREE
Senekai
Lindley
Newcastle
Vryheid
Winburg
Bethlehem
Brandwater
Harrismith
Glencoe
Dundee
Brandfort
Twcefontein
Fort Itala
Karee
Fouriesburg
Ladysmith
Elandslaagte
Siding
Bloemfontein
Roodebergen
Chieveley
Colenso
Fort
Thabanchu
Wittebergen
Frere
Prospect
Sannah's Post
Ladybrand
Estcourt
STATE
Bethanie
De Wetsdorp
NATAL
Wepener
BASUTOLAND
Pietermaritzburg
Bethulie
DURBAN
Aliwal
Herschel
North
Mordenaars Poort
INDIAN
Stormberg
Stormbergen
PONDOLAND
Junction
Eland's R
Dordrecht
OCEAN
Poort
Queenstown
TRANSKEI
Tarkastad
Kei R.
Great Fish R
L. East London
L. Port Alfred

N

50 kilometres

50 miles

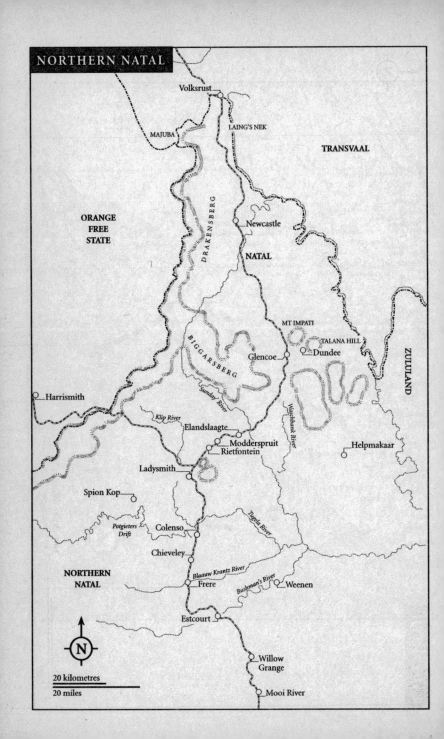

NORTHERN NATAL

Volksrust

MAJUBA

LAING'S NEK

TRANSVAAL

ORANGE
FREE
STATE

Newcastle

NATAL

DRAKENSBERG

MT IMPATI
TALANA HILL
Dundee

BIGGARSBERG

Glencoe

ZULULAND

Sunday River

Harrismith

Klip River

Elandslaagte

Waschbank River

Modderspruit
Rietfontein

Helpmakaar

Ladysmith

Spion Kop

Tugela River

Potgieters
Drift

Colenso

Chieveley

NORTHERN
NATAL

Blaauw Krantz River

Frere

Bushman's River

Weenen

Estcourt

N

20 kilometres
20 miles

Willow
Grange

Mooi River

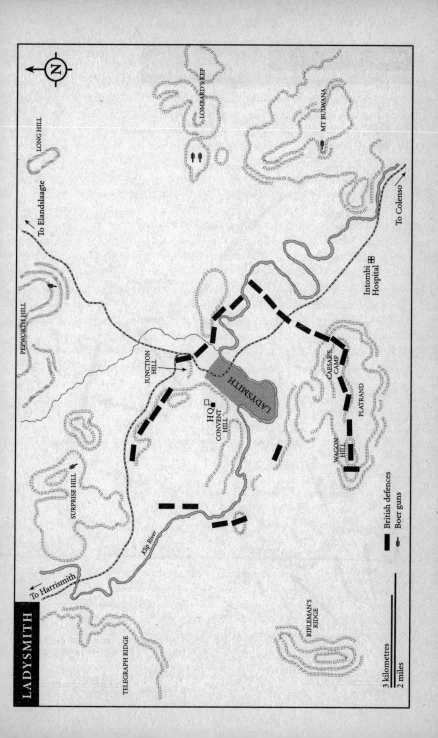

LADYSMITH

N

To Elandslaagte

LONG HILL

LOMBARD'S KOP

MT BULWANA

To Colenso

PEPWORTH HILL

Intombi
Hospital

JUNCTION HILL

LADYSMITH

CAESAR'S
CAMP

HQ

CONVENT HILL

PLATRAND

WAGON
HILL

SURPRISE HILL

Klip River

To Harrismith

TELEGRAPH RIDGE

RIFLEMAN'S
RIDGE

3 kilometres
2 miles

British defences

Boer guns

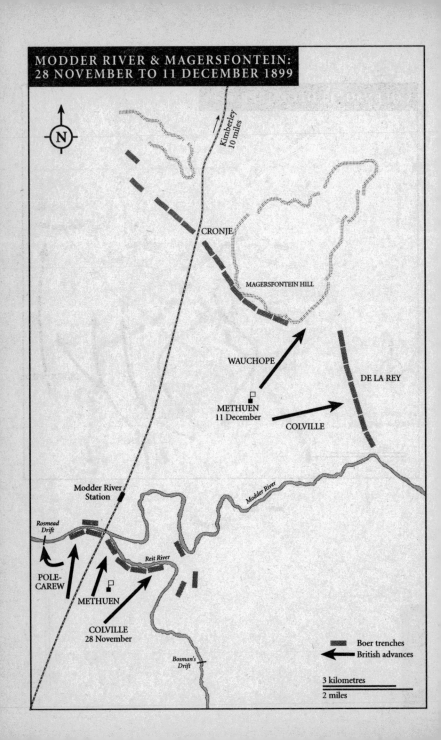

MODDER RIVER & MAGERSFONTEIN:
28 NOVEMBER TO 11 DECEMBER 1899

N

Kimberley
10 miles

CRONJE

MAGERSFONTEIN HILL

WAUCHOPE

DE LA REY

METHUEN
11 December

COLVILLE

Modder River
Station

Modder River

Rosmead
Drift

Reit River

POLE-
CAREW

METHUEN

COLVILLE
28 November

Bosman's
Drift

Boer trenches
British advances

3 kilometres

2 miles

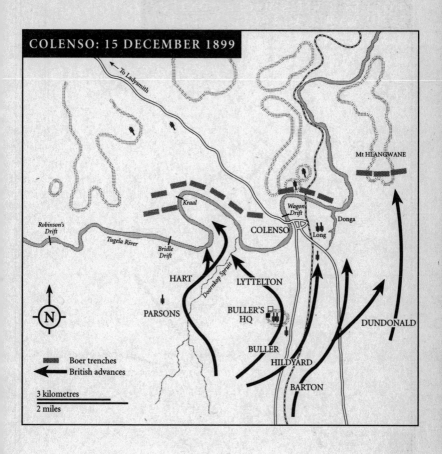

COLENSO: 15 DECEMBER 1899

To Ladysmith

Mt HLANGWANE

Kraal

Robinson's
Drift

Tugela River

Wagon
Drift

Donga

COLENSO

Long

Bridle
Drift

Doornkop Spruit

HART

LYTTELTON

N

PARSONS

BULLER'S
HQ

DUNDONALD

Boer trenches
British advances

BULLER

HILDYARD

3 kilometres

BARTON

2 miles

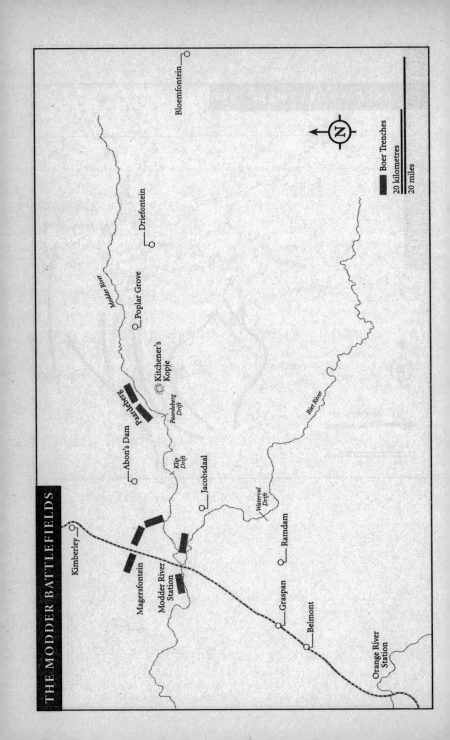

THE MODDER BATTLEFIELDS

Bloemfontein

Driefontein

Modder River

Poplar Grove

Kitchener's Kopie

Abon's Dam

Paardeberg

Paardeberg Drift

Klip Drift

Riet River

Jacobsdaal

Waterval Drift

Kimberley

Magersfontein

Modder River Station

Ramdam

Graspan

Belmont

Orange River Station

N

Boer Trenches

20 kilometres

20 miles

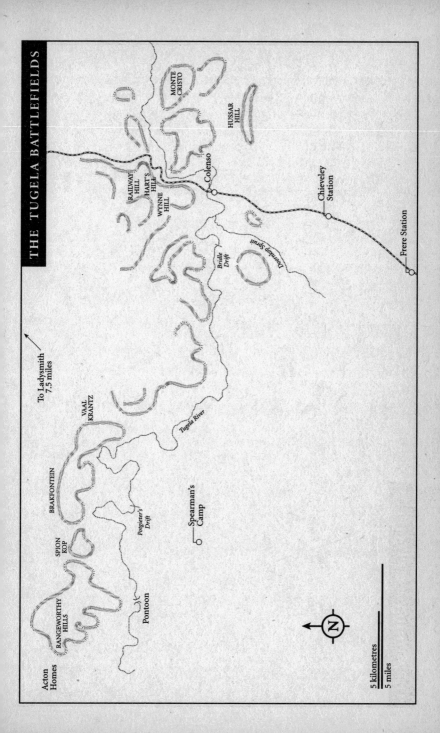

THE TUGELA BATTLEFIELDS

Acton Homes

To Ladysmith
7.5 miles

RANGEWORTHY HILLS

SPION KOP

BRAKFONTEIN

VAAL KRANTZ

Pontoon

Poegieter's Drift

Spearman's Camp

Tugela River

Bridle Drift

Doornkop Spruit

MONTE CRISTO

RAILWAY HILL

HART'S HILL

WYNNE HILL

HUSSAR HILL

Colenso

Chieveley Station

Frere Station

N

5 kilometres
5 miles

Bibliography

Amery, L. S. (ed.) *The Times History of the War in South Africa.* 7 Vols.
  London 1906–1909.
Belfield, Eversley. *The Boer War.* London 1993.
Maurice, Major General Sir Frederick, and Grant, M. H. *Official History of
  the War in South Africa, 1899–1902.* 4 Vols. London 1906–1910.
Pakenham, Thomas. *The Boer War.* London 1979.
Waters, Colonel W. H. H. and Du Cane, H. Translation of German
  General Staff Historical Section's *The War in South Africa.* London
  1905.

Index of Contributors

Ranks are those which, as far as can be ascertained, the contributors held at the time they are first mentioned. Names in square brackets which follow are those of copyright holders, whose permission has been obtained. Where there is none, it has not been possible to trace the holder. In those cases, the Museum would be pleased to hear from anyone who claims to be such, or knows the address of the person they believe to be the copyright holder. The figures in round brackets are the Accession numbers of the papers from which extracts have been taken.

Allen, Colonel R. E., East Yorkshire Regiment [Mr R. A. Allen] (1984-01-68)

Anonymous Sergeant, Royal Dragoons (1972-03-42)

Atlay, Lieutenant Hugh, Royal Artillery (1960-01-88)

Awdry, Lieutenant C. S., 1st (Wiltshire) Company, Imperial Yeomanry (1933-07-26)

Backhouse, Major (later Colonel), J. B., The Buffs (East Kent Regiment) (1976-02-48)

Baden-Powell, Colonel Robert (later Lieutenant-General Lord) [Lord Baden-Powell] (1971-01-23)

Balfour, Captain Christopher, The King's Royal Rifle Corps (known as the 60th Rifles) (1993-03-36)

Barnard, Trooper Charles, South African Constabulary [Mrs B. McGovarin] (1993-02-366)

Bellew, Captain R. W. D., 16th Lancers (1957-07-8)

Birdwood, Major William, XI Bengal Lancers (later Field Marshal Lord) [Lord Birdwood] (1967-07-19)

Bly, Private Frederick, Seaforth Highlanders (1973-10-850)

Britten, Lieutenant R. S., 37th (Buckinghamshire) Company, Imperial Yeomanry (1978-12-34)

General Index

The sub-entries for individuals are listed chronologically.

Figures in **bold type** refer to illustrations.

n = footnote.

References to units of the British Army will be found under Brigades, Divisions, and Regiments, and Royal Engineers, Royal Field Artillery, Royal Horse Artillery, etc.

Abbreviated ranks

The ranks given are those which the individual held when first mentioned in the book. Where known, the rank finally reached is also given.

Brig. – Brigadier
Brig.-Gen. – Brigadier-General
Col. – Colonel
Cpl. – Corporal
CQMS – Company Quartermaster-
    Sergeant
C/Sgt. – Colour-Sergeant
CSM – Company Sergeant-Major
FM – Field Marshal
Gen. – General
L/Cpl. – Lance-Corporal
L/Sgt. – Lance-Sergeant
Lt. – Lieutenant
Lt.-Col. – Lieutenant-Colonel
Lt.-Gen. – Lieutenant-General
Maj. – Major
Maj.-Gen. – Major-General
S/Sgt. – Staff-Sergeant
SSM – Squadron Sergeant-Major
Tpr. – Trooper